The Emergence and Development of English

An Introduction

This textbook provides a step-by-step introduction to the history of the English language (HEL), offering a fresh perspective on the process of language change. Aimed at undergraduate students, *The Emergence and Development of English* is accessibly written, and contains a wealth of pedagogical tools, including chapter openers, key terms, chapter summaries, end-of-chapter exercises, and suggestions for further reading.

A central theme of the book is "emergence," the key term from the study of complex systems, which describes how massive numbers of random verbal interactions give rise to regularities that "emerge" without specific causes. This unique approach encourages readers to incorporate complex systems into the mainstream coverage of HEL. Additional resources include examples of language from each period as well as appendices on terminology, online resources, and audio samples.

BILL KRETZSCHMAR is the Harry and Jane Willson Professor in Humanities at the University of Georgia, and also has an appointment at the University of Oulu (Finland). He is Editor of the American Linguistic Atlas Project, the oldest and largest national research project surveying how people speak differently across the country, and has provided American pronunciations for the online *Oxford English Dictionary* and other dictionaries in the Oxford US Dictionaries program. In 2014 he held an ACLS Digital Innovation fellowship, during which he developed a computer simulation to model language change. Recent works include the *Routledge Dictionary of Pronunciation for Current English* (2017) with Clive Upton, and *Exploring Linguistic Science: Language Use, Complexity, and Interaction* (2018) with Allison Burkette.

Cambridge Introductions to the English Language

Cambridge Introductions to the English Language is a series of accessible undergraduate textbooks on the key topics encountered in the study of the English Language. Tailored to suit the needs of individual taught course modules, each book is written by an author with extensive experience of teaching the topic to undergraduates. The books assume no prior subject knowledge, and present the basic facts in a clear and straightforward manner, making them ideal for beginners. They are designed to be maximally reader-friendly, with chapter summaries, glossaries, and suggestions for further reading. Extensive exercises and discussion questions are included, encouraging students to consolidate and develop their learning, and providing essential homework material. A website accompanies each book, featuring solutions to the exercises and useful additional resources. Set to become the leading introductions to the field, books in this series provide the essential knowledge and skills for those embarking on English Language studies.

Books in the series

Meaning in English Javier Valenzuela

The Sound Structure of English Chris McCully

Old English Jeremy J. Smith

English Around the World Edgar W. Schneider

English Words and Sentences Eva Duran Eppler and Gabriel Ozón

The Emergence and Development of English

An Introduction

William A. Kretzschmar Jr.
University of Georgia

CAMBRIDGE
UNIVERSITY PRESS

University Printing House, Cambridge CB2 8BS, United Kingdom

One Liberty Plaza, 20th Floor, New York, NY 10006, USA

477 Williamstown Road, Port Melbourne, VIC 3207, Australia

314–321, 3rd Floor, Plot 3, Splendor Forum, Jasola District Centre,
New Delhi – 110025, India

79 Anson Road, #06–04/06, Singapore 079906

Cambridge University Press is part of the University of Cambridge.

It furthers the University's mission by disseminating knowledge in the pursuit of
education, learning, and research at the highest international levels of excellence.

www.cambridge.org
Information on this title: www.cambridge.org/9781108469982
DOI: 10.1017/9781108555777

First published 2018

Printed in the United Kingdom by TJ International Ltd. Padstow Cornwall

A catalogue record for this publication is available from the British Library.

Library of Congress Cataloging-in-Publication Data
Names: Kretzschmar, William A., Jr., author.
Title: The emergence and development of English : an introduction /
William A. Kretzschmar Jr.
Description: Cambridge ; New York, NY : Cambridge University Press, 2018. | Series:
Cambridge introductions to the English language | Includes bibliographical references.
Identifiers: LCCN 2018007059| ISBN 9781108469982 (hardback) |
ISBN 9781108455114 (paperback)
Subjects: LCSH: English language – History – Textbooks.
Classification: LCC PE1075 .K89 2018 | DDC 420.9–dc23
LC record available at https://lccn.loc.gov/2018007059

ISBN 978-1-108-46998-2 Hardback
ISBN 978-1-108-45511-4 Paperback

Contents

Acknowledgments

This book has emerged from my own attempts over recent years to integrate complex systems in the History of the English Language (HEL) course I teach at my university. While I admire the rigorous analysis of traditional historical linguistics, which I learned at the hands of people like Sherman Kuhn and Fred Robinson, I have thought that it was time for a change in how we present HEL to our students today. We should not abandon traditional ideas and methods, but we need to explain our findings more comprehensively, more scientifically, for students who need information about English today. Some students will be teachers, some researchers in English language or literature, some in all kinds of careers – HEL regularly attracts all kinds of students. My first acknowledgment is to my students, who have put up with my efforts to teach them in a different way and who have made many suggestions for how to do it better.

Next, I am grateful to many anonymous readers for Cambridge University Press who offered a great many excellent suggestions. Of course, any problems that remain in the book are not their responsibility but my own. This book is supposed to be the "short" book on HEL, so it cannot compete in terms of the details of HEL with the many larger books in the area. And every teacher of HEL will have special interests not treated here. The CUP readers made me very aware of these facts, and I hope that I have found a middle path between the need for a brief treatment of HEL and the readers' expectations based on larger books.

Finally, I would like to thank my many friends from SHEL (the Studies in the History of the English Language conference), who have shown me a great deal about the English language that has shaped my views, among them the late Bob Stockwell and Dick Bailey, and Donka Minkova, Michael Adams, Anne Curzan, and Laura Wright.

Introduction

This textbook about the History of the English Language (HEL) is intended as a relatively brief volume designed for undergraduate courses in the area. *The Emergence and Development of English* is meant to be an all-in-one volume, and so it includes introductory treatment of basic terms and concepts for language study in two of the three appendices. It adopts a traditional organizational pattern of periods in HEL from Indo-European up to the present day, and at the end offers a chapter on what we mean by Standard English, and an appendix on the use of corpora, a relatively new and growing method for study of the language. The book is meant for students who lack training in English language studies, so the chapters are designed to leave nobody behind, and are not for advanced specialists. Finally, the book constitutes a brief tour of the subject, as appropriate for the Cambridge Introductions to the English Language series (CIEL), and so does not provide the kind of extended treatment found in some other HEL textbooks.

The key challenge for students and instructors in *The Emergence and Development of English* will be the incorporation of the science of complex systems into the mainstream coverage of HEL. If you are not aware of this, you might think that the title refers to the beginnings of English as a language at some moment in time, and to its improvement over time as it turned into the standard versions of the language we have today. Not so much. The book pursues a narrative thread throughout its chapters on "emergence," which is the key term from the study of complex systems. The science of complexity describes how massive numbers of random interactions can give rise to order, regularities that "emerge" from the interactions without specific causes. Complexity science is currently useful in physics, genetics, evolutionary biology, and economics, among fields that study large numbers of elements that interact with each other, but it is also a perfect fit for the humanities. People are talkers, and what we say depends on the people we interact with. The drive of twentieth-century linguistics to make the study of language more scientific, a logical system governed by grammatical and exceptionless phonological "rules," has never been as successful as linguists might have hoped. Speech, language in use, is first and foremost not a logical system but a complex system, as demonstrated from first principles and copious evidence in the author's *The Linguistics of Speech* (2009) and *Language and Complex Systems* (2015). Emergence in English is not once-and-done; it continues in every place where the language is spoken or written, in every locality and in every kind of conversation or text. Thus, in this book, while the text will apply the common terms and concepts of contemporary language study and linguistics, the story of the language will be about continual emergence and reemergence of lexical, phonological, grammatical, and discourse forms of English out of the interaction of its speakers and the contingencies of their history. The central aim is to produce a compelling account of HEL that does not leave out the people in favor of paradigms and rules, and that casts the important facts of the language as regularities that exist within a matrix of variation, subject to continual change both in the past, as we know has already occurred, and in the future.

The subject of complex systems is explained briefly and non-technically in Chapter 2; additional aspects of complex systems will be introduced in later chapters, but nowhere will students and their instructors be subjected to heavily mathematical or otherwise technical discussion. Complex systems can describe the process by which we perceive our language behavior to be associated with our communities and practices. Thus, the study of speech as a complex system addresses language as an aspect of culture that emerges from human interaction. The key point about the A-curve and the property of scaling, signs that a complex system has operated in a speech community, is that these are understandable on a conceptual basis, so that students and their teachers will not have to engage at all with the more technical aspects of complexity discussed in other sciences. As Chapter 2 will discuss in more detail, the A-curve is the frequency ranking of the different variants that exist in any community of speakers for anything we want to say: there are always a couple of very common variants, a few moderately common ones, and a great many rare variants. The property of scaling just means that we see this nonlinear A-curve pattern wherever we look, say when we consider English as a national language, or as the language of a particular region or city, or as the language of a small group of speakers who share a common interest. Whether we are interested in English overall or in small places or groups, we can rely on the same pattern being present, even if we do not try to do elaborate statistics on the frequencies of variants. Moreover, the book cannot replace normal linguistic terminology because the complex systems approach leads to discussion of emergence, and exactly what has emerged in the language must be described in linguistic terms. Basic discussions of linguistic terms and concepts are provided as Appendix 1 and Appendix 2. Appendix 3 is a little different, in that it explains how complex systems underlie what we understand as word meaning, and how modern corpus analysis can help us to see the bigger picture by using Big Data.

This volume follows the format of the CIEL series, and so each chapter includes the following sections: *In This Chapter, Chapter Summary, Key Terms, Exercises*, and *Further Reading*. The volume is also provided with online supplements. Readers and teachers can access three main resources online, which are referenced throughout this text book:

Moore, Knott, and Hulbert (1972), referred to throughout this book as the "Reference Grammar."

Moore and Marckwardt (1965), referred to throughout this book as the "Historical Outlines."

Audio samples from Bessinger and Bornstein (1973). Transcripts for the audio samples are also available online as a supplement to the often partial transcripts in the text itself. The audio samples available are listed in an additional section at the end of the relevant chapters.

These online resources replace things that are often found in longer, more extensive HEL textbooks, such as lists of sound changes (especially for early English in the Reference Grammar), paradigms (in the Reference Grammar and the Historical Outlines), and samples of texts from the earlier periods of the language. The Historical Outlines has particularly good coverage of the language of Chaucer, including phonetic transcriptions that will allow students to learn how to pronounce Middle English. While these resources could not be included in the book itself, many students and teachers will find them invaluable aids to studying HEL.

CHAPTER 1

Popular English: What We Think We Know

In this chapter

This chapter begins with what we already know about the English language. We have experience with the language that includes how it sounds and what words we expect. We know from our experience that people from different places sound and use words differently. People from different places also use different grammar, ways of putting words together. This is even true of what is often called Standard English. Our experience gives us all perceptions of how the language is used by different people, but these perceptions may not be very reliable when we come to describe how people actually talk. Linguists use a number of different approaches to describe the language, and such descriptions are always different from the prescriptions taught in schools.

1.1 **History and Variety**

The English language has a history. It's obvious once you think about it, yet the history of English is not something we think much about. All of us who use the language, wherever in the world we happen to live and work, whether we use other languages as well, and whether or not we consider ourselves to be fluent speakers of the language, use English in our daily lives in a kind of eternal present tense. English is now. English is what we say now and what we hear now from the other English speakers around us. How we got to where we are with the language does not enter into our conversations very much, we might think. And yet the history of English does enter into our talk and writing every day, without us being much aware of it. The history of English is more important to us than we might think because of the central fact about English, about all languages really, that the language changes over time. Your English will not be the same tomorrow as it is today. This book will introduce you to how the process of change works, and will tell you things about the history of the language that make a difference in how you use English today. Along the way, you will find out how you can describe aspects of English, so that you can mark the changes in the language and also talk in a more informed way about your own English today. You will find by the end of the book that you feel empowered to use English more effectively, both in the way that you understand how others speak and write the language and also in the way that you can express yourself. Once you know more about English and its history than most people do, you will be more in control of what you say and understand.

We are satisfied with our own impressions of English, instead of wanting to make a study of it, because our impressions are so clear. English has a certain concrete reality for us, based on our experience with people speaking English in comparison with people speaking what we consider to be other languages. Many of us around the world speak more than one language, and so we have a very personal and intimate experience with more than one language. We all have somewhat different experiences with English, too. Some of us learned English as children as our first language; some of us learned the language when we were children as a second language, one in addition to what we were speaking in our families; and some of us have learned English later in life, often with less opportunity for complete fluency. Many of us use English as a **lingua franca**, a common language among speakers of many languages, as for example between people from different parts of the European Union. Moreover, we all realize that our own English is not the same as the English used by somebody from another English-speaking country – even if we have never traveled far from home. The perennial James Bond of the movies (no matter the particular actor) just sounds different from us (no matter who we are), and that is part of his character. There are dozens of video clips of James Bond on YouTube, where you can hear that this is so. The directors of Bond movies often play up the difference through the introduction of an American colleague for Bond, typically a man from the CIA who shows a rough-hewn American persona as against Bond's British suavity. The CIA man sounds recognizably American, Bond recognizably British, and their ways of pronouncing words come to constitute a part of what we consider to be "rough-hewn" or "suave." Dame Judi Dench plays up the female side of "suave" as the character M in more recent Bond films. Different Bond movies also introduce speakers of English from Asia or Europe who have their own recognizable ways of speaking English, and their parts in the movies are sometimes large enough for us to associate the way they talk with a personality stereotype. We can take home the same impression from different musical artists when we hear them in interviews. While differences in pronunciation do not come through so clearly in the music itself, when we hear the singers and players talk, women and men, of many different ethnicities, we can wonder how (on the charts at this writing) Adele sounds so different from Lady Gaga or Beyoncé in an interview as well as in their music. Since we hear people's pronunciation all the while they are talking, it is only natural that this characteristic of speech, often called **accent**, becomes identified with the behavior of the people doing the talking.

Besides pronunciation, British English also contains words and expressions unfamiliar to Americans. These vocabulary differences (words and expressions in general are called the **lexicon**) can sometimes be difficult to decode, such as a British road sign that says "Unsuitable for Heavy Goods Traffic" when the American sign would say "No Trucks." Sometimes they can be pretty obvious: the British "Mind Your Head" sign to warn tall people about low ceilings is probably better than the American "Caution!" sign, even for Americans. Different words are, well, different, like British *windscreen* for American *windshield*, or American *parking lot* for British *car park*. Canadians can often call the same thing a *parkade*. The majority of differences in the lexicon are more subtle, words and expressions that are available for use in British and American English, and in other Englishes worldwide, but are simply used more often in one than in the other. Differences range from preferences, like American *mail* versus British *post*, to very subtle matters of endings we put on words to mark how they work in a sentence (called **morphology**) or other aspects of sentence construction (called **syntax**) or of the arrangement of chunks of language larger than sentences (called **discourse**). British speakers, for instance, may seem to you more likely to use the "have you (an object)" form of making a type of question, while Americans prefer to construct the question with "do you have (an object)." American workers want a *raise* in pay, while British workers want a *rise*. American students *review* material before a test, while British students *revise* it. Australians and New Zealanders tend to agree with Americans and Canadians in saying that they *studied* a subject, while the British *read* a subject at college. While the word *mistake* is quite common in world Englishes, the word *blunder* is much more common in Sri Lankan English than elsewhere.

As for whole discourses beyond the sentence level, British speakers seem more likely to inject qualifiers like *perhaps* or *sorry* than Americans would be. We all believe that such differences exist, and on them we base our belief in British English, as opposed to American English, or Australian English, or any other sort of English.

Differences between American English and British English come in for more comment than differences between either British or American English and any other world variety of English because British and American English are the varieties most familiar to English speakers around the world, but a list of differences might be drawn up between any two national varieties of the language. We can call the whole collection of features – pronunciation, lexicon, morphology, syntax, discourse – used by speakers from one place, or from one social group, a **dialect**. We have to be careful with the word "dialect," however, because when some people use that word they mean that there is something wrong with the speakers who talk that way. The same thing is true of the word **slang**, which describes words in common usage among some speakers which are not typically used in polite circles. A more neutral term for the collection of features used by some group of speakers is a **variety of a language**. All of these differences between varieties are the result of emergence, as we will see in the next chapter.

1.2 **Perception**

While many English speakers would find it difficult to cite particular differences in usage between, say, British and American English, most of them could also offer an imitation – more or less effective – of the speech of a British or American English speaker. Imitation here is not flattery but a declaration of differences: even people who give very bad imitations believe that there is a difference and can try to enact it. Dennis Preston has studied what he has called **folk linguistics** or **perceptual dialectology**. He has found that people are not slow to form perceptions of how other people talk, and that the perceptions are bound up with how these folk (by which Preston means nothing bad, just that his subjects are not trained to analyze speech) see themselves as English speakers. Thus, the "suave Brit" and "rough-hewn American" of the James Bond movies: the image is part of how the speech is perceived, and the speech helps to create the image portrayed by the actor. Speech and image are intertwined, as enacted by Sean Connery, George Lazenby, Roger Moore, Timothy Dalton, Pierce Brosnan, or Daniel Craig (or by the likes of Jack Lord, David Hedison, or most recently Jeffrey Wright for the CIA part) in Bond movies, and as enacted by every English speaker every day in every real conversation. Nelson Mandela sounded neither British nor American, and the way he talked was part of his identity, the image he conveyed. There are of course suave Americans and rough-hewn Brits (the Daniel Craig version of James Bond has his dark side), in other movies and in real life, but this does not in the least diminish the perception of difference between British and American English. We can accept individual people for themselves without abandoning our stereotypes. And we can maintain the stereotypes even if we cannot readily make a list of actual differences between them, whether in pronunciation or lexicon or syntax. This, then, is what most people mean by "a variety of English." For most people a variety of a language is constituted by the perception of a difference.

The boundaries of such a variety are usually convenient designations of linguistic borders, rather than accurate assessments of linguistic evidence. It is very convenient, for instance, to use national boundaries as definitions for varieties of languages, like British English and American English and Singapore English. The problem with attaching national labels in this way can be illustrated from the different actors who have played James Bond. Sean Connery, George Lazenby, Roger Moore, Timothy Dalton, Pierce Brosnan, and Daniel Craig do not speak with exactly the same accent. Brosnan, for instance, was born in Ireland, not Britain! We must allow for variation within national varieties, whether regional (Connery is Scottish, Dalton was born in Wales and grew up in the North of England, and Craig also has Welsh connections and grew up near the Welsh border, while Dame Judi Dench grew up in the North in York) or merely individual.

The problem remains even at the national level, as we can see from Canadian English. For British English speakers, Canadian English often gets lumped together with American English – rightly so, because Canada is also part of North America, and the USA need not, though in practice it usually does, grab the label "American" all for itself. "North American English" is a better term to apply to the English of Canada and the USA. While non-North-Americans perceive the pronunciation of Canadians to be essentially similar to that of the USA, American English speakers quite frequently think that a number of features of Canadian English remind them of British English – spelling, for one, in words like *labor/labour* and *center/centre*. The fact is that in many respects Canadian English, especially in the western part of the country, is very much like American English; on the other hand, especially in the eastern part of Canada, there are indeed a number of features that many Canadians share with British English. As R. E. McConnell (1979) puts it,

Canadian English is basically of the North American variety. But Canadians also share in the innovations and usages of the British . . . They learn to shift between such items as *first floor/ground floor, pants/ trousers, suspenders/braces, absorbent cotton/cotton batting/cotton wool* – and to recognize that *ladders*, as well as *runs*, can occur in stockings, and that *boaters* and *bowlers* can be hats.

If Canadian English is not to be recognized for itself by most non-specialist listeners (there are, after all, fewer opportunities for most English speakers around the world to gain experience with Canadian English than with American or British English), then it is plausible for people who hear Canadian English to connect it with either British or American English, depending on their point of view. Perceptions of linguistic differences, because they are defined by convenience and depend upon your point of view, are not very objective. They are, however, how most people lead their linguistic lives; they allow people to conceive of their linguistic experiences in a more ordered way.

We now can see that the idea that American English is "spoken in the United States" is problematic because what is "American" is defined less by the national border than it is by people's perception and point of view. We can say exactly the same thing about Australian English and Australia, or British English and Britain, or Canadian English and Canada, just to do our ABCs of English. Or about (New) Zealand and New Zealand English, to get all the way to *zed*, or *zee* as some of us would say.

1.3 Standard English

At the same time that we know, for certain, that English is a little different wherever you speak or write it, we also know, for certain, that there is such a thing as "Standard English." Describing a standard language might be thought to consist of the relatively simple act of writing down what people say, particularly what people say in the capital city where we all go to find the best and latest styles in many areas, not just language. Yes, London in England, but in the USA and other former colonies where English is spoken natively, the political capital may not also be the commercial capital, and there may be more than one important center whose language is influential (in the USA, you might think of New York, Chicago, Los Angeles, and Atlanta, among others, rather than Washington, DC). While some efforts to try to control variation may have been made earlier in history, the idea of a standard for language really got started in the Neoclassical period (starting in the seventeenth century in England and its dependencies), when there was new confidence that science and observation could find the causes behind the workings of the world around us. Great progress was made then on many fronts, for example Newton's formulation of our (neo)classical laws of physics. However, describing a standard language is not the writing down of what people do say and write, as the modern sciences rely on observation of facts in the world around us, but instead the formulation of rules for what people *should* say, often based on cultural factors like the political influence of the capital. In our contemporary world, higher education has taken the place of mere political influence, and the idea of a standard language is the particular province of the schools. Therefore, it is fair to say that Standard English is an institutional variety of the language, not one that emerges directly from the buzz and hum of language in use.

Standard English is real. You can find it in the grammar books used for teaching in the schools, and as the answers to language arts questions on standardized tests. And yet it is not complete, not anywhere, because the grammar books do not tell us everything about Standard English, and standardized tests do not ask us about all of it. We will consider what Standard English might be, and how it might be a little different from place to place, in a later chapter. In popular terms, we can say that the idea of Standard English is about **correctness**, the way that people *should* use English based on what is taught in school and included on standardized tests; this idea is also called **prescriptivism** because people who teach Standard English *prescribe* what we should say or write, in the same way that a doctor might prescribe medicine for an illness. We can also say that our perceptions of English tell us about the **rightness** of using the particular kind of English that belongs to people in any particular place and in any particular situation. Nobody teaches or tests whether you say the right kind of English; you just learn it in your family and your neighborhood and your workplace. In the popular view, then, what is right about someone's characteristic English, what makes people who use it sound right, like they belong to their groups, may at the same time sound wrong according to the idea of correctness. The popular idea of English thus has to endure an inherent contradiction between correctness and rightness, between what the school teaches and local authenticity.

1.4 Linguistics

There is yet another way to think about English, one that is not quite the same as our popular perceptions of English all around us, or the same as institutional Standard English either: **linguistics**. Academic linguists have competed strenuously over linguistic theory during the past century. Many linguists (but not all) share a commitment to the notion of a rule system for language. Under one approach, **structuralism** as developed by Leonard Bloomfield and others early in the twentieth century, linguists gather information about a language from one or two or some small number of speakers, and attempt to describe the system of the language from what they say. It is not necessary to talk to more than a few speakers, perhaps just one, because the structuralist assumes that the speakers of a language are more or less alike in that they share a rule system. Another major modern approach to linguistics is **generativism,** most associated with Noam Chomsky and beginning somewhat later, in the 1950s. Generativists take the creation of rule systems, by means of the assumption of a homogeneous speech community, to address our human capacity for speech and to contribute to the description of a "universal" system that people use in the formation of the rule system for our own particular language. Generativists focus on the creation of the smallest possible rule systems that could "generate" the acceptable sentences of a language, according to grammaticality judgments of its speakers. In Britain another approach, **systemic functional linguistics,** based on the work of J. R. Firth and developed by Michael Halliday in the mid twentieth century, does not make the same commitment to rule systems. Instead, functionalists focus on meaning in language, and describe a multidimensional framework for getting at the meaning of any utterance from different angles. These academic approaches, even though all of them are called "linguistics," have different assumptions and make different claims about language in general and about English in particular. This book is not particularly aligned with any of these three main approaches to linguistics.

What this book does share with all varieties of academic linguistics is a commitment to systematic observation of the facts of language, to the **description** of language as we find it and of the regularities we see in it (as opposed to social prescriptions of what we should do in language). The idea of a language is hopelessly entangled in perceptions, unless and until we can conduct a rigorous study of the parts of a language, of the features that speakers of the language commonly use. Features of pronunciation, lexicon, morphology, syntax, and discourse all come together to form the whole of a language. It would be impossible for anybody to take into consideration all of the actual conversations that people have, continuous interactions in language in actual use all around us. Instead we have to concentrate on the features of language that are constantly repeated to form those conversations, as we can derive them from examples of speech. The modern study of linguistics accepts five different ways for studying such features of a language, the names of which have already been

11

introduced: pronunciation (or accent), lexicon, morphology, syntax, and discourse. As for pronunciation, each language and variety has a range of sounds that are commonly used in the pronunciation of its words. There is also an inventory of words, a lexicon, that belongs to each language and variety, and a set of endings, its morphology, that we can attach to the words. Each language and variety has characteristic patterns, syntax, with which its words can be arranged in sentences. Finally, each language and variety has characteristic habits of arrangement of words and sentences to form meaningful discourse. Pronunciation, lexicon, morphology, syntax, and discourse, then, tell us where to look for particular features that can belong to English, and may be produced differently in different varieties.

There is the potential for great confusion between the popular notions of correctness and rightness of language and the academic views of linguistics, because everybody is using similar terms for quite different ends. What we think we know about English begins with our perceptions, with what we think of the language as it is used all around us. What we think we know about English is also strongly colored by our experience with Standard English. If you are reading this book you have been quite successful in school already, and you are likely to have strong feelings about correctness because of the trouble it took you to learn what you are supposed to say and write. And many readers of this book will have at least one additional layer of ideas about English, because of what we think we know about linguistics. The important thing to take away from this chapter is that *we are not all trying to do the same thing and getting it wrong*. Your perceptions of and your experience with English are just not going to be the same as everybody else's. Learning how to describe the language, rather than just perceive it, is the first step towards a more informed understanding of English. The trick in beginning to learn about the history of the English language is to realize that we all come at the subject from a slightly different place. The history will look a little different to each of us. And the fun is that we get to compare with each other what we think we know and what we can describe.

1.5 Chapter Summary

This chapter introduced the idea that, while we all have experience with the English language, our perceptions based on that experience will all be a little different and will not match exactly what linguists have to say about the language. We are aware of many different varieties of the language worldwide, even different variations in Standard English. Linguists are interested in describing the language, while the schools are more interested in Standard English, and individuals care about using the right English for their circumstances. Confusion can result from the contrast between the approach typically taken in schools, what we hear around us at home, and what linguists have to say about English.

Key Terms
accent
correctness
description
dialect
discourse
folk linguistics
generativism
lexicon
lingua franca
linguistics
morphology
perceptual dialectology
prescriptivism
rightness
slang
structuralism
syntax
systemic functional linguistics
variety of a language

Exercises

1.1 Write your linguistic autobiography. Where were you born, and where have you lived during your life? What about your immediate and extended family? What sort of jobs have you and your parents had, and what sort of social groups have you belonged to? If you are reading this book, you are likely to be involved with higher education, but again what about your family? Have you had experiences in life that you think have affected your language? Have you learned other languages besides your native language?

1.2 Think about the differences you have noticed between British, American, Canadian, and Australian speakers of English (or any other variety of English with which you are familiar). You know they are different, but can you name specific features that people from one or another of these places typically use? It will be easiest to name words that people use, even though you may think first of accent. Make a list of at least five such differences.

1.3 Can you think of specific differences between the standard forms of British English and American English? Who would use *in hospital* and who *in the hospital*? Make a list of at least five such differences.

1.4 Movies pay close attention to the accent of their characters, often hiring people to serve as dialect coaches. Can you think of movies where the accent of the characters is particularly well done? Particularly badly done? (You are more likely to be dissatisfied with movie accents if the movie is supposed to be taking place in your home town.) Famous examples of accents in the movies are *Steel Magnolias* and *Trainspotting*. Describe the accents you have heard in recent movies you have seen.

1.5 Make a list of at least three complaints that you have heard about your language. If you yourself have complaints about how people use the language, you can put them down. Who makes complaints? Are they about the difference between what the schools teach about language (correctness) and what people actually say outside of the school (rightness)?

Further Reading

www.imdb.org is the standard website for finding out about movies. It also covers TV and Hollywood celebrities. You can search for movie titles, but you can also search for plots, quotes, characters, and biographies of actors. There is an official website for James Bond movies, www.007.com.

Mitford (1951) is perhaps the most scholarly treatment of words particularly associated with America, but it is now over half a century old. Many standard dictionaries identify words as British or American, but their grounds for doing so are not clear. John Algeo has worked to produce a dictionary of Briticisms, which has so far not yet appeared, but you can look up Algeo to find his articles on differences between British and American English. Cassidy, Hall, and von Schneidermesser (1985–2012) cover words used in less than all of America and is available online at www.daredictionary.com.

Preston (1989; 1993); Preston and Niedzielski (2000). Preston has reinvigorated the idea that we should pay attention to what people think about language, not just how they say things differently. In particular, he has asked people where "correct" English is most likely to be found in America, and where the English in America is most "pleasant." The answers are quite different! And Preston has found that people have very different ideas about where regional dialects can be found, even if many people do name the same general areas (like the "South").

McConnell (1979) develops Canadian English, quite properly, as its own national variety of English. Her book is a classic in the field. A more up-to-date volume on Canadian English is Boberg (2010). There is an ongoing revision of the Dictionary of Canadianisms on Historical Principles online at www.dchp.ca/dchp2.

The brief survey by Schneider (2011) covers English worldwide, including historical treatment and an idea of how a language variety might develop in a new place. Kachru (2017) is the most recent book by another famous World Englishes scholar, the late Braj Kachru.

Dinneen (1967) provides a good history of linguistics for a general audience that goes all the way back to earliest ideas. Another history of linguistics that tends to be a bit more technical is Robins (1997). A good short history of linguistics with more attention to systemic functional linguistics is Chapter 12 in Bloor and Bloor (2013). No history of linguistics can be completely up to date, since linguistics as a field tends to change fairly rapidly.

Milroy and Milroy (2012) offers a fine account of the "complaint tradition" – how people write to complain about what they consider to be non-standard usage – and of the relationship between standards and normal usage in English. Another relevant title is Cameron (2012), about popular views of language and its regulation.

CHAPTER 2

Emergence

In this chapter

People are very good at group formation: we can find others who share our interests and beliefs. All the different groups we form create the culture in which we live – and also create variations in the language we speak. These patterns of variation in language emerge from all of the interactions between speakers, as we all learn to vary the way we speak or write in the different groups that we belong to. The process of emergence is best described in a new science called complex systems, which applies to situations where many individual components interact with each other and share information. Ants, for example, create complicated nests and behaviors even though no central authority tells them what to do. People are smarter than ants, but we are still affected by interaction in complex systems to create characteristic frequency profiles for the use of different features in every part of our language.

2.1 **Language and Culture**

Language and its structure are just one aspect of **culture,** a general term by which we can designate all the ways that people form themselves into groups and, as a consequence, develop particular habits in how they lead their lives. The American geographer Wilbur Zelinsky sees American culture to be involved in a "highly interactive world system," and he views regional culture areas as subject to different kinds of cultural behavior. Of course, England and every other English-speaking place are also involved in the same highly interactive world system right along with the Americans – whether they prefer to interact globally in this way or not. Geography has traditionally been the main source of culture areas because, historically, groups of people have usually stayed in one place, and these populations have developed separate cultural practices. In the United States, however, the English-speaking population has not been present and stable as far back in history as in England, but has been in the process of rapid expansion and development for only three hundred years or so. In the modern age, ease of travel and effective telecommunications tend to break down geographic barriers even in the Old World, not to mention the New. The English-speaking population of Australia and New Zealand has become established even more recently. English speakers in many countries around the world can count the time since English became an important local language, not in centuries but in decades.

What was always important about geography for culture, however, was not so much uncrossable mountains and rivers, but **group formation**, the way that people formed groups across the land. Political and religious views have effects on group formation and thus culture formation, for instance the long term differences between the Scots and the English within the UK, just as the topography of the land influenced groups and their culture. Plantation agriculture, and the culture associated with it in the American South, could not take place in mountainous areas, where only small farms created the culture of "yeoman farmers," and so two different cultures developed in these places. When geography and cultural components are brought together for analysis, we can think of alternative definitions of **culture regions**, such as the "voluntary region" where people have migrated out of common interest, such as Canadian "snow birds" to Florida (people who go south for the winter), or the "synthetic culture region" where people may live in clusters in several different physical locations and adopt a common cultural mode, such as "golf-course communities" or "gated communities." While the dimensions of culture should comprehensively include the processes of group formation, we must also allow for the possibility of individual, idiosyncratic behavior.

The individual person is the most basic constituent of human culture: no cultural groups can exist without people to be their members, adding up one by one to form the whole group, and no artifacts or ideas can exist without individual people, as members of groups, to make them or think them. And moreover, people are complex beings in cultural terms. Zelinsky (1992) has written that each person carries his [or her] own unique collection of cultural attributes, and may also be a participant in many subcultural groups. Imagine someone who is, among other things, a Czech-American Lutheran plumber, a member of the VFW [Veterans of Foreign Wars], an ardent Cleveland Indians fan, a radio ham, a regular patron of a particular bar, and a member of a car pool, the local draft board, the Book-of-the-Month Club, and the Republican Party, and a parent whose son attends a particular college.

It is not possible to say whether such a person is really only an Indians fan (or a Lutheran, or a bar patron), and that the rest does not matter. This complexity of association with different cultural entities is the nature of the modern human beast; while people outside of America may not share the particular attributes that Zelinsky cites, we could easily name parallel attributes from any country we name (a Polish Catholic plumber, a member of the Association of Wrens, an ardent Manchester United fan, and so on). Race or ethnicity is sometimes thought to determine someone's cultural status, but it is only part of the picture. People of any race or ethnic group can be Indians or Man United fans, or Catholics, or pub patrons, or hip-hop music devotees, and we should not ignore associations like these just to focus on race or ethnicity. So, while we often think of culture regions as places with their own populations, all of the individuals in every place belong to many different groups. Even within a culture region, not every person will share the property that dominates the culture region, and even the people who do share the dominant property will also have a wide range of other characteristics that associate them with different groups. Just because you are Asian, you do not have to follow the stereotype of being inscrutable, or the stereotype of being careful with a penny if you are Scottish. Each of us has our own collection of cultural associations, and that is what makes us individuals. Group formation is a multidimensional process everywhere you look, and every individual has a whole set of different interests and beliefs.

Just as membership in each of these groups brings with it certain physical artifacts or ways of thinking, so too it brings linguistic consequences. Association with different cultural groups makes special vocabulary available to the individual members, as for a sports fan ("home run!" in Cleveland, "goal!" in Manchester) or a plumber (with her *wrench* in Cleveland and her *spanner* in Manchester). Perhaps less obviously, association with different cultural groups makes special pronunciation or syntax available to the individual members; these different habits are often considered to be stylish. A good example is how those who like hip-hop or Afro-Caribbean culture, whether or not of African heritage, learn to carry stylish linguistic characteristics of rap or reggae over into their everyday speech, "keepin' it real" or "woke" (common as of this writing, no doubt to be replaced in future as such stylish words and phrases constantly change over time). All of these potential linguistic influences will be blended differently in different people, because it is rare for two people to share exactly the same set of cultural associations. Even if two people did participate in the same cultural groups, they would not necessarily use all of the same linguistic features that were available to them.

Some kinds of linguistic behavior do not come from association with any cultural group but are the property of the individual alone. Some people have missing teeth or another physical condition that affects speech; some have relevant brain or psychological conditions such as aphasia or stuttering or Tourette's syndrome. While these factors are usually considered to be abnormal, it is also true that each of us uses our "normal" vocal apparatus in slightly different ways and that, even though all human beings have the same kind of vocal tract, each of us has our own particular small variations in the vocal tract. That is why we can recognize voices, as we can recognize faces. We are all a little different, linguistically as well as physically, and happily so. It is also quite normal for all of us to be linguistically creative. We all make up words when we need to, or use words with new meanings, or create syntax that we have never learned or heard before. We do not often create new usages on purpose, but that does not mean that all such usages are just mistakes. Most of them are perfectly understandable. We need to recognize the fact that individuals are unique both in our cultural associations and in at least some part of our own linguistic behavior, in order to be able to make decisions about the relative contribution to linguistic behavior of cultural associations and individual characteristics. We need to give credit to individuality as well as to culture in order to provide a comprehensive classification of linguistic behavior.

2.2 **Emergence**

Even though we are all linguistic individuals, no two of us exactly alike, we can all readily accept that we have all become members of groups, regional and social ones but also groups based on common practices like hip-hop or playing cricket or being a lawyer. We see these groups all around us every day. However, it is one thing to accept groups as a part of our cultural environment, but quite another to try to understand how groups develop from all of our individual habits and behavior. It is another thing even beyond that to understand how we recognize any individual's linguistic

Figure 2.1 Ants in a line

behavior as being similar to the behavior we observe in a group. Groups are necessarily complex multidimensional constructs – we all belong to many groups at the same time, regional and social and practical. In order to explain how groups develop and how we recognize that individuals belong to them, we need a scientific model that can describe such a complex multidimensional situation. The process of development and recognition for all of these groups comes down to one word, **emergence**, as the term has been defined in the new science of **complex systems**.

Let's begin with something less complicated than human beings to see how emergence works: a line of ants.

Ants are not smart. They can only do a few things, like exploit food sources, build nests, and defend themselves against intrusions, but the queen ant does not tell the other ants to do any one of these activities (the queen is just needed for reproduction). Instead, ants just happen to be doing one of these tasks at any given time, following the instincts that belong to ants and the circumstances at the time. In searching for food, for example, ants wander around randomly; if they find some food, they leave chemical traces along their path to bring it back to the colony. Other ants can follow the traces, and leave more traces on their way back, till the path becomes a long line with lots of ants on it (as shown in Figure 2.1) to exploit the food resource. However, not all of the ants in the nest follow the path; some keep foraging and some stay home on nest and defense duty, again not because they are told to do so by the queen or some ant general. When ants come boiling out of a nest when it is disturbed, they are not reacting to a chemical trace but to touching the antennae of other ants and then they change their behavior from food or nest activities to defense. However, not all of the ants leave to gather food or rush to defense given the stimulus to do so. Some stay on nest duty during a provocation, and some ants look randomly for food when most have joined the line to a known food source. What looks to us like highly organized behavior is not controlled by any leader, and it is not absolutely determined by instinct or particular stimuli, but instead patterns of activity emerge from the genetic, instinctual behaviors of ants as they are conditioned by circumstances, the **contingency** of the moment. These patterns of activity, the result of the complex system of interactions among the ants, make the whole more than just the sum of a few instinctive behaviors. This is the defining characteristic of a complex system, when what we perceive as organized behavior in the ant colony just emerges from the process of interaction in reaction to the contingencies at the time (available food, disturbance of the nest, and many other possible situations). Finally, we can see that the complex system of the colony depends upon the continual motion of the ants. Each ant has to keep moving in order to allow the exchange of information that permits the colony as a whole to react to its current circumstances. It would literally be fatal for the ants to stop reacting to contingencies.

When we describe a complex system, then, we are engaging in a new kind of science. It does not replace the familiar kind of science, the cause-and-effect, action-and-reaction ideas that we have inherited from Isaac Newton. Newtonian mechanics work well for an individual interaction, like what will happen to a billiard ball if you hit it in a certain way with the cue ball, or what will happen to a pin struck by a bowling ball, or at the largest scale what will happen when a planet like the Earth is affected by the gravity of the Sun. However, Newtonian mechanics do not work when three or more bodies mutually influence each other, the so-called **Three-Body Problem**. Henri Poincaré proved in 1887 that there is no mathematical solution for what happens to the position, mass, and velocity of three or more bodies that interact over time. Thus, the science of complex systems. Instead of trying to calculate how every individual in a massive population influences every other individual, whether quanta in quantum mechanics or people in culture, the science of complex systems tries to understand the emergence of stable patterns from the interaction of large numbers of individuals that all interact with each other. The basic situation that is relevant for complex systems occurs around us all the time, whether in the cells of your body, the trees in a forest, or the animals in a (complex) ecological system.

People are not ants. We can choose what to do and how to do it, at least within the limitations of where we are and how we are set in life. Still, we are all members of a great complex system that we can call our culture, and our choices tend to bring us together. Bowling is not the sport for everybody, but keglers do find each other and share the game together. People who move from one place to another find neighbors who have the same religious preference. These choices are facilitated by specific places where people can go, like bowling alleys and churches, but many choices do not come with any specific place to go to join an activity. Man United fans may find a pub where they can watch matches with other fans of like mind, even if they are not in Manchester; in major American cities, graduates of distant universities often meet at a sports bar to watch football or basketball games with their fellow alumni. You can watch all kinds of Australian football in Honolulu bars. We are good at finding each other. If we walk into the wrong pub, say the one with hip-hop music in it when we were looking for jazz, we can walk out and try again in another one. Our choices may be quite specific: if somebody likes to get some exercise, the choices may involve how old or young the other people at the gym may be, or what equipment or activities are on offer, or even what time of day to go work out. The result of all of these choices and cultural interactions is the emergence of groups of like-minded people. Of course some of the people in the pub will not be there for music, and some of the people in the church or gym will still be seeking their best group, so emergence is not the same thing as uniformity. And some university graduates may prefer to watch their team at home, and some bowlers might come to prefer the video-game version in their living rooms to the actual lanes, so emergence does not attract all of the eligible people. Overall, however, we are good at finding people who make similar choices to our own and so cultural groups emerge within the complex system of our culture.

Complex systems have been discovered relatively recently, at least in comparison to the kind of cause-and-effect science that Isaac Newton championed in the seventeenth century. Complex systems were originally described in the physical (e.g., quantum mechanics) and biological (e.g., ecology, the immune system) sciences, and the definite procedures of information exchange have been explored in mathematics and computer science (e.g., Turing machines). Stephen Hawking included complex systems in his popular book about physics, *The Grand Design*; and Stephen Jay Gould and many others have pursued complex systems in evolutionary biology and genetics. Again, complexity science does not replace the more familiar kind of modern science that looks for particular causes for every effect, as when we expect that any action causes an equal and opposite reaction: if you drop a glass on the floor, it is still likely to break! However, we now know that some aspects of the world around us are not best described in terms of any simple cause for an effect. The emergence of order in a complex system cannot be computed as the sum of the small causes of every separate interaction in the process, even if we could track every interaction in a massive system of components, as Poincaré demonstrated. Individual interactions are unpredictable, subject to randomness just as we saw in the behavior of ants, and order in the system emerges as frequency patterns, not as uniform, homogeneous outcomes. Complex systems turn out to be a better way than causes and effects to understand many kinds of questions, from quantum physics to evolutionary biology to ecology. They are an excellent fit for human language. Because of how complex systems operate we cannot say *why* languages change, we cannot exactly specify the causes; instead, we can talk about *how* different spoken habits, and later written habits, emerge among groups of people who talk and write to each other.

There are just a few things that are most important to consider about complex systems of any kind, including human language. First, complex systems are always in motion; they depend upon continuing interaction among the elements of the system, for language depends on all of the speakers who are using it. If the system stops, it dies. So, for example, we call Latin a "dead" language because there is no longer any group of speakers who use it routinely for their daily communication (except perhaps some in the Vatican, though quite a few people do still read it). We might say the same thing about Old English (see Chapter 5), also a language without active speakers today – although there are groups of speakers who routinely use a more recent form of English, just as speakers of Italian, French, and Spanish are using more recent forms of Latin. Next, the speakers of a language notice, even if they do not notice consciously, how other speakers use their language in different groups and different settings, and speakers then adjust how they talk, even if they do so unconsciously, so that they tend to use the same words or pronunciation or grammar that other speakers do in the same groups or the same situations. So, for example, people who interact in the same local area or region, or who interact in the same social groups, tend to use the same words and pronunciation and grammar as the people they talk to. This leads to the last important characteristic of complex systems: **feedback** among the speakers who are busy interacting with each other leads to the emergence of stable patterns of language. People share information with each other in their interactions, just as ants share information with each other in theirs, and the feedback from sharing information leads to emergence. Such emergence gives us regional dialects, or different varieties of a language for social groups in the same place.

The great thing about complex systems is that they allow us to have many different varieties of a language, even at the same time and in the same place, not to mention across wide areas. We speakers are not stuck with just one kind of language. We can keep track of the different choices in language that we associate with different places and groups, and, consciously or not, we tend to use different features in different settings. Talk in the family is not the same as talk in the classroom, or talk in the courtroom, or talk on the factory floor. Some speakers are better than others at managing these different choices, but we all make them. The complex system of language is not once and done; the complex system continues to operate over time, as long as speakers keep talking to each other, so that every language continues to grow and change over time. This has been true of human language since its origins millennia ago, and it is true of English now. New linguistic habits emerge from the activity of the system in every group, in every place. You cannot stop change in language without killing it, or rather without loss of the population of speakers who use it. This we know from Latin and Old English, but also from endangered languages in our own time. The title of this book thus comes from complex systems: the "emergence of English" does not just mean how it first came to be recognized as a language, but how it continues to grow and change in its own right today.

So, we can sum up the process of all complex systems in just a few principles: 1) random interaction of large numbers of components, 2) continuing activity in the system, 3) exchange of information with feedback, 4) reinforcement of behaviors, 5) emergence of stable patterns without central control. These principles continue to operate according to the contingencies that occur over time, so that the stable patterns can change over time. For speech, the randomly interacting "components" are all of the different variant realizations of linguistic features as they are used by human agents, speakers. These "features" might be different pronunciations, or different words for the same thing, or different ways of saying or writing the same thing, really any aspect of speech that is recognizable for itself and therefore countable. The activity in the system consists of all of our conversations and writing. The exchange of information is not the same as sharing the meaningful content of what we say and write (which is exchange in a different sense), but instead our implicit comparison of the use of different components by different speakers and writers, as they use them in different kinds of conversations and writings. Feedback from exchange of information causes reinforcement, in that speakers and writers are more likely to employ particular components in future occurrences of particular circumstances for conversations and writing. Human agents, unlike ants, can think about and choose their words, but that does not change the basic operation of feedback and reinforcement; we all make choices inside of the complex system of speech, in relation to current circumstances. The order that emerges in speech is simply the configuration of components, whether particular words, pronunciations, or grammatical constructions, that comes to occur in the local communities, regional and social, and in the occasions for speech and writing in which we actually communicate. The fact that complex systems react to contingencies means that the order we can see in speech at any time, whether among regional or social groups of speakers, will change to go along with new circumstances. The process at work in complex systems just explains better what we already knew: we tend to talk like the people nearby, either physically near or socially near, or both, and we tend to use the same linguistic tools that others do when we are writing or saying the same kind of thing.

2.3 **Emergence in Language**

Just as an example of what emerges from our linguistic interactions, we can consider all the different words that Americans use to describe a heavy rainstorm (Figure 2.2). These answers come from a survey of 1162 people in the Eastern USA, in the middle part of the twentieth century. All of this data, and much more like it, is freely available at the Linguistic Atlas Project website, www.lap.uga.edu. Figure 2.2 gives the top-ten list of words people used for the survey overall, and then separately for the men and the women in the survey. The next rows of Figure 2.2 then give the top-ten list for three different age groups, and for three different regional groups. To be clear, each of the top-ten lists has the same survey answers from the same people, just sorted out by gender and age and place; the numbers in the tally thus look larger for the survey overall than they do for each subgroup. The numbers in the top-ten lists do not add up to the same totals because the subgroups are not exactly the same size, and even if they were, there are many less frequent words not shown in addition to those that made the top ten in each list. The word *cloudburst* used to be very popular, but now about fifty years after the Eastern States survey many younger Americans do not even recognize it; these are the most common words at the time of the survey – including *gully washer*, which may also seem strange to many readers.

The first thing to see is that not everybody used the same word; moreover, many words were commonly used not only overall but in every subgroup. Our vocabulary is more varied in common use than we might ever have believed. Some lists have words not in the other lists (can you find *trash mover*, *pouring rain*, and *pouring down rain?*), but most of the top-ten lists have the same words on them. Another thing to see is that the lists are not in quite the same order for all of the groups, and that not one of the subgroups has the words in the same order as the list for the survey overall. For example, men and women reverse the order of *cloudburst* and *downpour* at the top of the list, and there is a big difference in the tally between the first- and second-place words for men and women, while the top two are nearly equivalent in the survey overall. Thus, the process of interaction and emergence has

All	2052	Men	1441	Women	611
cloudburst	345	cloudburst	260	downpour	151
downpour	332	downpour	180	cloudburst	85
heavy rain	171	heavy rain	132	hard rain	43
hard rain	146	hard rain	103	heavy rain	39
gully washer	120	gully washer	83	gully washer	37
big rain	84	flood	68	big rain	28
flood	84	big rain	56	hard shower	24
pourdown	61	pourdown	43	pourdown	18
hard shower	57	heavy shower	38	flood	16
heavy shower	47	hard shower	33	shower	10

Younger	678	Middle	739	Older	624
downpour	172	downpour	103	cloudburst	86
cloudburst	162	cloudburst	95	heavy rain	59
heavy rain	55	heavy rain	57	downpour	56
hard rain	42	hard rain	56	hard rain	48
gully washer	36	gully washer	48	gully washer	35
hard shower	20	flood	39	big rain	33
big rain	17	big rain	33	flood	30
pourdown	16	pourdown	25	pourdown	20
flood	14	hard shower	23	heavy shower	15
heavy shower	14	trash mover	19	hard shower	14

Northern (NY/NJ/PA)	517	Midland (WV/MD/DE/DC/VA)	459	Southern (NC/SC/GS/FL)	1072
cloudburst	140	downpour	94	downpour	144
downpour	94	cloudburst	77	cloudburst	128
heavy rain	41	hard rain	47	gully washer	89
heavy shower	32	heavy rain	43	heavy rain	87
hard rain	23	gully washer	29	hard rain	76
flood	21	pourdown	28	big rain	58
hard shower	21	hard shower	22	flood	49
pouring rain	11	big rain	21	trash mover	36
pourdown	10	flood	14	pourdown	22
big rain	7	heavy shower	8	squall	17
		pouring down rain	8		

Figure 2.2 Words for a heavy rainstorm, Eastern USA, mid twentieth century (Linguistic Atlas Project, www.lap.uga.edu)

created somewhat different **frequency profiles** for the survey overall and for each of the subgroups.

When we look at all the survey responses (Figure 2.3), not just those in the top ten, we find that a great many words were only collected from one or two people. Still, there are very few of those 184 terms for heavy rain that we have trouble understanding. Many of them appear to be short phrases containing more than one word, but deciding what to call a "word" can be

All	2052						
cloudburst	345	downfall	7	a-pouring down	2	squash up	1
downpour	332	pourdown rain	7	awful shower	2	big fresh	1
heavy rain	171	rainy spell	7	deluge of rain	2	big hard washing	
hard rain	146	washout	7	fresh	2	rain	1
gully washer	120	frog strangler	6	good shower	2	big lot of rain	1
big rain	84	heavy downpour	6	hard storm	2	big pour of rain	1
flood	84	lighterd knot		heavy downpour		big rainfall	1
NA	62	floater	6	of rain	2	big storm	1
pourdown	61	terrible rain	6	heavy pourdown	2	bottle washer	1
hard shower	57	washing rain	6	heavy weather	2	chunk mover	1
heavy shower	47	washup	6	lighterd knot		clay soaker	1
NR	45	big shower	5	mover	2	cloud	1
trash mover	37	powerful rain	5	lightwood knot		cloudburster	1
squall	25	rain	5	floater	2	devil of a shower	1
deluge	21	ground soaker	4	mighty hard rain	2	ditch maker	1
shower	20	heavy rainstorm	4	pour	2	dog mire	1
freshet	15	raining cats		pourdown of rain	2	drencher	1
pouring rain	15	and dogs	4	pouring down	2	dropdown	1
pouring		soaker	4	rainfall	2	flash flood	1
down rain	14	trash lifter	4	raining hard	2	flash shower	1
flood of rain	9	very heavy rain	4	storm	2	flash storm	1
good rain	9	big heavy rain	3	stump lifter	2	flood down	1
rainstorm	9	downpour of rain	3	torrential rain	2	flood rain	1
torrent	9	downspout	3	waterfall	2	flop down	1
water spout	8	hell of a rain	3	ant mire	1	godsend	1
wet spell	8	quite a shower	3	awful hard rain	1	good big heavy	
awful rain	7	raining bullfrogs	3	awful heavy rain	1	rain	1
gully mover	1	toad strangler	3	awful rainstorm	1	good seeding	1
gully rinser	1	trash piler	3	big fall of water	1	gully buster	1
gully wash	1	large rain	1	pretty good rain	1	gully digger	1
gush	1	lighterd knot		pretty heavy rain	1	storm rain	1
gushing rain	1	lifter	1	quick rain	1	temperance	1
hard falling		lighterd knot		rain pourdown	1	flood rain	
down rain	1	soaker	1	raining	1	temperance rain	1
hard mild rain	1	liquid sunshine	1	raining pitchforks	1	terrible big rain	1
hard rainstorm	1	log mover	1	real heavy rain	1	terrific rain	1
hardest rain	1	long rain	1	regular deluge	1	toad frog	
hasty	1	lot of rain	1	regular flood	1	drownder	1
heap of rain	1	main coast storm	1	regular pouring		toad frog	
heavy dash		mighty lot of rain	1	down rain	1	strangler	1
of rain	1	milldam buster	1	right smart rain	1	trash floater	1
heavy fall		near flood	1	root soaker	1	tremendous rain	1
of water	1	nice rain	1	sand sifter	1	tub soaker	1
heavy flood		old time rain	1	set rain	1	very hard rain	1
of rain	1	potato bed soaker	1	severe rain	1	very heavy	
heavy rainfall	1	pour out	1	sharp shower	1	shower	1
heavy storm	1	pouring	1	shower of rain	1	watergall burst	1
hell of a		pourout	1	sight of rain	1	wet weather	
downpour	1	pours	1	sky	1	shower	1
knot floater	1	powerful shower	1	soak	1	young flood	1
		pretty big rain	1	soaking rain	1		

Figure 2.3 All the different terms collected for 'heavy rain', edited to merge plural forms with singular forms, to group finite verbs and prepositional phrases, and to remove initial articles; NA = Not Asked, NR = No Response (adapted from Linguistic Atlas Project, www.lap.uga.edu)

troublesome: in Figure 2.3 many of the terms are compound words, and many others might well be, like *gully washer*, so we might well count them as single terms.

At the same time, there is the same basic pattern in the tallies for each group, whether overall or a smaller group: there are a few words at the top that are very common, but the numbers pretty quickly decline to much smaller numbers. Figure 2.4 shows graphs of the frequency profiles of the terms, arranged from the most frequent to the least frequent. For the survey overall, the graph of all the information in Figure 2.3, we see a sharp curve, which we can call an **A-curve** (short for asymptotic hyperbolic curve),

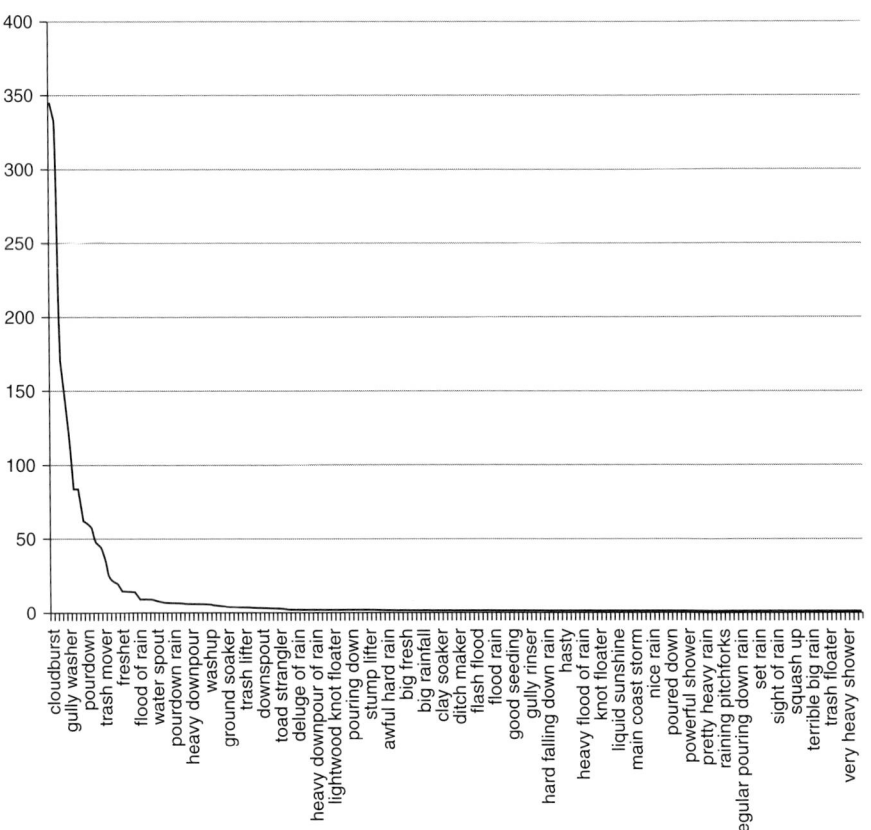

The whole survey

Figure 2.4 Graphs of the frequency profiles of terms for 'heavy rain' (adapted from Linguistic Atlas Project, www.lap.uga.edu)

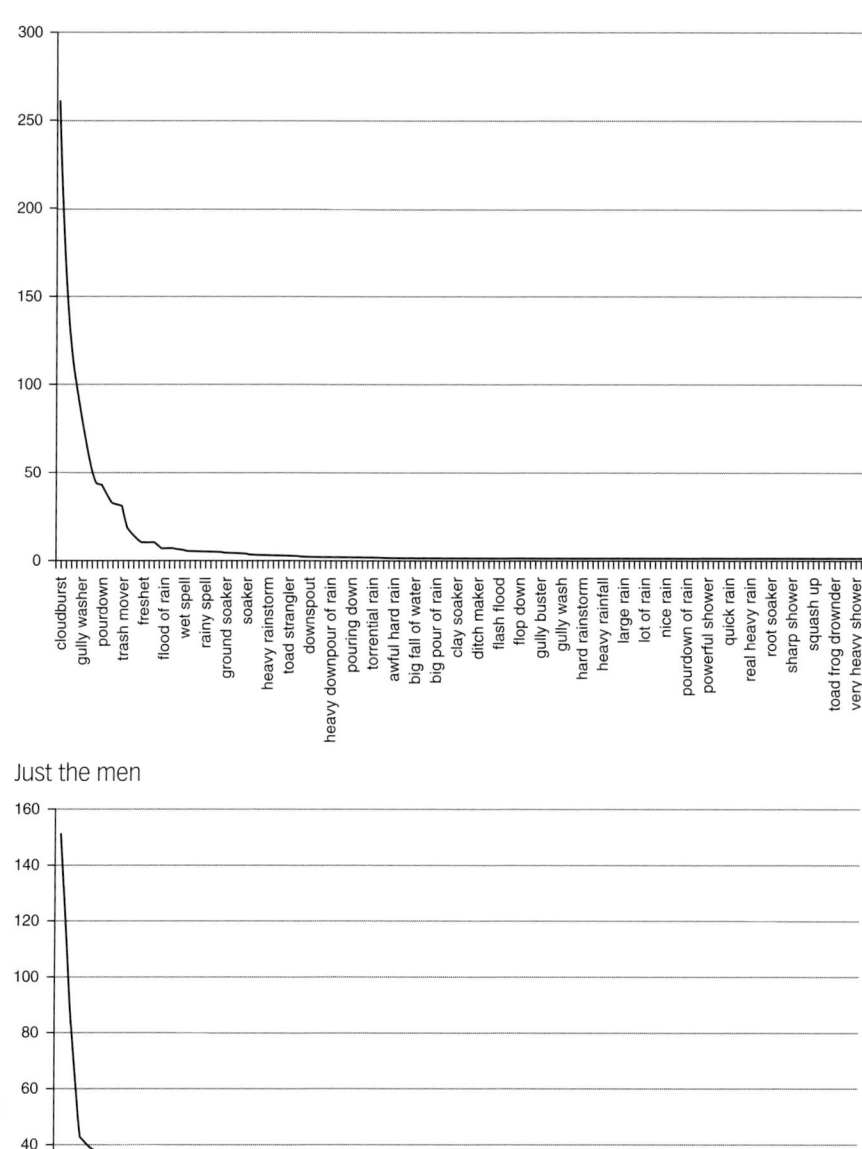

Just the men

Just the women

Figure 2.4 (cont.)

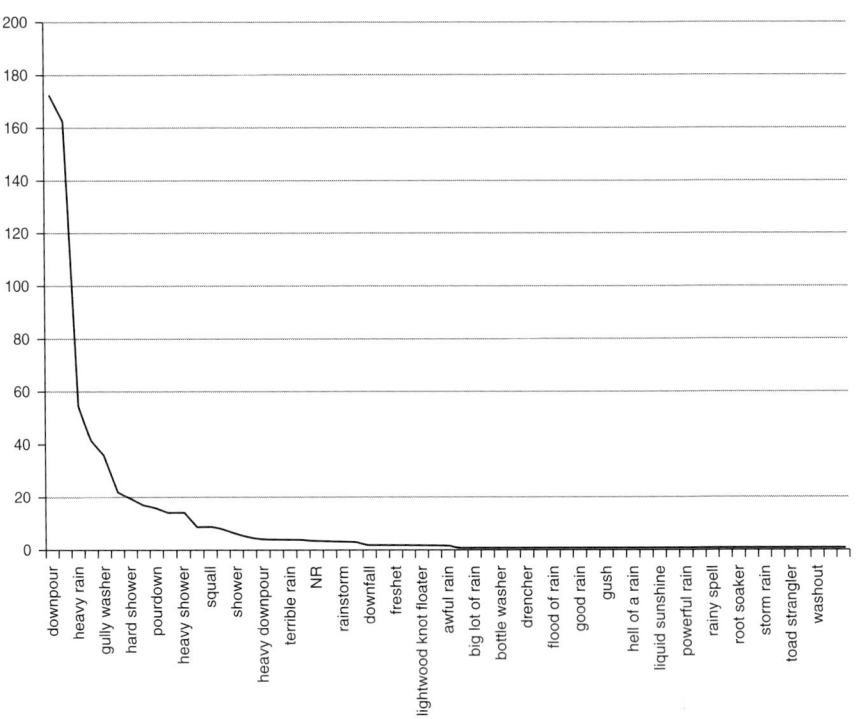

Just the younger speakers

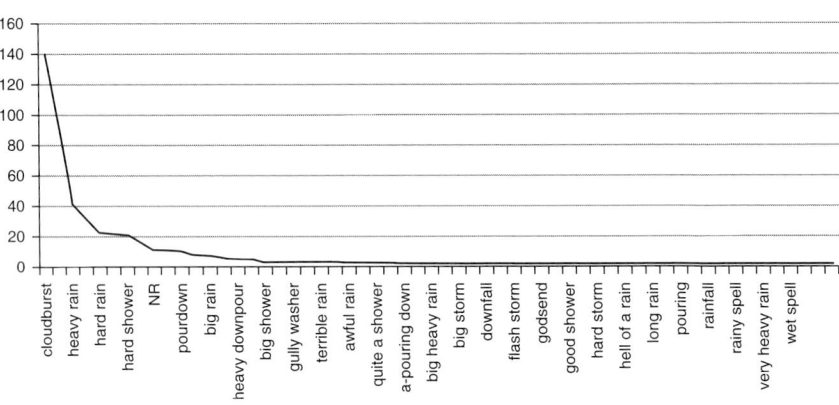

Just the Northern speakers

Figure 2.4 (cont.)

formed by the few very common words at the left declining to a long tail at the right of all the words that the survey only collected from one speaker. Each of the other subgroups from the survey shown in Figure 2.2 also have the same kind of curve, as shown in Figure 2.4 for the men, the women, the younger speakers, and the Northern and Southern speakers. This shows

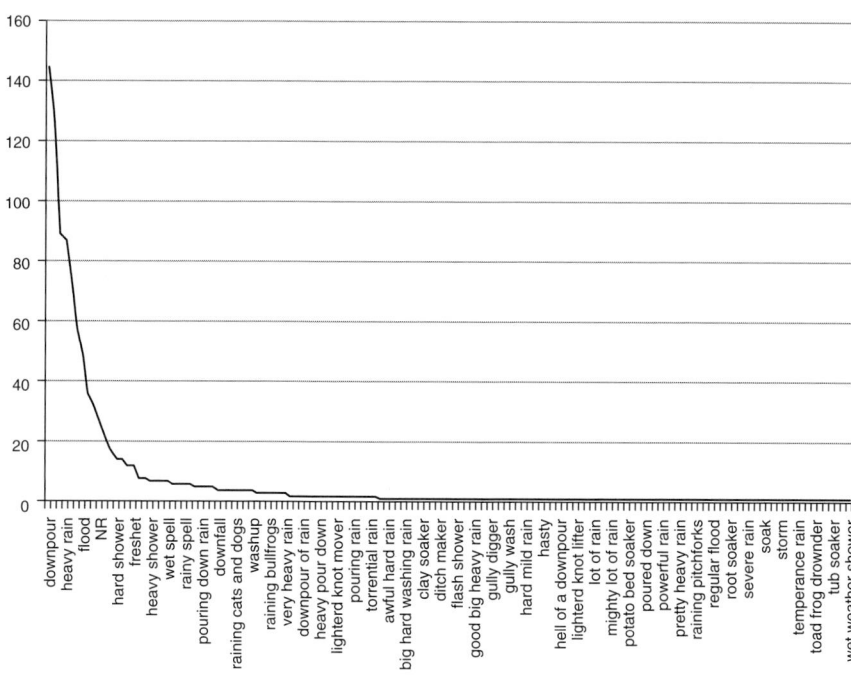

Just the Southern speakers

Figure 2.4 (cont.)

the characteristic **scaling** behavior that occurs in complex systems, where the A-curve pattern is repeated over and over in every subgroup of the data as well as in the data set overall. The A-curve and scaling properties that we see in speech are known in mathematics as a **fractal** pattern with **self-similarity**.

Thus, we see the complex system of speech in action. A few words emerge as the most frequent ones, while whole lists of words are still in use less frequently. The pattern may not seem complex; the complexity in complex systems comes from the interactions of all individuals, not from the pattern that emerges. Most of the different words in the list only occur once or twice among the large population of speakers interviewed for this project. The existence of the A-curve pattern demonstrates that speakers of English simply do not agree on what to call things, and we tolerate a wide variety of choices in our lexicon as names for things and ideas. Even though all of the speakers surveyed were Americans, they did not use exactly the same words at exactly the same rates from region to region and from age group to age group. Men and women are different, too, but not so different that we are likely to misunderstand each other – at least when we talk about heavy rain – and the same can be said of the different regions and ages.

31

The cultural interaction that creates these frequency profiles in word use is a process that takes time, and as we now know from the word *cloudburst* that is no longer recognized by younger Americans, the process does not stop. Some changes like this can go very fast, like the decline of *cloudburst*, but others can take a very long time to emerge. Language change does not always proceed at the same rate. Continuing cultural interaction between people keeps the process going so that new frequency profiles continue to emerge all the time, both overall for a large national group like American speakers and for every subgroup within it, like those for gender, age, and region.

The same A-curve pattern, with its scaling property, occurs for every word, pronunciation, and grammatical arrangement in English. What we have seen for heavy rain is also true of what to call a dragonfly or of familiar names for parents. It occurs for how to make plurals: think of the differences between *desks, houses, sheep, oxen,* or the fact that some people say *three mile* when others say *three miles.* In the Eastern US survey, interviewers recorded 243 different ways to pronounce the vowel in the word *fog* in a fine phonetic transcription, and there are still thirty-four different pronunciations of the vowel in a broad IPA transcription without diacritical marks (see Appendix 1 for information about the IPA). Grammar may not seem like it could have A-curves, since the point of a grammar is to make a generalization about how words are put together, but if we consider not the generalization but the words used in any grammatical construction, the different words will occur in an A-curve. For instance, if you think of the different verbs that could be used in a construction like "We went there," forms of *go* would be most common, and we could make an A-curve with *go* at the top and alternates like forms of *drive, walk, run, fly, crawl,* and a great many other verbs further down the curve. Every aspect of English is subject to change owing to interactions between speakers in the complex system, and the A-curve pattern emerges for many variant ways to say something at every level of scale.

When we consider A-curves for the same topic over time, we can see that particular variants move up and down the curve. Burkette (2001) considered words for bedroom furniture (e.g., where you keep your socks) over time by using the earlier Eastern States survey and a smaller survey by Johnson (1996) from fifty years later. Johnson only interviewed people in American Southern states, so differences in Burkette's comparison might come from the difference in time, or might come from the difference in place, but here let us think about the difference in time. Figure 2.5 shows the two lists of variants and the two A-curves. In both surveys, large and small the A-curve that we expect does appear. The thing to note is the order o

Mid 20th Century, Eastern States		Late 20th Century, Johnson	
bureau	1104	dresser	18
dresser	380	chest of drawers	17
chest of drawers	227	bureau	5
chest	42	chest	5
sideboard	34	washstand	2
washstand	30	highboy	2
highboy	27	dresser drawers	1
chiffonier	22	bachelor's chest	1
trunk	22	chest on chest	1
drawers	19	dressing table	1
bureau drawers	19	linen press	1
commode	17	press	1
dressing table	9	vanity dresser	1
box	8		
stand	7		
lowboy	5		
chest on chest	4		
vanity	4		
desk	3		
case of drawers	3		
dresser of drawers	3		
stand of drawers	2		
set of drawers	2		
blanket chest	1		
cabinet	1		
checkrobes	1		
chest upon a chest	1		
clothes stand	1		
clothespress	1		
chifforobe drawers	1		
cupboard	1		
bookcases	1		
cabinet table	1		
kast	1		
vanity dresser	1		
wardrobe	1		
wash hands stand	1		

Figure 2.5 Words for bedroom furniture, Mid versus Late Twentieth Century (adapted from Burkette, 2001)

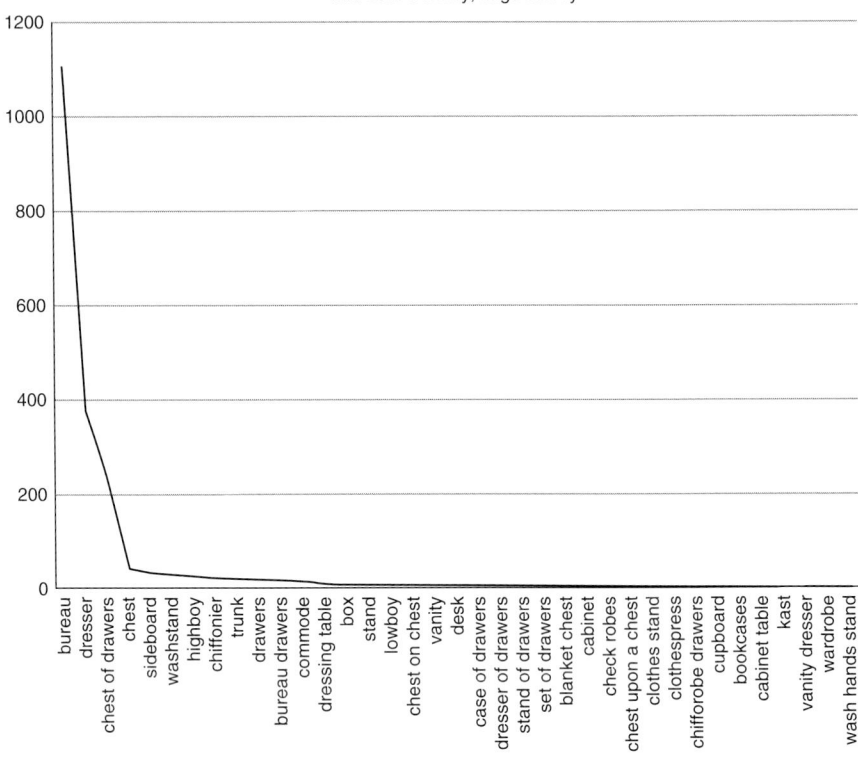

Mid 20th Century, large survey

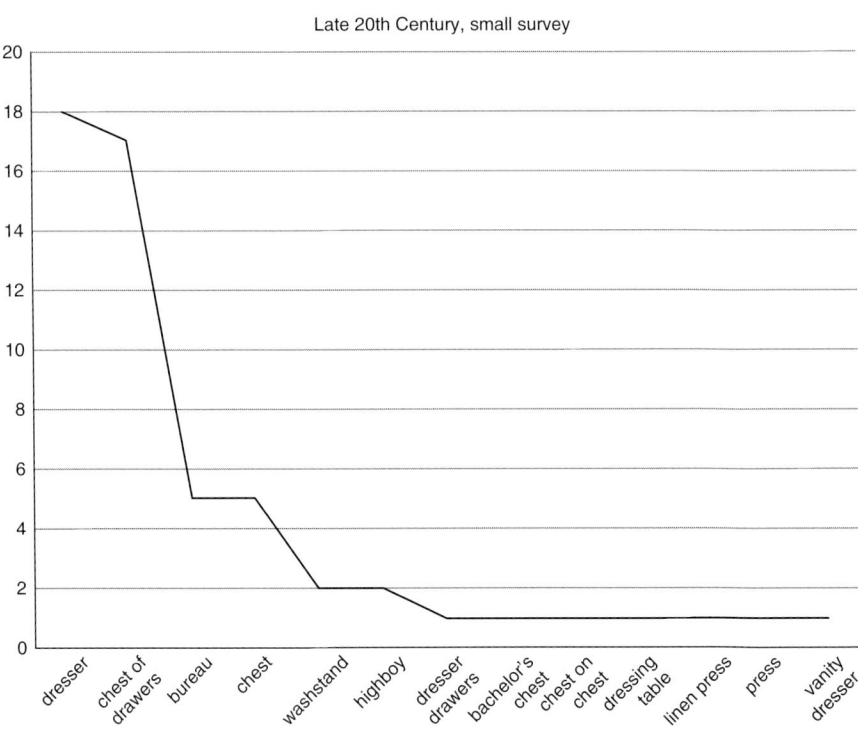

Late 20th Century, small survey

Figure 2.5 (cont.)

variants on the lists. *Bureau* has gone from the top-ranked variant in the earlier survey down to the third-ranked variant in the later survey. *Dresser* and *chest of drawers* have each climbed up the curve. *Chest*, which had been further down the curve in the earlier survey, is now at the same level as *bureau* in the later survey. If we consider time to be the cause of these differences, then we can see that a linguistic change is really a change in the frequency profile. *Dresser* has not replaced *bureau* entirely, just climbed up the curve to take the top rank while *bureau* has fallen down in rank. The difference in frequency is not small: *bureau* was three times as common as *dresser* in the earlier survey, and in the later survey *dresser* is about three times as common as *bureau*. Changing just one or two steps in rank is a big change at the top of the A-curve, and just a small change in the long tail at the bottom. For the history of the English language, then, we should understand that a language always maintains a large number of variants for any feature, whether names for bedroom furniture or realizations of sounds in the language or grammatical usages. We will want to be thinking about changes at the top of the A-curve at any moment in time from earlier times, and we will understand that it is easy for words or other linguistic features to enter an A-curve as variants towards the bottom in the long list of variants.

There is an old song written by George and Ira Gershwin, "Let's Call the Whole Thing Off," with famous lyrics about whether you say *tomato* [təmeɪtoʊ] and I say [təmɑtoʊ] (see Appendix 1 for how to read the IPA phonetic symbols that tell the difference in the pronunciation here). The Gershwins just expressed the popular understanding that choices between words, or between pronunciations, are all or nothing, that we have to choose one way or the other way. In fact, as our survey data shows, we do not have such simple choices in language. The romantic song has a happy ending because one singer gives up *pajamas* [pədʒɑməz] to say [pədʒæməz] and thus saves the relationship. In real life, we can just choose to say one thing in one set of circumstances and another thing in a different set of circumstances: [təmeɪtoʊ] and [pədʒæməz] to keep the peace at home, and [təmɑtoʊ] and [pədʒɑməz] when we go out to buy them. The complex system of speech gives us many choices – not just the two illustrated by the Gershwins – and we can use them as we think best to fit the circumstances of the conversation or writing.

The existence of complex systems in our cultural interactions allows us to be diverse, and at the same time allows us still to show ourselves through our behavioral choices to be members of our regions and groups at every level. Complexity science thus describes the process by which we perceive our language behavior to be associated with our communities and practices; it is the underlying process for the creation of what we call language varieties or dialects. Complex systems science, therefore, offers a model that can explain the multidimensional layering of cultural regions and groups described by Zelinsky (1992). The complex systems approach accommodates the decisions that speakers make about their language in every kind of conversation and occasion for writing and by extension their participation in every recurrent cultural situation. Complex systems allow us to recognize and honor the linguistic and cultural decisions that every individual has to make, and at the same time to understand how such decisions result in local and larger cultural patterns. Complex systems also gives us a good way to understand the historical information about the English language that we are about to see.

2.4 **Chapter Summary**

This chapter focused attention on all of the different groups that people form in our culture, whether regions or groups defined by interests or behavior. Individuals all have a wide range of different beliefs and interests, and they all participate in many different cultural groups. Complex systems was explained as a new kind of science that can explain how we can maintain such a multidimensional array of different groups. The operation of the complex system of human language has left frequency profiles in our language that correspond to different subgroups within an overall population. The scaling property of this fractal pattern is what allows us to have somewhat different language in all of the different groups to which we belong.

Key Terms
A-curve
complex systems
contingency
culture
culture region
emergence
feedback
fractal
frequency profile
group formation
scaling
self-similarity
Three Body Problem

Exercises

2.1 How many groups do you belong to? Make a list of them, including regional and social groups, and also including activities in which you participate. Don't forget that some groups are big and other groups are quite small.

2.2 Think about areas of your experience besides language (or ants) where you think complex systems may operate. Can you think of other insects or animals that create noticeable patterns without central control? Can you think of situations where massive numbers of participants interact with each other?

2.3 Make a list of the different words for heavy rain that you think you use. Try to think of things that you might occasionally say, not just the word or two that you usually use. When you really think about it, is your list composed of just one or two terms? Have you heard other people use terms other than the ones you would use? You can look up information from the Eastern States survey of American English at www.lap.uga.edu, under the LAMSAS project. More information, this time from the Southern States, is available from the same source under the LAGS project.

2.4 How many of the different terms (whether words or short phrases) for heavy rain do you recognize in Figure 2.3? How many do you think you have used yourself? Do you have any terms for heavy rain that do not occur in the list? You can look up information from the Eastern States survey of American English at www.lap.uga.edu, under the LAMSAS project. More information, this time from the Southern States, is available from the same source under the LAGS project.

2.5 Consider other common aspects of life besides heavy rain. Can you think of different terms people might use to refer to the following things: pancakes, athletic shoes, the drink made with milk and ice cream, the drink that is fizzy and usually sweet and often sold in cans or bottles, the piece of furniture in the bedroom where you keep small items of clothing like socks? If you can only think of one word for these things, you should ask other people what they say. Make a list of all the terms for these things. You can look up information from the Eastern States survey of American English at www.lap .uga.edu, under the LAMSAS project. More information, this time from the Southern States, is available from the same source under the LAGS project.

Further reading

Zelinsky (1992). First published in 1973, this brief, classic textbook of cultural geography both outlines the field and comments on American culture. Part Three contains Zelinsky's rethinking after twenty years of many of his original ideas, with some generally pessimistic comments on developments in American culture. Readers may or may not agree with the later comments, but will find no clearer presentation of the structures and patterns of American culture. Treatments of the cultural geography of other English-speaking countries are of course also available. A treatment of language and region that develops Zelinsky's ideas is Kretzschmar (2011).

A good, readable introduction to complex systems is Mitchell (2009): the ant section of this chapter is derived from Mitchell's book. Complexity science arose in the second half of the twentieth century, one landmark being the foundation of the Santa Fe Institute in 1984 (see www.santafe.edu). For a foundational study of complex systems and language, see Kretzschmar (2009), and for applications of complex systems to many fields within linguistics see Kretzschmar (2015). For an introduction to complex systems and language, see Burkette and Kretzschmar (2018). Many linguists have developed ideas that approximate some aspects of complex systems as described here, and the particular value of complex systems is that, as a scientific model, it can associate them together.

Burkette (2001) connects all the different names for bedroom furniture to colonial American pattern books for carpenters. Johnson (1996) reports on a large number of different items, not just furniture.

For those interested in complex systems as they apply in other sciences, there are a number of books that are not too technical for non-specialists. The application of complex systems to quantum mechanics is described, with panache, in Hawking and Mlodinow (2010). A readable application of complexity to financial markets occurs in Mandelbrot and Hudson (2004): the most recent printing includes comments on the 2008 economic crash. Mandelbrot (1982) is the originator of fractals, the mathematical basis for the A-curve and scaling described in this chapter. Mandelbrot applies fractals to many fields; the mathematics in the book may be daunting to many readers, but the pictures are attractive for everyone. For the view of complex systems from computer science, see Holland (1998). For broad coverage of complexity versus reductionism in science from the point of view of an evolutionary biologist, see Gould (2003).

CHAPTER 3

Indo-European

In this chapter

This chapter is about the ancient history of language before the English language existed. We can know little about the origin of human language, but we know that our language must have emerged as a new characteristic kind of behavior belonging to the human species. Indo-European is the name of the language family to which English belongs, from a time before written records but still long after the first emergence of human speech. Today we need to reconstruct what Indo-European must have been like in order to explain the differences in lexicon and pronunciation on the different branches of the Indo-European family tree. The Germanic branch, to which English belongs, emerged from its Indo-European beginnings with its own characteristics, and yet we still need to remember that Germanic was part of a great language continuum all across Europe.

3.1 The English Oak

English belongs to a process of change in our language that began over a millennium ago, when we could first recognize something that we can call English, and continues to this day. The most common metaphor to describe language development is that of the branching tree, perhaps a good old English oak: a single trunk appears to separate into large boughs as we look up the tree at the results of growth over time. Each bough in turn separates into smaller branches, which again separate into yet smaller branches, until we finally see the myriad of tiny twigs that make up the great canopy of the tree. As we have seen in Chapter 1, varieties of a language are not so concrete and easy to distinguish as are the branches of a tree, yet nonetheless the tree metaphor does illustrate at least how our perceptions of difference can take shape in a historical process. After a long period of development in Britain, other branches emerge a good way up the English tree, and then in their turn form their own different branches.

The next chapters will trace the development of these different English voices. First, in this chapter, we need to know about the trunk of our English oak: where English came from, what it was like until the point that other English voices began to branch off, and what circumstances influenced the branching process. Emergence in human language, to return from the tree metaphor to science, started long before there was anything like what we call English. The metaphor of the branches of the tree represents the different groups of people whose choices in language emerged over time as they talked, and much later wrote, to each other and came to give them speech habits that characterize the different groups. The tree metaphor also does a good job of representing the continuity of the process: language patterns among population groups did not just emerge once but keep emerging, keep branching, from ancient times until the present day and beyond. What makes the tree a good metaphor, of course, is that real trees are themselves complex systems, and their real branches emerge in just the kind of patterns we saw in the complex system of speech in Chapter 2.

3.2 Ancient History

The English language is historically related to a family of languages called **Indo-European**. Nobody knows exactly where or when the actual people lived who spoke the first form of Indo-European, perhaps 6000 years ago, now reconstructed (there are no written records from that far back) as Proto-Indo-European. Indo-European was not the original human language. The origins of our most human characteristic are hidden in the far past, probably in Africa where our species, Homo sapiens, emerged. Yes, evolutionary biology is also a complex system in which patterns, which we call species, come to emerge over time. We do not know when our species began to use human language as such, as distinguished from the simpler communicative behavior of many kinds of animals. William Golding's novel *The Inheritors* (1955) offers a fictional portrayal of contact between Neanderthal people (another branch of the Homo genus, Homo neanderthalensis) and Homo sapiens in which the emergence of complex language plays a role. Paleontologists have found evidence of Neanderthal culture from as far back as 300,000 years ago, which is still much more recent than the first emergence of a human-like, tool-using ancestor of man, Homo habilis, about two million years earlier. Some theories propose that Homo sapiens began to act substantially like we do (what anthropologists call "behavioral modernity," including art, music, cooking, and trade over long distances) about 50,000 years ago, and Derek Bickerton (1990) has suggested that the new mode of behavior is associated with the origins of complex human language. Because the evidence of the most recent Neanderthal populations comes from only 30,000 years ago, contact between Neanderthal and Homo sapiens populations could have occurred as Golding imagined. Indeed, there is evidence of Neanderthal DNA in the present human genome, which suggests crossbreeding. Emergence is neither sudden nor exclusive, whether in complex systems of evolutionary biology or of language, so populations of different species and speakers with different frequency profiles of language features can certainly coexist and interact.

Written records from the Indo-European language family only go back as far as about 2000 BC, so what we identify as Indo-European itself must have emerged from the speech of earlier populations. Our earliest records of a written language, Sumerian, survive from about 3000 BC, for example, and Sumerian is not a member of the Indo-European family. In the last few decades one line of research has attempted to connect Indo-European itself as a branch language with a larger family of languages known as **Nostratic**. This hypothesis would connect Indo-European historically with various South Indian and Asian languages, and perhaps even with Native American languages. Its branches include the Afroasiatic, Kartvelian, Indo-European, Uralic (which includes Finno-Ugric), Dravidian, Altaic, and Eskimo-Aleut language families. Sumerian and Etruscan, which have been thought to be examples of an **isolated language** (i.e., a language that does not have a language family), may also possibly be members of the Nostratic family. Proto-Nostratic, the beginnings of Nostratic, would have been spoken about 15,000 years ago. However, "deep reconstruction" of languages this old (anything over 10,000 years) has not won consensus among historical linguists, and so the idea of a Nostratic family of languages remains controversial.

Of course the term **language family** is also a metaphor, like the tree metaphor, that represents the simultaneous existence of populations of speakers in which different language habits have emerged. To use the term "family" emphasizes the relationship between the different populations of speakers, just as the tree metaphor emphasizes the continuous process of development and emergence of populations with different habits. Whether

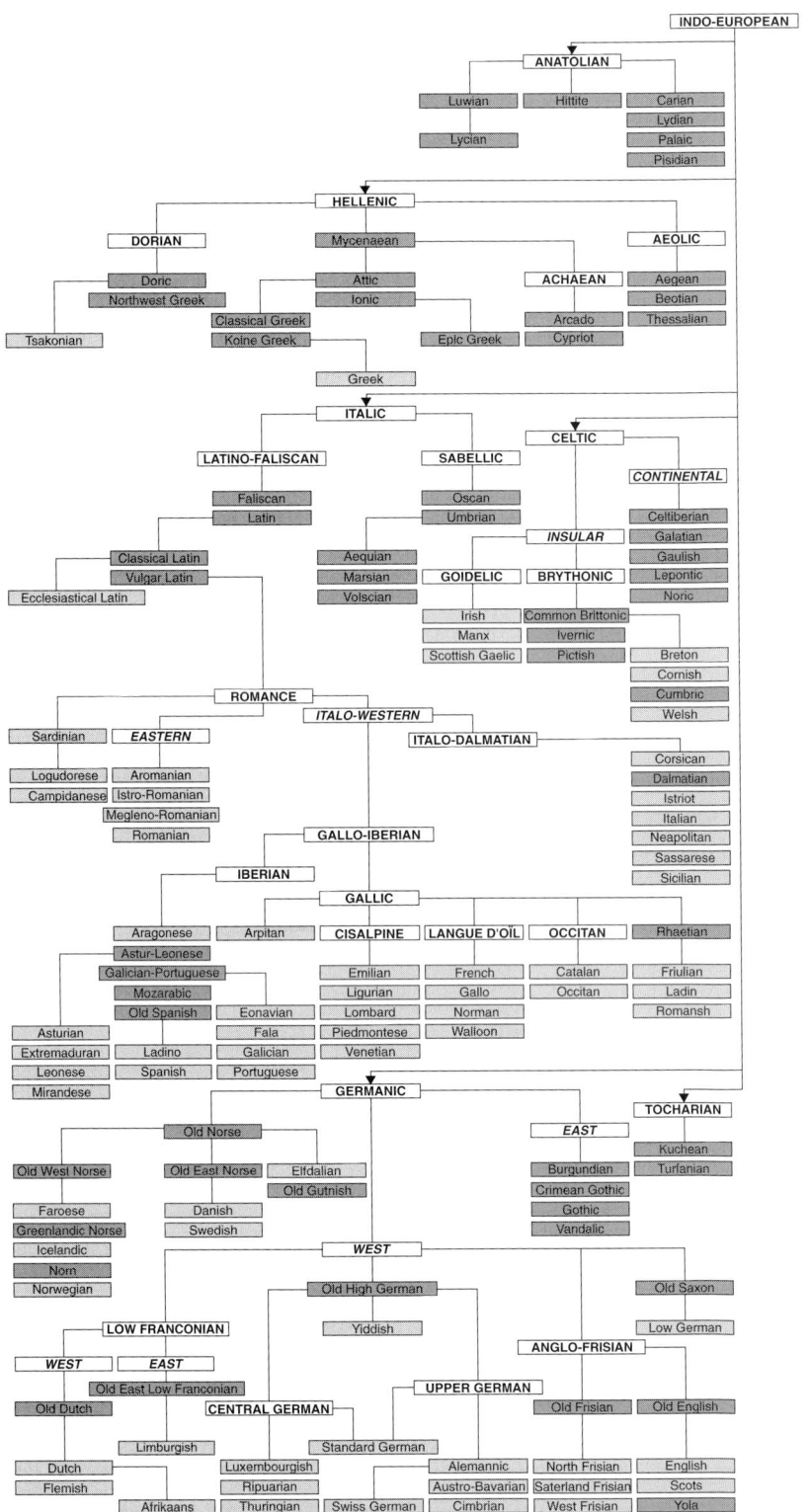

Figure 3.1 *Stemma* of the Indo-European language family. (left side) (Wikipedia commons, viewed from www.ancient.eu/image/1028/)

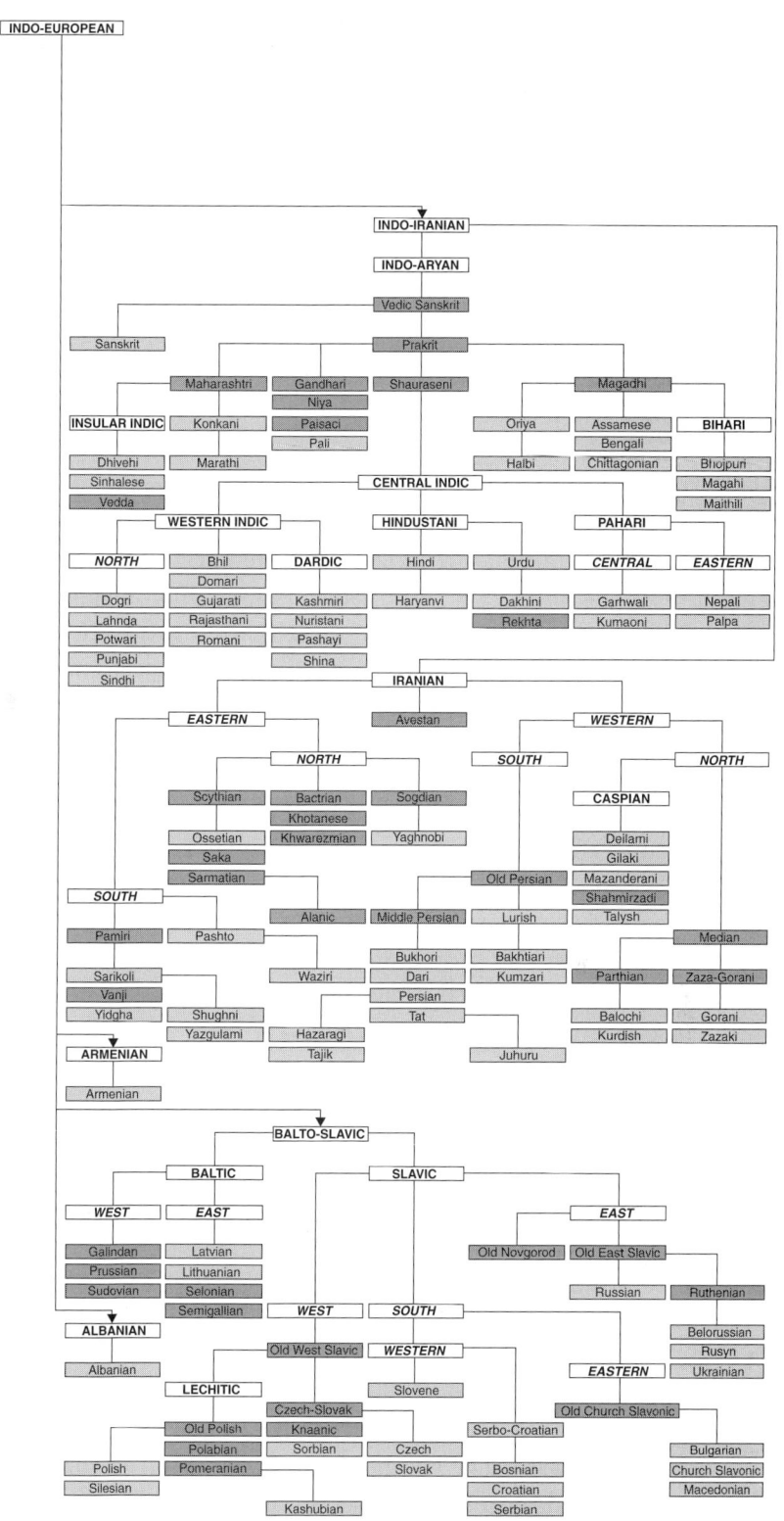

Figure 3.1 (cont.) *Stemma* of the Indo-European language family. (right side) (Wikipedia commons, viewed from www.ancient.eu/image/1028/)

or not we choose to believe the Nostratic hypothesis, it is certain that Indo-European was one language group among many, not the sole ancestor for human languages. When we think about the history of human language, it is always good to think about both the differences and the similarities between different languages.

By 2000 BC the emergent Indo-European language had already begun to branch into what have become its main constituent language groups: Indian, Iranian, Armenian, Hellenic, Albanian, Italic, Balto-Slavic, Germanic, Celtic, Hittite, and Tocharian. Many of these groups in turn branched and rebranched, in the continuing process of emergence, into languages familiar in the modern era; some, like Hittite and Tocharian, became dead languages when they no longer had living communities of speakers. Figure 3.1 shows a **stemma** (the Latin word for a genealogical chart, or **family tree**; dark boxes indicate languages no longer spoken) of the development of the Indo-European languages. To consider an example of what happens as populations of speakers continue to grow and change, the Italic group includes Latin (now no longer spoken by any living community but still taught as a historical language), which in turn developed into Romance languages such as Italian, French, Spanish, and others. Of course today people speak Italian, French, and Spanish in different communities all over the world, and just as for English today, the language habits of those speakers are a little different wherever you go. The existence of languages like Italian, French, and Spanish is good evidence for the operation of the complex system of speech, as Latin emerged from an earlier Italic population of speakers and the different Romance languages emerged from Latin – and as new patterns continue to emerge worldwide today. We should also keep in mind that Latin was not the only language spoken on the Italic peninsula (where Italy is today). Etruscan was another, non-Indo-European language that coexisted for a time with Latin but died out early in the Christian era. Latin "died" when other daughter languages emerged from it in an expanding population, and Etruscan "died" when its population of speakers disappeared. Languages can die in the complex system of speech as well as continue the process of emergence.

The next branch towards English from Indo-European is the **Germanic** languages (at the bottom left of Figure 3.1), which arose in the northwestern part of the Indo-European area. The beginnings of the Germanic languages are still too old for there to be any written records. What must have happened, over great periods of time in the process of emergence, is that the success of the Indo-Europeans in their original homeland caused their population to grow and in turn created the need for them to occupy more territory. The **Kurgan hypothesis** proposes that the original home of the Indo-Europeans was in the Central Asian steppes and the

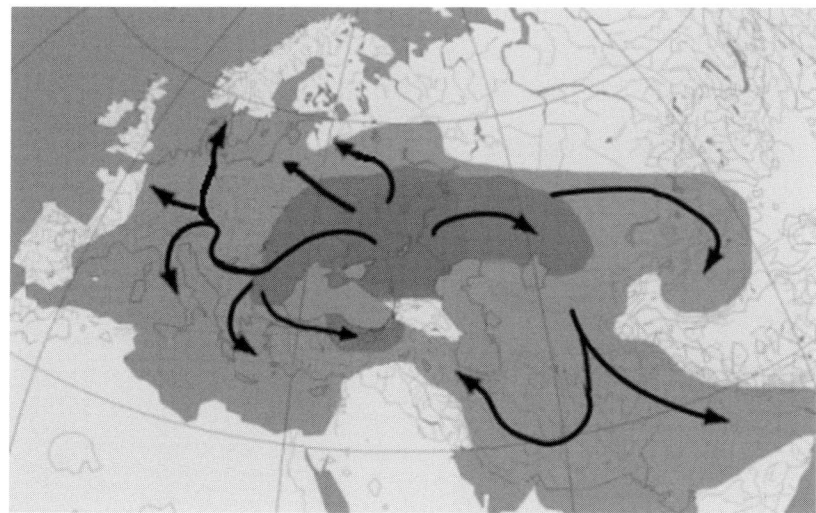

Figure 3.2 Kurgan hypothesis for the spread of the Indo-Europeans (Wikipedia commons)

Indo-European population spread out from there, as shown in Figure 3.2. This proposal is currently the most popular, but controversy remains. Those who prefer to work with the Nostratic hypothesis think that the Indo-Europeans may actually have originated in Northwestern Europe (perhaps Denmark), the general location of the Germanic language family.

Whatever the origin of the Indo-Europeans, the various branches of the Indo-European language family, including Germanic, emerged with different language patterns as a result of differential language change as people moved to settle new areas. That is, when groups of Indo-Europeans moved away from their original homeland, the members within each group would interact more, talk more to each other than they would to members of other groups. Thus, the habits of speech that developed over time within any single group would be different from the habits that developed in any of the other groups. That is, the frequency profile of the linguistic choices that people made in one group became different from the frequency profile of the choices people made in another group. Figure 3.3 shows this process schematically.

The **daisy model** shows schematically how the habits of speech that developed over time within any one of the groups would be different from the habits that developed in any of the other groups. The groups were never entirely separate, however, and people at the edges of the daisy petals could understand each other, as suggested by their overlapping edges. Of course, the daisy is another kind of tree in that it has a branching structure, but this model suggests how the emergence of different varieties of speech in different

45

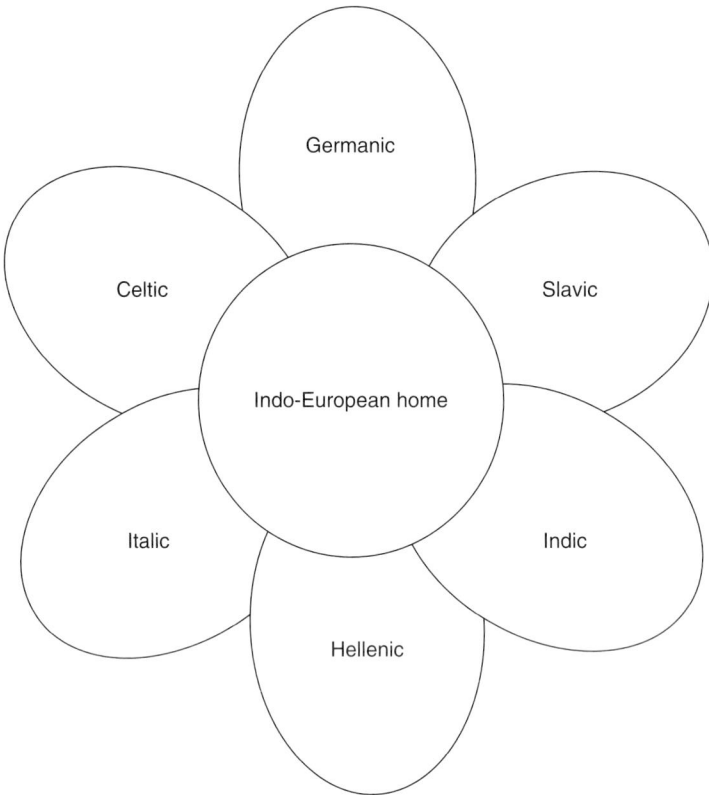

Figure 3.3 Daisy model of Indo-European branches (Author's image)

groups can have continuities, not just separation. It is also the case that population groups did not just move in a regular pattern like the schematic daisy model. For example, the eastern branch of the Germanic people migrated south and west until one Germanic group, the Ostrogoths, ended up in what is now Italy, and another group, the Visigoths, ended up in what is now Spain and Portugal. Such population movements created more opportunities for interaction between population groups. As we will see below, it is also possible for speakers in different branches/petals to borrow words from each other. What is important to remember is that the proximity of speakers interacting with each other makes a big difference: speakers close to each other will have more of an effect on each other than speakers far away.

The central fact of language change is that people are always developing new frequency profiles of how they say things, sometimes consciously but most times not through any deliberate intention. It happened for the Indo-Europeans and their descendants, and it is still happening today. Then and now, these emerging habits tend to follow the residential and other cultural groups to which people belong. The Germanic branch of Indo-European developed in just this way as the generations passed among the ethnically Indo-European people who moved towards and settled the northwest (before some of them kept moving elsewhere). The same thing happened to Indo-Europeans who settled in other directions. The language habits of the Indo-European people who lived south of the Germanic group became **Celtic** or **Italic**, again with the passage of great stretches of time, and the language habits of the Indo-European people who lived east of the Germanic group in time became **Slavic**. The Indo-Europeans expanded from their homeland, wherever it actually was, to cover almost all of the area of modern Europe, as far as India where Sanskrit was the ancestor of several modern Indian languages. In Europe today there are only a few languages not in the Indo-European family, including Finnish, Estonian, and Hungarian from a language family called Finno-Ugric, and Basque, an isolated language that remains from pre-Indo-European times.

3.3 Comparison of the Branches

Historical linguists can trace the population movements that must have occurred by comparing the modern languages that belong to each of these groups. Of course the modern languages are the product of many changes in the intervening thousands of years since the first emergence of these groups from Indo-European, but still there are similarities that offer clues. For example, it is possible to see tantalizing correspondences between languages from different language branches within Indo-European. (The lists in Table 3.1 are adapted from **Carl Darling Buck's** (1949) dictionary of synonyms among the Indo-European languages for many common words.)

It is most often the case that the words for the modern languages grouped together in the same branch are more similar to each other than they are to the words in other branches of Indo-European. The words for *foot*, for example, pattern nicely by language branch according to the initial sound of the words, as do the words for *flower*. English, however, has borrowed the Romance word *flower* as well as keeping the Germanic word *bloom*. There is a little more variation within the branches for *father* and *fish*. Gothic, the eastern component of the Germanic branch, has the word *atta* for 'father,' influenced by the Slavic words to the east. The Romance words for *fish* show the effects of extensive sound changes. Comparisons like these provide the information we need for **reconstruction** of what changes must have occurred from earlier forms of each language and branch.

Between the Indo-European branches there are clear differences in the initial sounds (sometimes the entire word is different), but a closer look will show that some of these differences in initial sounds appear to be systematic. For instance, words that start with /p/ in the Italic languages tend to start with /f/ in the

Table 3.1 *Comparison of Words in Indo-European Branches*

Italic/Romance		Celtic		Germanic		Slavic	
Foot (Buck 4.37)							
Latin	*pes*	Irish	*traig*	Gothic	*fotus*	Slavonic	*noga*
French	*pied*	Welsh	*troed*	Swedish	*fot*	Russian	*noga*
Spanish	*pie*			English	**foot**	Polish	*noga*
Father (Buck 2.35)							
Latin	*pater*	Irish	*athir*	Gothic	*atta*	Slavonic	*otici*
French	*père*	Welsh	*tad*	Swedish	*fader*	Russian	*otec*
Spanish	*padre*			English	**father**	Polish	*ojciec*
Fish (Buck 3.65)							
Latin	*piscis*	Irish	*iasc*	Gothic	*fisks*	Slavonic	*ryba*
French	*poisson*	Welsh	*pysgodyn*	Swedish	*fisk*	Russian	*ryba*
Spanish	*pez*			English	**fish**	Polish	*ryba*
Flower (Buck 8.57)							
Latin	*flos*	Irish	*blath*	Gothic	*bloma*	Slavonic	*cvetu*
French	*fleur*	Welsh	*blodyn*	Swedish	*blomma*	Russian	*cvetok*
Spanish	*flor*			English	**flower, bloom**	Polish	*kwiat*

Adapted from Buck (1949)

Germanic languages. Correspondences like this led in the nineteenth century to the proposal for the **Germanic Sound Shift (Grimm's Law)** (see Table 3.2), under which some original Indo-European consonants are said to change systematically into different consonants in the Germanic branch (see Appendix 1 for how to read the IPA phonetic symbols used to represent the consonant sounds here).

Of course, the Indo-European consonant values are reconstructed: we have no evidence for how early Indo-European speakers actually pronounced things. Our first written evidence of Germanic comes from Bishop Wulfila's translation of the Bible into Gothic, as late as the fourth century AD. However, comparison of sets of words like those presented in Table 3.1 allows us to make a good guess about how early Indo-European speakers most likely pronounced things, and how their pronunciation changed

Table 3.2 *Grimm's Law*

Indo-European		Germanic
/p, t, k/	become	/f, ð, x/
/b, d, g/	become	/p, t, k/
/bh, dh, gh/	become	/b, d, g/

in each of the later branches in the Indo-European language family. In the online Reference Grammar (Moore, Knott, and Hulbert, 1972), §201 to §216 describe Grimm's Law in more detail, as well as other reconstructed changes between Indo-European and Germanic. The regularity of correspondences like this, called **sound changes**, led the great school of nineteenth-century historical linguists called the **Neogrammarians** to proclaim that "sound change operates without exception." The Neogrammarians promoted the idea that languages are systems that can be described and studied scientifically.

One famous sound change between Indo-European and Germanic is called **umlaut**, when words pronounced with [e] in one syllable and followed by an [i, ɪ, j] in the next syllable change so that the first syllables are pronounced with [ɪ]. So, Latin <medius> from the Italic family still has the <e> in the first syllable with an <i> following, while in Old English the word is spelled <midd> with an <i> (even though the following syllable with an [i, ɪ, j] was lost between Germanic and Old English). Modern English still has *mid*, and also *middle*. This is the kind of change we see in Carl Darling Buck's tables, and it accounts for a spelling difference between Latin and both Old English and Modern English.

Besides sound changes, Indo-European and Germanic came to differ in other characteristic ways. Germanic developed a pattern of strong stress on the first syllable of words, a change that would eventually lead to changes in the following syllables, notably the weakening of inflectional endings (that is, they no longer sounded different from each other; see Appendix 2 for information about inflections) which undermined the complex Indo-European system of cases. **Case** is a set of grammatical categories, a different number of them in different languages, where each category reflects the grammatical function of a word in a phrase or clause. Indo-European had eight or nine cases, but the Germanic languages had only four (nominative, accusative, dative, genitive), with some evidence for two more (locative, instrumental), having lost completely three cases (ablative, vocative, allative). Germanic also simplified the number of verb tenses from Indo-European, so that only a present tense and a past tense remained. Verbs and adjectives came to have "weak" inflections, simplified sets of endings from those found for "strong" adjectives and verbs. The words "weak" and "strong" just designate parallel inflectional systems in the same language, not anything inherently weak or strong about the endings. Finally, Germanic also developed a pattern of having the verb come second in the word order of a sentence. This was the beginning of word order as a significant way to know what words are doing in sentences, rather than reliance on case endings (modern English has mostly lost its case endings). As early as we can reconstruct differences between Indo-European and Germanic, we see changes in speakers' habits that would eventually lead to the even greater changes that are characteristic of English.

Buck's tables also show that, as Indo-European words changed over time to the forms they hold in different language branches, sound correspondences do not tell the whole story. As suggested earlier, sometimes different branches adopted different words from Indo-European, and sometimes words that were not originally Indo-European came to be used. The Slavic word for *foot* comes not from the Indo-European root *ped (as reconstructed – reconstructed forms are marked with a *), but instead from a word that meant 'claw.' Slavic also replaced the Indo-European root for *father* with a different word. The words for *fish* in the different branches also come from different places. Moreover, sometimes the languages in the different branches can share words. The word for *fish* is related in the Italic and Germanic families, and is also connected to the word used in Welsh, a Celtic language. Correspondences and differences like these led the early twentieth-century linguist **Jules Gilliéron** to proclaim that "each word has its own history," just the opposite position from the Neogrammarians but a theory equally subject to scientific study and description. Neither way of thinking can be ignored: there are important systematic correspondences between languages and language branches, at the same time that word histories sometimes take their own way and need to be addressed outside of any mechanical system of correspondences. Such is always the case with habits, which is what the differences between language branches really come down to. Sometimes our habits, including language habits, are very regular and systematic, and sometimes they are more idiosyncratic, whether for individuals or for whole groups of people. As we saw in Chapter 2, the regularities emerge from the operation of the complex system of language, in which there is room for a great many choices for words and sounds and in which, at the same time, speakers do come, most of the time, to make similar choices.

3.4 **Difference and Continuum**

The detective work in dictionaries and grammars that we call historical Indo-European linguistics had its great age of discovery only as recently as the nineteenth century, and work continues today to unravel what must have happened to create the range of language branches and language habits existing today in the Indo-European region – and in all of the places to which Indo-European languages have been carried around the world. Most of this work attempts to explain the *differences* between language groups and languages, to make the branches of the Indo-European tree appear more separate and distinct, because people perceive that modern languages are separate and distinct (as discussed in Chapter 1). It is important to keep in mind, however, that all of these groups and languages are still historically related to Indo-European and to each other. The language habits of the Germanic group are not entirely different from those of the Celtic group or the Slavic group. If they were completely different, nobody could tell that these language groups were historically related to each other. The same is true for modern languages. There are systematic differences between them, to be sure, but there are also many similarities that testify to the connections between languages within branches and to the connections between branches within the Indo-European family. Consideration of the similarities and connectedness (as opposed to differences) focuses attention on the **linguistic continuum** within the Indo-European territory. Both then and now, people who live near to each other tend to be able to understand each other, as they must in order to carry on their daily affairs with each other. National boundaries even today most often do not prevent neighbors from talking to each other, and talking more like each other than might be predicted from their respective national languages as taught in schools or printed in books. The historical development of the Indo-European languages was no different: near neighbors talked to each other, and the differences between particular branch languages, and by extension the major Indo-European language branches, can be observed to emerge by historical linguists only as a function of the distance between the people who spoke them – we see the branches as more different when we consider languages as they are spoken in their heartlands or capitals, not along the borders of the territories or countries in which they are spoken.

Knowledge of the existence of a linguistic continuum has importance for English because, historically, people who spoke the branch languages that emerged from Germanic could often communicate with each other better than might be implied by the separate branches that historical linguists draw as emerging from the Germanic family. Speakers developed different speech habits in the East, North, and West portions of the Germanic region, but as they did so they could still talk to each other as the occasion arose. East Germanic (Gothic in particular) is chiefly known from Bishop Wulfila's translation of the bible (originally from the fourth century AD, with surviving manuscript fragments only from the sixth century and later), and thus not much evidence exists for contact between Eastern speakers and Northern and Western speakers of Germanic. But historical records document the fact that, at least at some times and for some purposes, speakers of North Germanic (which developed into the modern Scandinavian languages) could still talk to and understand speakers of West Germanic (which developed into English and German, among other modern languages). A poetic example comes from the poem *The Battle of Maldon* (of uncertain date, surviving in a manuscript copied as late as the eleventh century), in which the invading Norsemen are said to negotiate with the defending Englishmen before they did battle in the late tenth century.

The ancient history of human language offers us a complex story of different peoples and cultures. English is not *the* endpoint of a process of development that began in Africa thousands of years ago, but instead just *one* outcome of the complex system of human speech that continues to operate today. Will English eventually disappear and turn into something else, like Indo-European and Germanic did? It seems unlikely today, but the change of Latin into the Romance languages must have seemed an unlikely prospect to the Romans at the height of their empire. Language development and change can play out over very long periods of time, and we cannot predict how it will come out because it depends on continual interactions of huge numbers of speakers as they are affected by the contingencies of their times. We can, however, predict that change over time will always continue as long as there are groups of active speakers.

3.5 **Chapter Summary**

This chapter described the process of language development and change over very long periods of time. Human language probably began in Africa, in association with the emergence of our human species, and it changed differently over time in the different populations of speakers who spread out over the world. Indo-European is the language family from which English eventually emerged, and this chapter discussed what and how we know about prehistorical varieties of language. The tree model emphasized the continuity of development over time and the differences that emerged between branches, while the daisy model emphasized continuities between populations across the linguistic continuum.

Key Terms
*
Carl Darling Buck
case
Celtic
daisy model
family tree
Germanic
Germanic Sound Shift (Grimm's Law)
Jules Gilliéron
Indo-European
isolated language
Italic

Kurgan hypothesis
language family
linguistic continuum
Neogrammarians
Nostratic
reconstruction
Slavic
sound change
stemma
umlaut

Exercises

3.1 What does the term "Neanderthal" mean to you? It describes one of the branches on the way to the human species, but we still use the word today to refer to other things. Why do you think the word means what it does today?

3.2 Look up one of the languages on the Indo-European stemma (Figure 3.1), such as "Balto-Slavic," and find out how many different languages are attributed to that branch. Where do people speak them?

3.3 Compare the map of the Kurgan hypothesis in Figure 3.2 with the daisy model in Figure 3.3? Did people really leave the Indo-European in particular directions? Did people always move in straight lines? Were these population movements simple and uncomplicated, or did people move, and then move again, and then have other people move in with them? You will need to look up language branches online to find the answers.

3.4 Look up Verner's Law in the Reference Grammar (Moore, Knott, and Hulbert, 1972) online, and describe how it relates to Grimm's Law. What problem does it solve? How does it solve it? Do you think that Verner's Law really agrees with the Neogrammarian principle that "sound change operates without exception"?

3.5 Find a translation of *The Battle of Maldon,* and locate the passage where the Viking invaders are talking to the English defenders. What did the Vikings say to the English? What did the English say back to them? If they were speaking their own languages, and if they did understand each other, what do you think of the exchange?

Further Reading

The ancient history of languages has fascinated many an imagination. See, among many other scholarly offerings, Bickerton (1990). Among literary treatments of the subject, notable is Golding (1955). A book that considers the big picture of human cultural evolution, including a chapter on language, is Wade (2006).

Kaiser and Shevoroshkin (1988). The Nostratic hypothesis began early in the twentieth century with Holger Pederson, and was greatly developed by a number of Russian scholars beginning in the 1960s. The Nostratic hypothesis still has a following today (see, for example, the writings of Allan Bomhard), but many traditional comparative and historical linguists remain opposed to it on grounds that it is unrealistic to expect to be able to go that far back in time to do linguistic reconstruction. Still, there must have been other language families besides Indo-European at that time, and it is useful to be able to present an organized account of what they might have been.

The daisy model is the author's version of a kind of visualization also developed by others. See Modiano (1999) and Werner (2016).

Buck (1949); Watkins (1985). It is fascinating to look at the evidence for comparative linguistics in Buck, and to read Watkins' dictionary made from the evidence that shows how Indo-European roots remain in languages across Europe today. Other books on Indo-European include Fortson (2010), Clackson (2007), and Watkins (1995). On the Germanic languages, see Nielsen (1989) and Robinson (1992).

Townend (2005) treats in detail the possibilities for language contact between Norse and English speakers in the Viking age, as depicted in The Battle of Maldon.

The Neogrammarians can be credited with making linguistics into a science, in contrast to earlier treatments that favored Biblical or spiritual or magical bases for language (for a contemporary example, consider Harry Potter and the word-curses that magicians throw at each other). Perhaps the best modern defense of Neogrammarian principles, but a very difficult one to understand, occurs in Labov (1994). A more readable book that draws heavily upon Labov's work is Tagliamonte (2011).

CHAPTER **4**

Origins of English

In this chapter

This chapter discusses how the history of English is usually divided into different periods, and then treats the beginnings of English about AD 450. English was not the language first spoken on the island of Britain, and English emerged as the language of the Germanic people who conquered the population on the island. The history of this time, the Prehistoric Old English period, tells a story of the loss of civilization, and then how it began to come back. It also tells the story of how a collection of Germanic groups from the continent came, eventually, to change their habits of speech over time so that English could first be described as a separate language.

4.1 **Periods for the Study of English**

Unlike most other languages, English can date its origins with fair precision to about AD 450. No written records of the language from that time still exist; the earliest written records of English come from about AD 700. Still, between the "internal" history of the language (reconstruction of regularities in the features of a language of the sort discussed in Chapter 3 for Indo-European and Germanic) and historical records "external" to the language (cultural circumstances that affected the speakers of a language, and thus the conditions for change in the language), modern observers can

Table 4.1 *Periods in the History of English*

Old English	AD 450 to AD 1100
Prehistoric Old English	AD 450 to AD 700
Early Old English	AD 700 to AD 900
Late Old English	AD 900 to AD 1100
Middle English	AD 1100 to AD 1500
Early Middle English	AD 1100 to AD 1300
Late Middle English	AD 1300 to AD 1500
Modern English	AD 1500 to the present
Early Modern English	AD 1500 to AD 1700
Modern English	AD 1700 to AD 1950
Contemporary English	AD 1950 to the present

build a decent picture of what must have been happening before written records are available as evidence. The history of English is conventionally divided into three **periods**, each with subdivisions (Table 4.1).

Thus, while it is common today to hear people call the language of Shakespeare "Old English," that description is not accurate for those studying the history of the English language: Shakespeare died in 1608, and so historians of English would say that he was a speaker of **Modern English**. Clearly Shakespeare's language is not the same as today's Modern English. These three periods are really just rough divisions in the history of English. Change in the language is continuous, both within the periods and across them. Of course, the language was not uniform across all of its speakers at any one time, either, so a time period must necessarily be a generalization across regional and social differences.

More specific references to the condition of the language often apply the labels "early" or "late" to the period name, and so Shakespeare's stage of the language is often called **Early Modern English** (usually considered as coming from AD 1500 to AD 1700). What we speak today is now often called **Contemporary English** (considered as beginning in the Information Age, roughly after the Second World War). The earliest form of **Old English** is often called **Prehistoric Old English** (usually considered as coming from AD 450 to AD 700). In time it may become necessary, because of continuing change in the language, to create a new period in the history of English that comes after Modern English. In the field of English literature the "Modern" period is considered to be long finished and the "Contemporary" period to be well underway, so Contemporary English may come to be the name for a new major period in the history of the language and not just a subdivision of Modern – but even if it does, it will not be the last name for a period because change in English continues unabated and will do so as long as there are living groups of people speaking it. English has a well-defined origin, but no foreseeable end.

4.2 **Origins of English**

Before the origin of English, the island of Britain was first populated by a prehistoric culture whose language remains undocumented, but members of the Celtic-speaking branch of the Indo-Europeans came to settle there and were the inhabitants at the dawn of our recorded history. Julius Caesar invaded Celtic Britain in 55 BC, and Emperor Claudius conquered the island and made it part of the Roman Empire in AD 43. Although Britain was at the edge of the Empire, it still received the benefits of Roman civilization: roads, new cities with some advanced features like public baths with central heating, literate culture (as opposed to the oral culture of the Celts), new forms of religion (including, in time, Christianity), and defensive walls and garrisons to protect the Romanized citizens from unRomanized Celts (the **Scots**) and **Picts**, population groups who lived in the North of Britain. Wales and Cornwall, to the far West and far Southwest, also retained Celtic populations without much Roman influence. Thus, in the first few centuries of the historical era many inhabitants of Britain came to speak both their Celtic **British** language and also Latin, from the Italic branch of the Indo-European family. Others, especially those outside the centers of Roman influence, spoke only British, and still others, those beyond Roman control, spoke other Celtic languages like the Scots, or spoke Pictish (whose relationship to Indo-European is not well defined), in active resistance to Roman control.

Rome fell (for the first time) in AD 412. Such trouble at the core of the Empire caused the Romans to withdraw their garrisons, so that the Romanized British were no longer protected from the Scots and Picts. As one of the Romanized British, **Gildas**, wrote in his *De Excidio Brittaniae* (Giles, 1841) in the sixth century AD:

> No sooner were they gone, than the Picts and Scots, like worms which in the heat of midday come forth from their holes, hastily land again from their canoes . . . differing one from another in manners, but inspired with the same avidity for blood, and all more eager to shroud their villainous faces in bushy hair than to cover with decent clothing those parts of their body which required it . . . [The British put their own garrison on the Roman Wall, but] the hooked weapons of their enemies were not idle, and our wretched countrymen were dragged from the wall and dashed against the ground. Such premature death, however, painful as it was,

saved them from seeing the miserable sufferings of their brothers and children . . . They left their cities, abandoned the protection of the Wall, and dispersed themselves in flight more desperately than before. The enemy, on the other hand, pursued them with more unrelenting cruelty than before, and butchered our countrymen like sheep, so that their habitations were like those of savage beasts; for they turned their arms upon each other, and for the sake of a little sustenance, imbrued their hands in the blood of their fellow countrymen.

Gildas, writing in Latin in the colorful style of a lament for his society, reported no less than the end of civilization as he knew it. He saw the calamity as God's vengeance upon a sinful people. But it got worse still.

The leaders of the British attempted to replace their own ineffective defenses with the same mercenaries that the Romans had employed to defend Hadrian's Wall at the northern border of Roman Britain, that is, members of Germanic groups from across the North Sea on the continent. **Hengest** and **Horsa** were the leaders of the Germanic mercenaries who were invited to settle in Britain (on their own isolated territory, the Isle of Thanet in the southeast) in AD 449. They did repel the Picts and Scots, but after they had done that they first complained about their agreements with the Romanized British, and continued to pick quarrels and to invite more of their countrymen to come to Britain, until they began their own invasion of all Britain. As Gildas wrote (again in colorful and graphic language) about a century after the arrival of Hengest and Horsa,

For the fire of vengeance, justly kindled by former crimes, spread from sea to sea, fed by the hands of our foes in the east, and did not cease, until, destroying the neighboring towns and lands, it reached the other side of the island and dipped its red and savage tongue in the western ocean . . . So that all the columns were leveled with the ground by the frequent strokes of the battering ram, all the husbandmen routed, together with their bishops, priests, and people, whilst the sword gleamed and the flames crackled around them on every side. Lamentable to behold, in the midst of streets lay the tops of lofty towers, tumbled to the ground, stones of high walls, holy altars, fragments of human bodies, covered with livid clots of coagulated blood, looking as if they had been squeezed together in a press; and with no chance of being buried, save in the ruins of the houses or in the ravening bellies of wild beasts and birds; with reverence be it spoken for their blessed souls, if, indeed, there were many found who were carried at that time into the high heaven by the holy angels.

Gildas, translation by Giles (1841)

It took the Germanic invaders nearly two centuries to complete their occupation of Britain, lacking only Scotland, Wales, and Cornwall, where some of the Romanized British sought haven with their ethnic relatives (often not safely). Other British speakers resettled across the Channel in what is now known as Brittany, part of modern France. This exodus gave rise to the King Arthur legends among the Celtic population, about a hero who faced the challenge and was eventually defeated but not without hope of a return, the "once and future king." It used to be thought that the British population was slaughtered by the Germanic invaders, but now there is evidence that many British people remained in England as second-class citizens, without the same rights or value as Germanic residents, as some early Germano-British legal codes show. What is certain is that the Romanized civilization of Britain came to an end at this time, and the benefits of Roman civilization were lost. Today contemporary works of science fiction often like to consider what would happen if civilization were lost – and the history of Britain provides a graphic historical example.

4.3 First Emergence of English

The English language originally emerged from the speech of the Germanic mercenaries, not the early Romano-British. Indeed, there are very few influences in English from the Celtic British language, which is one reason the Germanic invaders were long accused of genocide. The Germanic mercenaries-cum-invaders were members of a number of West Germanic groups, **Angles, Saxons, Jutes,** and **Frisians,** each certainly with their own speech habits but each able to understand speakers from the other groups. The names **England** and **English** come from the name of one of these groups, the Angles, but the fact is that the Angles were historically no more important than the other groups. The speech of the modern-day Frisian population, who live in the northeastern part of the Netherlands and on islands off its coast, is often said to be the language closest to English, though such a judgment is more a matter of perception than science.

What became English, as an identifiable branch of the larger Germanic branch of Indo-European, started with the speech of Hengest, Horsa, and their compatriots. The mixture of speech habits from these different ethnic populations combined and changed in the complex system of speech, until something we might call English emerged on the island of Britain. Emergence was uneven across the island, with somewhat different habits becoming common in different regions we still talk about today: the North, the Midlands, and the South. *The **Anglo-Saxon Chronicle**,* a historical

59

record maintained in several locations from the ninth century to the end of the Old English period (and thus not very reliable for earlier periods – a source written earlier is Bede's *Ecclesiastical History of the English People*), says that Angles occupied the eastern coast of Britain, as in the area of modern East Anglia, and that the Saxons came to the south, as in the area of modern Sussex (there are other places with the *-sex* derived from the name Saxon – Middlesex and Essex, further north, and Wessex further west). Uneven settlement by the original Germanic groups no doubt contributed to the emergence of regional differences in speech. Overall, English grew more identifiable over time as something in itself, as something distinct from other West Germanic branches, as the various members of the Angles, Saxons, Jutes, and Frisians, along with Germanic hangers-on in fewer numbers from other groups, together waged war against the British and came to settle most of the island of Britain.

In linguistic terms, these Germanic speakers came, in time, to share particular language habits as a result of their regular communication together, while at the same time they had less chance for communication with Germanic speakers still on the continent. The habits of speech among the Germanic people in Britain thus came to resemble each other more than they resembled speech habits among any of the continental Germanic groups. The first step in this process of change separated the West Germanic languages from the North and East Germanic branches. One of the important changes was **gemination**, the doubling of any single consonant except *r* when it occurred between a short vowel and an [i, ɪ, j] sound, which is how we got many of the doubled consonants we still have today in English. So, for example, Germanic <*sætjan> becomes West Germanic <*sættjan>. As we saw in Chapter 3, an [i, ɪ, j] sound also caused umlaut to occur, so that <*sættjan> becomes <settan> 'set' and <*fulljan> becomes <fyllan> 'fill.' Others include West Germanic <*sandjan, *dohtri> becoming Old English <sendan, dehter> 'send, daughter.' The fact that an [i, ɪ, j] sound is involved in both umlaut (from Chapter 3) and gemination does not mean that an [i, ɪ, j] is required for all changes. On the contrary, sound changes often occur in very specific environments, and historical linguists have described a great many of them. Unfortunately for modern observers of sound change, the [i, ɪ, j] sound was later lost, which makes it harder to recognize when i-umlaut has occurred. The strong stress on the root syllable in the Germanic language branch eventually resulted in the loss of many final *i* and *u* sounds, but only after umlaut had occurred. The sequence of changes is important: gemination occurred before i-umlaut, which occurred before the loss of the [i, ɪ, j] sound.

The online Reference Grammar (Moore, Knott, and Hulbert, 1972) covers the emergence of West Germanic in §217 to §223. As you refer to the Reference Grammar you should notice the special marking for the class of long vowels. Appendix 1 says that vowel length can be significant in English pronunciation; it is usually still marked in transcriptions of British English but not in American English. Long and short vowels developed differently in the history of English, so as an aid to students and readers the editors commonly distinguish <ǣ, ā, ē> and other long vowels from <æ, a, e> and their other short-vowel counterparts. The line over the vowel is called a **macron**.

The next step in the process separated Old English from other West Germanic languages. For example, many words that in West Germanic were pronounced with an /ɑ/ vowel, as in Modern German *tag* 'day,' came to be pronounced in the earliest form of English with an /æ/ vowel, as in Old English *dæg* 'day,' which today in Modern English we pronounce /deɪ/ owing to later changes in pronunciation. Similarly, some West Germanic words pronounced with an /o/ sound, such as Modern German *wolle* 'wool' or *vol* 'full,' came early to be pronounced in English with an /ʊ/ vowel still used in Modern English *wool* and *full*. Changes like these are not world shaking in themselves, and some English speakers today may sometimes pronounce *wool* as /wol/, but the fact that different pronunciations like these became widely shared as habits among the ethnic Germanic speakers in Britain helps to mark the emergence of English as a newly recognizable branch on the historical Indo-European tree. In the online Reference Grammar, §224 to §240 cover changes from West Germanic to early Old English, and §241 to §263 cover changes that occurred during the Prehistoric Old English period before AD 700.

The Germanic invasion and occupation of Britain was largely complete in the sixth century, as Gildas reported. At the end of the sixth century the Roman world returned to Britain, now bringing Christianity. A mission from Rome, led by **St. Augustine**, arrived in England in AD 597. Before that, Christian monks from Ireland had landed in the North, beginning with **St. Columba** in AD 563, who established an outpost on the island of Iona among other islands off the western coast of Scotland. The conversion of the English was a long, slow process, lasting through the seventh century and beyond. The northern and southern missions to the English eventually met to unify their practices at the Synod of Whitby in AD 664.

The cultural importance of these missions was more than religion: the language of the church was Latin, and people trained by the church were literate, unlike most of the English. Thus, besides religion the Christian missionaries brought literacy back to Britain. Civilization, then, in the form of late Latin culture, did return to Britain after the Germanic invasion, but on new terms. Latin became the language of many early documents, as the early English kings made use of the literate Christians. Literacy was

Figure 4.1 Bede as represented in the Nuremberg Chronicle, 1493 (public domain)

quite limited, however, so the general population continued to speak only English, not Latin. Centers of Christian culture, cathedrals, monasteries, and abbeys at places like Canterbury, Lindisfarne, York, and later Winchester, were retreats from the daily life of the English (the separated monastic pattern of living had been established in Italy as a consequence of the fall of the Roman empire) and were also storehouses of books, surviving documents from Roman culture as well as religious texts. **Bede** wrote the best period history, in Latin, *Historia ecclesiastica gentis Anglorum* (*Ecclesiastical History of the English People*). The *History*, completed in AD 731, stands as a monument to the return of literate culture to the English, if not in English. It was dedicated to Ceolwulf, King of Northumbria, who may even have been able to read it. Nearly three hundred years after the Germanic invasion, the English-speaking population had rejoined European culture. Unfortunately, by the end of the eighth century the **Vikings**, North Germanic raiders, had attacked the monastery at Lindisfarne which had been established in AD 634, and then the monastery at Monkwearmouth and Jarrow, founded in AD 674, that had been home to Bede. A new Germanic group had arrived to threaten civilization in Britain.

4.4 Chapter Summary

In this chapter we heard from Gildas, a sixth-century British historian, how Germanic groups who had been mercenaries for the Romans were invited to Britain to help defend the Romanized British population after the Roman garrisons left. We also heard how the Germanic groups did not stop by defeating the Picts and Scots, but instead eventually came to occupy almost all of Britain. In speech, the different Germanic groups began with different habits but as they interacted with each other, changes in their West Germanic languages made it possible to describe English for the first time. By the end of the Prehistoric Old English period, some civilization had returned to the island when Christian missionaries brought literacy as they attempted to convert the English people.

Key Terms
Angles
Anglo-Saxon Chronicle
Bede
British
Contemporary English
Early Modern English
England
English
Frisians
gemination
Gildas
Hengest
Horsa
Jutes
Late Modern English
macron
Middle English
Modern English
Old English
period
Picts
Prehistoric Old English
Saxons
Scots
St. Augustine
St. Columba
Vikings

Exercises

4.1 The notion of a "period" exists not just for the English language but for ranges of time in many other areas. Can you name various literary periods? Can you name different historical periods? Are these sharply bounded time ranges, or do they flow from one into the other? What is the value of talking about periods?

4.2 Look up the fall of Rome. Who were the first outside people, "barbarians," to conquer the city? How many times did Rome fall? How is it that Rome fell, and yet St. Augustine's mission to convert the English originated in Rome?

4.3 In the online Reference Grammar there are many more changes than just those reported in the chapter. Changes are often reported according to what sound preceded the changed sound, and what sound followed it. Look at the changes in the Prehistoric Old English period (§241 to §263), and make a list of the preceding sounds involved in changes, and of the following sounds involved in changes.

4.4 Consider the problem of stressed syllables in the Germanic languages. Read §208 and §253, and write a description of the effects of Germanic stress on sound changes.

4.5 The Christianization of the English came from both the North, from Irish monks, and the South, with a mission from Rome. Differences between the Northern and Southern missions were resolved at the Synod of Whitby. Look up the Synod of Whitby in Bede's *Ecclesiastical History of the English People*, describe the practices that had to be resolved, and discuss the importance of the Synod.

Further Reading

Pryor (2005), based on a 2004 Channel 4 series; Pryor (2004; 2006). Francis Pryor has published a series of readable books on the archaeological history of Britain. He is an archaeologist who often appears on UK TV on the Channel 4 Time Team program.

Giles (1841) is a translation of the works of Gildas. As will be clear from the excerpts quoted above, Gildas had a polemical point to make when he told the story of the coming of the Germanic mercenaries. The rest of the story is part sermon and part history, in the genre known as a "lamentation."

Bede (1994). Bede's account, originally in Latin, here translated by Judith McClure and Roger Collins, is one of the best period sources for the early history of the Anglo-Saxons.

CHAPTER 5

Old English

In this chapter

This chapter introduces Old English sounds, inflections, and characteristics of the lexicon. Paradigms show the different possibilities for inflections for different stem classes, and for strong and weak verbs. Old English dialects are illustrated alongside West Saxon and in conjunction with Norse settlement, with discussion of the emergence of English regions that still exist today. Cædmon's Hymn shows the relation between poetic and prose text, and also indicates how much of Old English constitutes recognizable core English vocabulary.

5.1 Inscriptions and Manuscripts

Some of the first physical evidence we have for the Old English language comes from a time long after Hengest and Horsa, even long after Gildas: from the late seventh / early eighth century, in about AD 700. The Franks Casket (Figure 5.1) now in the British Museum, is a small box from about that time with pictures to decorate it, but also an inscription written in **runes** at the top, sides, and bottom of the panel.

Figure 5.1 The Franks Casket (Granger Historical Picture Archive / Alamy Stock Photo)

Runes are symbols from a writing system whose "alphabet" is known for Old English as the **futhorc** from the first symbols in the list, in the same way that our word *alphabet* comes from the first two letters in our list (alpha and beta, if you speak Greek at least). Runes were used among the Germanic peoples even before Hengest and Horsa, typically for inscriptions; the style of the letters, which may have been adapted early on from Greek, features straight lines in the symbols, easier to carve than curves. The first word of the inscription is *fisc*, the Old English word for *fish*; you can find the runes on the list in Figure 5.2 and match them to the inscription at top left in Figure 5.1. The rest of the inscription offers a riddle, something the English loved, about what the casket is made out of: *hronæs ban* 'whale bone.'

At about the same time, the English were also preparing books. Figure 5.3 shows the beginning of the gospel of Matthew from the early eighth-century Lindisfarne Gospels. Writing a book at that time was expensive: the pages were not made of paper but of **parchment** (called *vellum* when of the best quality), an animal product, and the text was all written by hand since printing would not be invented in Europe for another seven centuries. In books even more expensive than normal, there were colorful drawings called **illuminations**, sometimes separate pictures but often, as here, decorations of the initial capital letter of a section of the book, an **illuminated capital**.

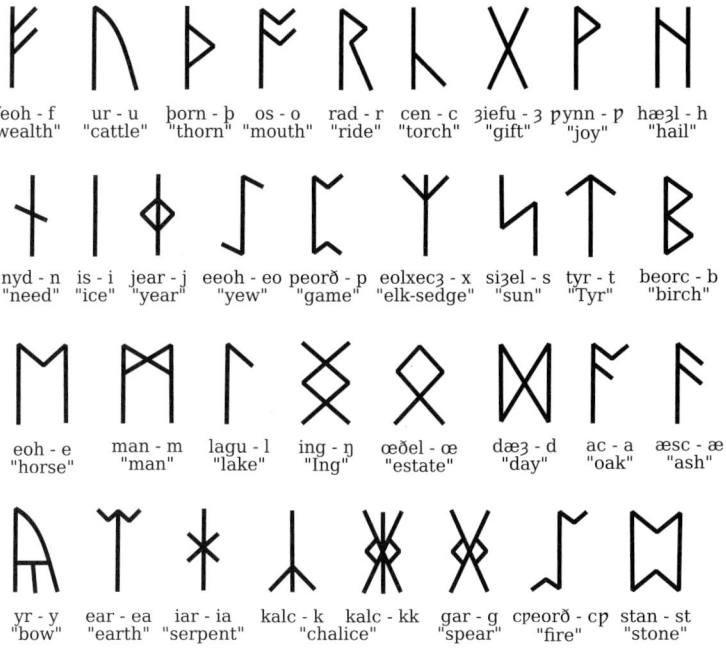

ᚠ	ᚢ	ᚦ	ᚩ	ᚱ	ᚳ	ᚷ	ᚹ	ᚻ
feoh - f	ur - u	þorn - þ	os - o	rad - r	cen - c	ȝiefu - ȝ	pynn - p	hæȝl - h
"wealth"	"cattle"	"thorn"	"mouth"	"ride"	"torch"	"gift"	"joy"	"hail"

ᚾ	ᛁ	ᛄ	ᛇ	ᛈ	ᛉ	ᛋ	ᛏ	ᛒ
nyd - n	is - i	jear - j	eeoh - eo	peorð - p	eolxecȝ - x	siȝel - s	tyr - t	beorc - b
"need"	"ice"	"year"	"yew"	"game"	"elk-sedge"	"sun"	"Tyr"	"birch"

ᛖ	ᛗ	ᛚ	ᛝ	ᛟ	ᛞ	ᚪ	ᚫ
eoh - e	man - m	lagu - l	ing - ŋ	œðel - œ	dæȝ - d	ac - a	æsc - æ
"horse"	"man"	"lake"	"Ing"	"estate"	"day"	"oak"	"ash"

ᚣ	ᛠ	ᛡ	ᛣ	ᛤ	ᚸ	ᛢ	ᛥ
yr - y	ear - ea	iar - ia	kalc - k	kalc - kk	gar - g	cþeorð - cþ	stan - st
"bow"	"earth"	"serpent"		"chalice"	"spear"	"fire"	"stone"

Figure 5.2 Runes: the Old English (Wikipedia commons)

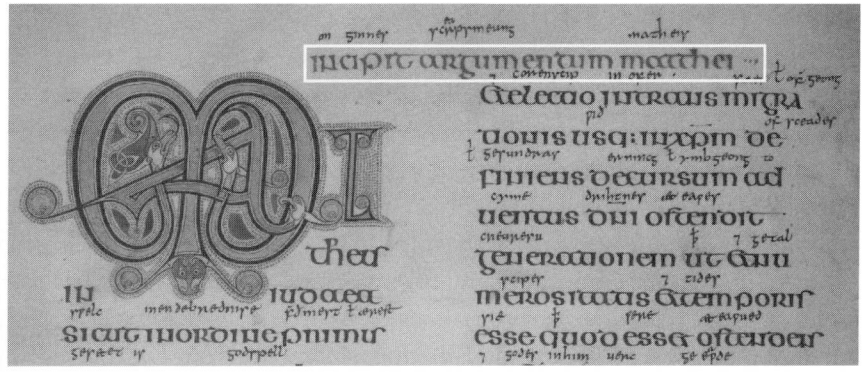

Figure 5.3 Incipit for the Gospel of Mark, Lindisfarne Gospels (image from the British Library, www.bl.uk)

The red letters at the top say that this is the beginning of the book of Matthew – in Latin. Old English was what most people then spoke, but they did not write it much. Latin was the language of the church in Britain, and it was the language used for literate purposes more generally. Many of the earliest writings remaining to us in Old English are religious in character. This does not mean that most of what the early English talked about was religion, but instead that literacy and books were more common in church settings and such books were more likely to survive over the great stretch of time.

The illuminated capital continues in Latin, "Mattheu in iudaea …" If you look carefully, you can see that the capital M is interwoven with the second letter, a, and that the tails of both letters end in beasts (for the M) and a bird (for the a). This artistic style, **interlace**, often appears in medieval jewelry and other objects from this time across Northern Europe. The alphabet used for the normal writing in the book is a form of **uncial**, a letter style used in manuscripts where curves were natural to produce with a quill pen. The tiny writing between the lines of the book is a **gloss**, a translation into Old English added about two hundred years after the first composition of the book. The gloss for the red Latin word "incipit" is the Old English word "on gynneþ," 'begins' in Modern English. The letter style of the gloss is called **minuscule**, not because it is tiny but just as a name for this kind of writing, which is less formal than the style used for the main book text. There was also a letter style called **majuscule**, letters used for inscriptions that featured more straight lines, and these have become what we call capital letters, while the minuscule letter style is now often called lower case (a term derived from the history of printing). We now use the word "font" (another term derived from the history of printing) to label design differences between letter styles, and, as shown by the differences in letter shapes between the glosses and the book text, the appearance of our alphabet could be quite different from place to place and across time. There is a long history of different letter styles across a thousand years of medieval manuscripts before the invention of printing, covered in the field of **paleography**, and an equally long history of how manuscripts were made, copied, and used, covered in the field of **codicology**, also called **history of the book**. These fields both contribute to what we know about Old English and other pre-modern periods of the language, because we need them to describe our historical evidence for the language. As Saussure once wrote, writing is not a garment but a disguise for language, because writing conventions may obscure what is happening in the spoken language, but until very recently writing is the only evidence we can use to tell the history of the language. Every old text is a semiotic exercise (**semiotics** is the study of signs and symbols), in that the book is the product of, and a sign of, its own particular environment. Along with semiotics, we also need to consider **philology**, the history of the transmission of a text as it is copied over time, often in different places from its origin and always by different people.

While the Roman alphabet has various letter styles, in the Old English period there were also some different letters than what we have today. Some of them can be seen in this part of the Cædmon passage discussed later in this chapter: "Þa he ða þas andsware onfeng . . . þe he næfre gehyrde." Letters þ 'thorn' (capital Þ) and ƿ 'wynn' (capital Ƿ) come from the futhorc; thorn is used where we would use <th> in Modern English spelling, and wynn is used where we would use <w> in Modern English spelling. The letter æ 'aesc' (capital Æ) comes from Latin, and can still be seen occasionally in words like *encyclopædia*; in Modern English spelling we would use <e> or <a> for it. Letters ȝ 'yogh' (capital Ȝ) and ð 'eth' (capital Ð) came from Irish Latin; yogh is used where we would use a <g> or <y> in Modern English spelling, and eth is used where we would use <th> in Modern English spelling. These letters are on Windows and Macintosh computers, part of the Unicode standard for characters. You will find them in the extended character sets that come with the Times New Roman font (and many other fonts, too), and you have to use the "Insert Symbol" command in a word processing program to put them in a document. Besides the letters, a symbol that resembled the modern Arabic number 7 was used as an abbreviation for 'and.' Some modern letters were not used in Old English: <v, z, q, j>. So, we can say that the Modern English alphabet and fonts that we use today have emerged over time from different character sets and letter styles. Some letters like eth and thorn are no longer in use for English (Icelandic still uses them, though), and some characters like aesc have limited use in English, while at the same time new letter symbols can continue to emerge. How about @ ? Have you seen it used to help spell a word, perhaps in place of <at>?

One thing different about Old English manuscripts for modern readers is that modern punctuation has not yet emerged. Modern editors usually insert it in their editions of Old English texts. Another thing inserted by modern editors of Old English is the macron for long vowels. A modern edition that retains as much as possible of the presentation of text from the manuscript (e.g., no modern punctuation, no macrons) is called a **diplomatic edition**, but these are uncommon. Editors also frequently **normalize** the texts they edit to remove dialect differences (see below), or **emend** the text to repair what they believe to be errors in the copying of the manuscript. Readers need to pay attention to what the editors have done and how they present the text to their audiences! We could get the impression that Old English was as regular as Modern Standard English from normalized texts, but that was certainly not the case. Some writers about Old English refer to a **West Saxon** "standard," and there were some institutional efforts to standardize Old English late in the Old English period, but the appearance of greater regularity in later Old English arises chiefly because most of our surviving manuscripts come from the Wessex region. We should be cautious about applying a modern notion to the language at an older time. "Caveat lector!" is an old-fashioned way to say "Let the reader beware!"

Another difference for modern readers about Old English, even in heavily normalized and emended editions, is that even familiar words are spelled differently. Old English is at an earlier stage in the emergence of contemporary English pronunciation practices, and Old English was written at a time before standardized spelling, so writers tended to write down words as they said them. Thus, different spellings over time tend to suggest changes in pronunciation. We have no written records surviving from Indo-European or Germanic or even West Germanic, the last stage in development before Old English. Once we get to Old English, we do have written records as of about AD 700, and we continue to have them after Old English until the present day, so we are always in the position of comparing the spellings that we have from different times and different places.

A set of vowel changes between West Germanic and Old English begin to account for some of the characteristic differences between English vowels and those of Indo-European daughter languages on the continent. As mentioned in Chapter 6, West Germanic [ɑ] becomes Old English [æ], except before a nasal consonant or a back vowel, yielding Old English <dæg> 'day' (but also Old English <dagas> in an inflected form), <hæfde> 'had,' and <æcer> 'iron.' Another such change is called **diphthongization after initial palatals**, in which West Germanic [æ] becomes Old English [ea], and West Germanic [e] becomes Old English [ie] after [j, tʃ, ʃ]. So, West Germanic <*cæster > becomes Old English <ceaster> ('camp'; see below about the town of Chester). These are all reasonable generalizations of sound changes that mark the differences between stages in the development of English, and yet we must remember that they are, after all, generalizations. These new habits of speech emerge over time in the populations that use them. We know for a certainty that there was variation in each of these populations, as some people kept using older forms, or used the new forms in somewhat different environments. Since we have no written evidence before Old English (and none for the earliest stages of Old English), these reconstructions capture the big picture of emergent change while they tend to hide the process of change that must have occurred. The online Reference Grammar lists changes from the historical Old English period in §264 to §273.

5.2 Emergence of Regions

By the time we have evidence of Old English, four regions had emerged among the English, as shown in Figure 5.4. British populations remained in Wales and Cornwall in the West, and the Scots were still in the north. In

(a)

(b)

Figure 5.4 English Regions in the Old English period (base maps from the UK Ordnance Survey)

about AD 700 English kings ruled in the north in **Northumbria**, in the midlands in **Mercia**, in the southeast in **Kent**, and in the southwest in **Wessex**. Beginning about AD 790, however, the Vikings began to raid in the northeast and during the next century they conquered and settled much of the area north and east of **Watling Street**, the old Roman road from London to Chester on the Welsh border (the town name is related to the Latin word *castrum* 'camp'). The Vikings also raided and settled on the continent, in France in Normandy ('land of the North men'). The Vikings were Norse people, the northernmost branch of the Germanic people in comparison with the West Germanic English people. As was true of the English when they conquered the British, the Vikings began to come in bands and families, and only became more unified as a political and cultural group over a long period of time.

King **Ælfred** (849–899) was the fourth of his brothers to take the throne of the West Saxons (871–899), and he battled with the Vikings. By the winter of 878 Ælfred was reduced to a camp in a Somerset swamp, but in spring 878 he rallied and defeated Guthrum and the Vikings. About 880 he negotiated a treaty to divide the kingdom and create the **Danelaw**, where the Vikings held sway, and Wessex, the territory of the English, divided by

71

Watling Street. Conflict with the Vikings created renewed interest among the English in an overall king, the *bretwalda* 'ruler of Britain' originally discussed by Bede. Ælfred did unify the English throne and held off the Vikings from taking over completely, but he did not rule all of Britain. By the time of his death in 899 England still existed in two parts, and later weaker English kings eventually gave way to Viking-heritage kings like Cnut in 1016. Beginning in the tenth century the English made payments to the Vikings to avoid war, which later came to be called Danegeld (and which we might call 'tribute' or even 'ransom').

The significance of the four regions, and of the coming of the Vikings, cannot be overstated. We can still see the effects of those original English regions today, when we commonly speak of the North, the Midlands, and the South in England (with a distinct difference between the Southeast and the Southwest), although the center of England's national political gravity has moved from Wessex, in the time of King Ælfred, east to London. So, too, the effects of population mixture of the English and the Vikings in the northeast have given us options in our language that will be discussed in the next chapter.

Again, we can say that these regions in England emerged over a long period of time, while families and bands of Germanic English people slowly took over Britain from the British, and the smaller English groupings grew into four kingdoms. The **Anglo-Saxon Chronicle**, begun in the time of King Ælfred and maintained for a long time afterwards in some locations, documents the volatile shifts in political power during this time, proceeding year by year, with fewer details (some of them no doubt apochryphal) in the early years and more details in the time of Ælfred and thereafter. In the previous chapter, we heard the report of the Roman-British author Gildas about the coming of the Germanic groups who eventually became the English people. Here is what it says in the *Anglo-Saxon Chronicle* for the year 449 (you can listen to this passage if you go online to the website for this textbook):

> 449: Her Martianus 7 Ualentinus onfengon rice. 7 rixadon.vii. winter. 7 on þeora dagum geladode Wyrtgeorn Angel cin hider. 7 hi þa coman on þrim ceolum hider to Brytene. on þam stede Heopwines fleot. Se cyning Wyrtgeorn gef heom land on suðan eastan ðissum lande. wiððan þe hi sceolon feohton wið Pyhtas. Heo þa fuhton wið Pyhtas. 7 heofdon sige swa hwer swa heo common. Hy ða sendon to Angle, heton sendon mara fultum. 7 heton heom secgan Brytwalana nahtscipe. 7 þes lands cysta. He ða sona sendon hider mare weored þam oðrum to fultume. Þa comon þa men of þrim megðum Germanie. Of Ald Seaxum. of Anglum. of Iotum.

Here Martianus and Valentinus seized the kingdom, and reigned seven winters. And in their days Vortigern invited the Angles here. And they came here to Britain in three ships, in the harbor called Heopwinesfleet. King Vortigern gave them land in the south-east of this country, on condition that they should fight against the Picts. Then they fought against the Picts, and had the victory wherever they came. They then sent to the Angles, ordered them to send more help, and had them told of the worthlessness of the Britons, and the virtues of the land. Then they soon sent here a larger army as help for the others. Then came men from three tribes in Germany, from the Old Saxons, from the Angles, from the Jutes.   From the *Anglo-Saxon Chronicle*

This passage is not a lamentation like Gildas wrote. It describes events more succinctly, but still includes the political statement that the Angles did fight and win against the Picts and that the British people were "worthless." They sent news of an opportunity back to the continent, reporting the "virtues of the land" in their request that more of their Germanic tribespeople reinforce them in Britain. This is the stock from which the English people emerged and eventually formed four kingdoms. The *Anglo-Saxon Chronicle* says that the Jutes settled in Kent and Wessex, that the Old Saxons settled in Essex, Sussex, and Wessex, and that the Angles settled in Mercia and Northumbria. We should expect, however, that a mixture of Germanic peoples lived in all of these areas (since settlement proceeded by tribal/family groups focused on individual leaders, not as an organized mass migration), and that other Germanic groups such as the Frisians also participated in settlement, so that it is not possible to connect any of the four kingdoms exclusively with any Germanic group.

The political, cultural, and linguistic emergence of the English in Britain did not stop with the four kingdoms and the Danelaw, but through the continuing interaction of the English people and others, it continues to this day in the changing face of Britain. The regions that emerged long ago in the complex system of cultural interaction in Britain have, however, remained quite similar over very long periods of time, which illustrates how stable order emerges and continues to emerge in a complex system in which all of the elements continue to interact over time.

In the surviving writings in Old English we can see the effects of these regions in differences in the language. Today we recognize four dialects of Old English following from the four kingdoms – West Saxon (from Wessex), **Kentish**, **Mercian**, and **Northumbrian** – although these are not so much separate branches of the language as sets of habits that blend into each other across the land. The people who talked to each other in the western and eastern regions of the south, in the midlands, and in the north, had their own features emerge at the top of their regional A-curves, and if we put these habits together we get the A-curves for Old English as a whole, not identical with any of the regions. We must remember that our evidence, old books, may have been written in one place by a scribe from another place, or that a book could be carried from one region to another and copied so that the copy might keep some characteristics from the old region and change some for the new region. Each of the manuscripts that has survived from the Old English period requires different paleographic, semiotic, and philological interpretation. That said, we can make sensible generalizations about regional language variation, which comes about because a language changes differently over time among the different groups of people who use it. So, words in West Saxon like <dǣd> 'deed' may appear in texts from the rest of England as <dēd>. The two spellings (remember that the macron is not original, but we know that the word for *deed* had a long vowel at this time) suggest a **differential change** in pronunciation. In this case, we can suggest that an earlier West Germanic vowel <ā> changed over time into the <ǣ> we see in West Saxon (except before the consonants w, p, g, or k), and that this new pronunciation continued in Wessex while it underwent a further change to <ē> elsewhere in England. Our earliest surviving documents in Old English show us the process of emergence, differential change, as it was happening in the different regions.

5.3 Features of Old English

The pronunciation of Old English is easy: pronounce every letter if you read aloud. Vowels are pronounced with continental values, the same ones you might use for French, Spanish, or German. Consonants are the same as they are in Modern English with just a few exceptions. The combination <sc> in spelling is pronounced [ʃ]. The <cg> spelling is pronounced [dʒ]. The letter <k> was not yet used in Old English, so the letter <c> is pronounced [k] in all cases except before high front vowels, where it is pronounced [tʃ] as in *cidan* 'chide.' The same is true for letter <g>, which has its modern pronunciation in all cases except before high front vowels as in *giefan* 'give' in Old English pronounced [jɪəvɑn]. The <ng> spelling was pronounced in Old English as [ŋg] as it is today by natives of Long Island: [lɔŋgaɪlənd]. If a consonant was doubled by gemination, you give it a longer pronunciation. Finally, <f, s, þ, ð> are all pronounced with voicing when they occur between vowels and voiced consonants. You can hear the sound of Old English, as performed by a modern reader, on the website accompanying this textbook.

The last difference about Old English for modern readers is the fact that it is an inflected language. This means that there were different endings on noun and adjective **stems** to mark **number** (singular, plural), **gender** (**masculine, feminine, neuter**), and **case** (**nominative, accusative, genitive, dative**). Gender is grammatical gender, not natural gender, which is not very predictable from what kind of thing a noun names. The case endings match whether a word is used as a subject or object, or in those relationships that we now encode with a variety of prepositions (*of, to, from*, and many others). If you want to read Old English, as opposed to just looking at it in this book, you have to learn the **paradigms** for what all the different endings are. If every slot in the paradigm had a different ending, this would mean learning the endings for the different combinations of number, gender, and case, a total of twenty four (2 x 3 x 4). What makes the task harder is that there is a different paradigm for each of a number of stem classes. All of the paradigms and inflections are listed in the online Historical Outlines. Some differ because of the vowels or consonants that occur in them, some because the endings themselves are **strong** (ideally a different ending for each slot, in practice just a more differentiated paradigm) or **weak** (a less differentiated paradigm). Pronouns have the most fully inflected paradigms, as they still do in Modern English.

What makes the memorization task easier is that Old English was already on the way to substantially limiting the differences in the endings. Indo-European was thought to have had eight cases, not just four like Old English; there were still traces of the **instrumental** case in Old English, and also traces of inflections for the **dual** number (two of something, to stand alongside just one or more than two). Indo-European was not as inflected as some languages: modern Finnish, a member of the Finno-Ugric language family, has fifteen cases! So, we can say that, while the inflections in Old English may be unusual for contemporary English readers, there were already fewer than Indo-European, and nowhere near what the Finns have to learn. Of course, the Finns can complain about all the prepositions and articles in English!

Verbs in Old English also had endings, and thus also paradigms. If you want to learn to read Old English, you must learn to **conjugate** them, which means both endings and changes in the vowel of the stem, for **person**, number, **tense** (present, past), and **mood** (indicative or subjunctive). There are three categories of person, each of which can be singular or plural, called **first** (I, we), **second** (you, you plural), and **third** (he/she/it, they). Like nouns, verbs also came in strong (more differentiated paradigm) or weak (less differentiated paradigm) classifications. All of the paradigms for verb conjugations are also listed in the online Historical Outlines. The strong verbs have seven classes that make changes in the stem vowel across the **principal parts**. This kind of change across the paradigm, called **ablaut**, is not the same thing as the sound change over time that came from a

Table 5.1

Paradigm for *sprecan* Infinitive	2nd Sing. Pres.	3rd Sing. Pres.	1st Sing. Past	Plural Past	Past Participle
sprecan	spricst	spricð	spræc	spræcon	sprecen

following [i, ɪ, j], called umlaut. The principal parts of the verb that vary across the strong verb classes are the 2nd person singular present tense, 3rd person singular present tense, the 1st person singular **preterite** (preterite just means past tense) indicative, and the plural preterite indicative. The **infinitive** and the **past participle** are also principal parts, things to be learned. The paradigm for the verb *sprecan* 'to speak, to say,' to offer one example, is found in Table 5.1.

In the past, and sometimes still in old titles or language that is supposed to sound old-fashioned, you may still see alternation in the vowel of *speak: speak/spake/spoke*. We still have remnants of strong verbs in Modern English in verbs like *sing/sang/sung*, although most verbs have fallen in with the weak class. The good thing about Old English weak verbs for Modern English readers is that they add *-(e)de* for preterite and *-ed* for the past participle without changing the verb stem, quite similar to how we do it in Modern English.

Once you know about inflections and conjugations, it is much easier to recognize vocabulary in Old English. Germanic vocabulary was carried over from Indo-European roots, of course allowing for characteristic sound changes and for the selection of particular word forms. The most basic vocabulary of Modern English comes to us from Old English, about 2000 words, the ones that we tend to use most frequently. Some words have been lost or replaced, but there are still a great many that we can recognize if we allow for minor differences in pronunciation. So, in the following sentence from a story by **Cædmon** (see Section 5.4 for a longer extract),

> Wæs he se mon in weoruldhade geseted oð þa tide þe he wæs gelyfdre ylde
>
> Was he this man in world-hood settled until the time that he was of advanced age   From Bede's *Ecclesiastical History of the English People*

we can recognize most of the words. Some have small changes in sounds (wæs/was, weoruldhad/world-hood), and sometimes a word has become more specialized in meaning now than in Old English (tide/time), and sometimes both at once (yld/eld). A few words are clearly different (se/this, oð/until, gelyfdre/advanced), but the ones we recognize outnumber them so we can just look up the ones we do not know already. One curious aspect of Old English poetic vocabulary is the tendency to put words together in compounds, to make **kennings**. The name of the most famous Old English epic poem, *Beowulf*, is one such. *Beo* is the word for 'bee' and *wulf* is the word for 'wolf,' and so the question is, what is it that acts like a wolf with bees? Perhaps a bear? Other kennings are more transparent, like "whale-road" meaning 'sea.' The Germanic languages in general have frequently made compound words, though these are only called "kennings" in Old English poetry.

Besides the words that Old English carried straight through from Indo-European, some words were borrowed from other language families. Borrowings from Latin lead that list, for the simple reason that the Romans played such a big role in the history of the region. The Germanic people had already borrowed some Latin words before they came to Britain, so-called **continental borrowings**: *camp, wall, street, cheap, pound, wine,* and others. The English did not borrow many words from the Romanized British, mainly place names. But in later years the English borrowed more and more words from Latin. Some were words for the new Christian religion (*abbot, altar, angel, candle, hymn, mass, pope, priest*). Others came from everyday life, whether foods (*beet, cherry*) or other things (*sock, purple, chest, school, gloss, anchor*). The main thing to remember about these borrowings was that they were everyday words, not terms involved in intellectual or legal affairs where Latin was still the language of choice.

5.4 Cædmon

In order to illustrate Old English, let us take up a portion of the Cædmon story, which you can listen to if you go online to the website for this textbook:

> Wæs he, se mon, in weoruldhade geseted oð þa tide þe he wæs gelyfdre ylde, ond næfre nænig leoð geleornade. Ond he for þon oft in gebeorscipe, þone þær wæs blisse intinga gedemed, þæt heo ealle sceolden þurh endebyrdnesse be hearpan singan, þonne he geseah þa hearpan him nealecan, þonne aras he for scome from þæm symble, and ham eode to his huse. Þa he þæt þa sumre tide dyde, þæt he forlet þæt hus þæs gebeorscipes ond ut wæs gongende to neata scipene, þara heord him wæs þære neahte beboden, þa he ða þær in gelimpricre tide his leomu on reste gesette and onslepte, þa stod him sum mon æt þurh swefn ond hine halette and grette ond hine be his noman nemde, "Cedmon, sing me hwæthwugu." Þa ondswarede he ond cwæð, "Ne con ic noht singan, ond ic for þon of þeossum gebeorscipe ut eode, and hider gewat, for þon

ic naht singan ne cuðe." Eft he cwæð, se ðe mid hine sprecende wæs, "Hwæðre þu meaht me singan." Þa cwæð he, "Hwæt sceal ic singan?" Cwæð he, "Sing me frumsceaft." Þa he ða þas andsware onfeng, þa ongon he sona singan in herenesse Godes Scyppendes þa fers ond þa word þe he næfre gehyrde, þara endebyrdnes þis is:

Nu sculon herigean   heofonrices Weard,
Meotodes meahte   ond his modgeþanc,
weorc Wuldorfæder,   swa he wundra gehwæs,
ece Drihten,   or onstealde.
He ærest sceop   eorðan bearnum
heofon to hrofe,   halig Scippend;
þa middangeard   moncynnes Weard,
ece Drihten,   æfter teode
firum foldan,   Frea ælmihtig.

He was, this man, settled in worldly life until he was quite old, and he never learned any poetry. And because of that often during beer drinking, when there was a happy occasion so that they should all sing to the harp in order [around the table], when he saw the harp come near him, then he arose for shame from the feast and went home to his house. When he did that on one occasion, he left the house with the beer drinking and went out to the cattle shed where he was supposed to keep watch that night, when in good time he set his limbs to rest and slept, then someone stood before him in a dream and hailed him and greeted him and called him by his name, "Cædmon, sing me something." Then he answered and said, "I don't know how to sing anything, and so I went out from the beer drinking and came here, because I don't know how to sing anything." Then he said, the one talking to him, "But you can sing for me." Then he said, "What shall I sing?" He said, "Sing to me about creation." When he had this answer, he immediately began to sing in praise of God the Creator a verse and a word that he had never heard of which the order is this:

Now we shall praise   the Guardian of Heaven
The power of the Measurer   and his forethought
The work of the Father of Wonders   as He each of the wonders
The Eternal Lord   first established.
He first shaped   for the children of the earth
Heaven as a roof   the Holy Creator,
Then middle earth   the Guardian of Mankind
The Eternal Lord   afterwards created
A fold for men   the Lord Almighty.

        From Bede's *Ecclesiastical History of the English People*

The first part of the story is in prose. Old English is often called a **synthetic** language because it is an inflected language: it does not have to have any fixed word order because the inflections say what role each word plays in a sentence. However, Old English does not have completely distinctive inflectional endings for all persons, numbers and cases, or for persons and tenses for verbs. Old English is thus part of the way from a fully inflected synthetic language (like Finnish) to Modern English as an **analytic** language that uses word order, auxiliary verbs, and prepositions to organize its sentences. We can see this in the word order of the Cædmon passage. The subjects tend to be near the beginning of each clause, often with an auxiliary verb. The verb can be reversed in order with the subject, as in "wæs he" and "aras he." Participles and inflected verbs tend to fall toward the end of the clause, as they do today in Modern German, as with "geseted" in the first clause and "geleornade" in the third one. We see some use of prepositions along with case endings. We see the same tendencies in the reported speech of the dream angel and Cædmon himself: " 'Ne con ic noht singan' . . . 'Hwæðre þu meaht me singan.' " This is not so different from Modern English.

Prose writing in Old English was used for all sorts of purposes. Laws and wills were commonly written in Old English. The *Anglo-Saxon Chronicle* and some other historical works were written in Old English. What passed for science could be written in Old English, like the *Enchiridion* of Byrthferth of Ramsey. And there was preaching in Old English prose, as in the homilies of Ælfric. The Cædmon story itself is a good example of the use of multiple languages in Britain: the story comes originally from Bede in his *Ecclesiastical History of the English People*, written in Latin. The Old English version is actually a translation from Latin.

The second part of the passage is set as a poem. Cædmon is the legendary originator of Old English poetry, as Bede told the story. As the later Old English translation of the *Ecclesiastical History* reports,

> Ond eac swelce monige oðre æfter him in Ongelþeode ongunnon æfæste leoð wyrcan; ac nænig hwæðre him þæt gelice don meahte, for þon he nales from monnum ne þurh mon gelæred wæs, þæt he þone leoðcræft leornade, ac he wæs godcundlice gefultumed and þurh Godes gife þone songcræft onfeng.

> And also many others after him among the English people began to make religious poetry; but none might do it like him, because he was not taught by men or through a man that he learned the craft of poetry, but he was divinely inspired and through God's gift adopted songcraft.

From Bede's *Ecclesiastical History of the English People*

Old English poetry was highly formal, arranged in **half-lines** with a pause in the middle of each line called a **caesura**. The two half-lines were connected by alliteration, by specific consonants or by any vowel. So, in the first line, we see *herigean* and *heofonrices* connecting the half-lines; in the second line we see *Meotodes meahte* connecting with *modgeþanc*. In the fourth line vowels make the connection, *ece* with *or onstealde*. The alliteration falls into one of five metrical "types" (with variants), usually with two stressed syllables but sometimes with one ("light") or three ("heavy") stressed syllables. Word order tends to be much more free in poems than it is in prose. Cædmon's Hymn, as it is generally known, makes extensive use of apposition, eight different names, in order to describe different aspects of God in nine short lines: guardian of heaven, a measurer, the father of wonders, eternal lord, creator, guardian of mankind, and almighty lord. Cædmon also takes us from the thought of the Creator, to the creation of heaven as a roof, to the creation of the world, middle earth, as the place for mankind, a sort of "fold" or pen under His protection. This is a worthy start for English poetry.

Poetry in English came originally from the "oral" tradition of composition for sagas like *Beowulf* that tell the story of families through significant events. Homer's *Iliad* is the same sort of thing, from centuries earlier in Greece. We have some idea about how preliterate cultures sponsored such oral productions, somewhere between history and literature, from Albert Lord's study of Caucasian singers in his *Singer of Tales* (Lord, 1960; Mitchell and Robinson, 2011). Of course, poetry in Old English comes to us in written form, as Homer's does in Greek, and so we need to consider how an originally oral production comes to be written down and preserved. Heroic traditions for poems like *Beowulf* were carried over from continental Germanic roots. As the Roman writer Tacitus (see the 2010 translation) reported of the Germanic people, "As for leaving a battle alive after your chief has fallen, that means lifelong infamy and shame. To defend and protect him, to put down one's own acts of heroism to his credit – that is what they really mean by allegiance." Another common aspect of Old English poetry is fate: "fate often saves the undoomed man when his courage is good" (*Beowulf*). Old English poetry can have its dark side. On the other hand, about half of Old English poetry is on religious subjects. There were biblical subjects and saints' lives, and various other religious poems (such as *Dream of the Rood*). Old English poems like *Genesis* and *Exodus* clearly do not come from oral composition but from the Bible. Poems like *Andreas* (about acts of the apostle Andrew), *Juliana* (about the life of St. Juliana, who lived during the Roman Empire), and *Elene* (about St. Helena's discovery of the true cross) also come from previous written sources. For poems like these, we need to consider why and how Old English writers might want to remake Latin writings into Old English poems. We have already seen how the Cædmon story was translated back into Old English from Bede's Latin, and this movement back and forth between Latin and Old English is characteristic of the times.

Old English, then, at first sight looks like a different language, but when you look more closely it has much in common with Modern English. The biggest task for anyone who wants to know more about Old English is to learn about the culture of the time, with its tumultuous relations between Scandinavian and English populations.

5.5 **Chapter Summary**

This chapter discussed the Old English language from its first historical appearance about AD 700. Alphabets are an issue in the inscriptions and books of the time, and Old English used some letter forms that are not used today. Old English had regional varieties corresponding to ancient kingships, and the northeastern area of Britain was under Viking control most of the time. Old English had inflections and conjugations that are mostly lacking today. Old English vocabulary gives us our most frequent words today, so it is easier than one might think to recognize words in passages like the Cædmon story.

Key Terms

æ (capital Æ), 'aesc'

ȝ (capital Ȝ), 'yogh'

þ (capital Þ), 'thorn'

ð (capital Ð), 'eth'

ƿ (capital Ƿ), 'wynn'

ablaut

accusative

analytic

Anglo-Saxon Chronicle

Cædmon

cæsura

case

codicology

conjugate

continental borrowing

Danelaw

dative

differential change

diphthongization after initial palatals

diplomatic edition

dual

emend
feminine
first person
futhorc
gender
genitive
gloss
half line
history of the book
illuminated capital
illumination
infinitive
instrumental
interlace
kenning
Kent
Kentish
King Ælfred
majuscule
masculine
Mercia
Mercian
minuscule
mood
neuter
nominative
normalize
Northumbria
Northumbrian
number
paleography
paradigm
parchment
past participle
person
philology
preterite
principal parts
rune
second person
semiotics
stem
strong
synthetic
tense

third person
uncial
Watling Street
weak
Wessex
West Saxon

Exercises

5.1 Use the futhorc list in Figure 5.2 to try to decode the inscription on the Franks Casket in Figure 5.1. NB: this is not an easy task!

5.2 Read about Old English dialects in the online Historical Outlines, Chapter 3, §27. Describe how different you think the main dialect regions might have been from each other. Would people have had difficulty understanding each other? Compare the differences between Old English dialects with differences in English accents today.

5.3 Make a list of as many strong verbs as you can think of in Modern English (there about 35 of them). Compare the principal parts of these verbs (e.g., sing/sang/sung) with ablaut series in the seven Old English verb classes (see the chart in Chapter 3 of the online Historical Outlines), and see how many of your verbs match one of the historical ablaut series.

5.4 Make a list of the English words you think you can recognize in the passage from the *Anglo-Saxon Chronicle* or prose portion of the Cædmon story. Can you understand most of what is happening (without peeking at the translation below)?

5.5 Look at the word order in the poem section of the Cædmon story, and make a list of all of the cases where the order does not match what you expect the order to be in Modern English. Are the words "scrambled" so that you have to rely on the inflections to know what they are doing in the sentences?

Audio Samples
Anglo-Saxon Chronicle
Cædmon
Beowulf (poetic language from an oral-formulaic source)
Ælfred, Pastoral Care (the king's letter to accompany a translation of the Pastoral Care)
Ælfric, Homily (about St. Gregory's decision to convert the Anglo-Saxons)
Wulfstan, Sermo Lupi ad Anglos (a sermon about Viking incursions)

Further Reading

There are numerous editions of the *Anglo-Saxon Chronicle*, which still exists in nine manuscripts, each one different. Whitelock, Douglas, and Tucker (1961) align translations of several of the manuscripts. A recent translation is Swanton (1998).

The engaging book by Parkes (1993) describes the history of punctuation, something we no longer notice – unless we get it wrong.

Blair (2003) is the classic account of Anglo-Saxon culture. A compendious resource, over 600 pages and 700 articles, is Lapidge et al. (2013).

Baker (2012); Mitchell and Robinson (2011); Campbell (1959). The first two books are popular introductions to Old English, both in advanced editions. Campbell is still the standard Old English reference grammar. A fine new Old English reader, with an introductory chapter on Old English, is Marsden (2015).

The *Dictionary of Old English*, at doe.utoronto.ca, was from the start based on the complete collection of Old English texts, now represented in the *Dictionary of Old English Corpus*, which is searchable online. The dictionary is completed for letters A-H (at this writing), and is also now available online.

Lord (1960) and the second edition (Lord, 2000). Oral-formulaic poetry was a feature of many preliterate cultures. Lord's account was influential for discussion of the orality of Old English poetry. A more recent account is Foley (1985). Still more recent is Amodio (2005). You can read Tacitus's history of the Germanic people in Tacitus (2010), edited and translated by James Rives and Harold Mattingly.

CHAPTER 6

Early Middle English

In this chapter

This chapter describes another invasion, this time by William the Conqueror from Normandy. The transition of the nobility brought Norman French to England, with strong effects on vocabulary formation. Norse vocabulary also appears in English from the former Danelaw. A literary example from *Ancrene Wisse* illustrates changing modes of writing.

6.1 **Norman Conquest**

When **William the Conqueror** took the English throne in 1066, it changed the course of emergence for English. Perhaps it should not have done so. William was the Duke of Normandy – of course "Normandy" means 'land of the North Men,' the same Vikings who had settled that region of France about the same time they were settling in the north and east of Britain – and thus William had his Norse heritage in common with many Englishmen. But change did come because William, as a conqueror and not merely a successor, changed the nobility of the English state, and thus

Figure 6.1 Section of the Bayeux Tapestry: William taking ship (public domain)

put speakers of **Norman** French into positions of authority all across Britain. While the common people in England continued to speak English, they now had to contend with an aristocracy that did not speak their language, and the consequence is a massive influx of French words that have come into English. The **Middle English** period thus continues the changes that were already underway in Old English, such as loss of inflections, but adds on top of that the disruptions caused by a French nobility that, over the course of the period, comes to use English again.

In 1066 England had no heir to the throne. In 1014 the Vikings had forced the English king into exile, and Æthelred took refuge with his in-laws in Normandy. After about three years of further fighting, there began a twenty-five year stretch of Norse kings in England ending in 1042. At that point, however, Æthelred's son Edward, known as the Confessor, reestablished the English line of kingship and held the throne for twenty-four years. When he died childless in January 1066, three people competed for the throne. Harold, the Duke of Wessex and most powerful lord in England at the time, also Edward's brother-in-law, was elected king the day after Edward's death by the *Witenagemot*, an assembly of the chief nobles and clerics in the country. However, Harold's estranged brother, Tostig, invited Harald Hardrada, King of Norway, to challenge for the English throne, and Harold had to defeat Tostig and Harald at the Battle of Stamford Bridge in Yorkshire in September of 1066. Meanwhile, William the Conqueror also claimed the throne, and landed his own army in the southeast while Harold was fighting in the north. Harold marched south as quickly as possible after Stamford Bridge and engaged William's army at Hastings in October 1066. The story is told on the famous Bayeux Tapestry (Figure 6.1 shows William taking ship).

Harold's force was holding the high ground and winning the battle at Hastings but, when part of the Norman army appeared to retreat, part of the English army pursued them and was attacked by the Norman cavalry outside their defensive position. The Normans then pretended to retreat again, and then again, with the same effect. Somewhat later Harold was killed in battle and William won the field. However, he was not immediately

Figure 6.2 Tower of London. The original White Tower is in the center (image from Wikipedia)

accepted by the English nobility – the Witanagemot initially elected a distant relative of Edward the Confessor, Edgar the Ætheling, who was never crowned – and after more fighting it took until Christmas 1066 for William to be crowned King of England. In the following five years raids and rebellions erupted across Britain as foreign claimants to the throne and English earls contested William's sovereignty, but in the end he was able to defend his claim and gain control of England.

In order to secure it, William and his sons, William and Henry, and their successors for the next two hundred years, "fillden þe land ful of castles" ('filled the land full of castles,' as the Peterborough continuation of the *Anglo-Saxon Chronicle* put it in reference to the reign of King Stephen, in the annal for 1137). The first castles were built by the new king in key strategic locations, including Cambridge, Lincoln, Nottingham, and York. Subsequently castles were built by the major land holders and then by the lesser ones on their new estates. Castles began as military fortifications, but over the centuries evolved into luxurious residences for the nobility. The **Tower of London** (Figure 6.2), for example, was begun by William the Conqueror in 1078 and was used as a residence, and later it was greatly expanded so that it came to have the concentric walls still visible today.

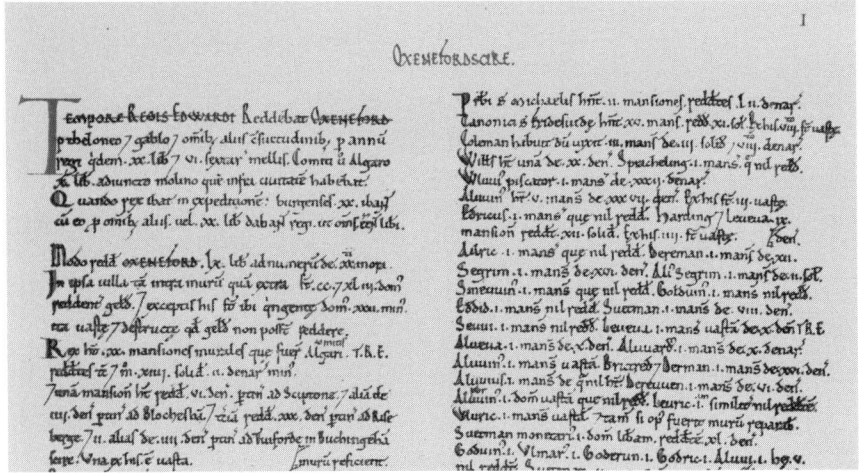

Figure 6.3 Domesday Book, a portion of the first page for Oxfordshire (Domesday data created by Professor J. J. N. Palmer and George Slater, University of Hull. domesdaymap.co.uk/book/oxfordshire/01/)

Over time the Tower of London also came to be used as a prison, the Royal Mint, and now as the home of the Crown Jewels. Another way that William tried to secure his kingdom was with accounting. Near the end of his reign he ordered an inventory called the **Domesday Book** (Figure 6.3), a list of all the properties and their value across the country. In so doing William greatly advanced the cause of government bureaucracy.

6.2 Anglo-Norman and English

By the mid 1070s, then, William had defeated the English earls, and replaced all of them with his own Norman associates. Not just the highest nobility but also lower ranks in the feudal hierarchy, as well as high church appointments like bishops and abbots, were occupied by Normans, and thus arose the group in England who spoke **Anglo-Norman**, the kind of Norman French used in England. Each of these central figures would have been accompanied by retainers, whether soldiers or members of the household, so the Anglo-Norman population, while never larger than about 2 percent of the overall population of England, was large enough to change the flow of linguistic interactions in the country. While the chief figures continued to speak Anglo-Norman with their close associates, the retainers who had to make the arrangements for daily life must by necessity have had to speak with the

English craftsmen and peasants, who were always in the great majority. It was these interactions, not the power or wealth per se of the new Norman lords, that eventually allowed so much French to emerge as part of our English language. The first Norman king of England who understood English was Henry II (1154–1189), but the first post-Conquest king actually to speak English was Edward I (1272–1307), two full centuries after William the Conqueror.

Relations between Norman and English were not always smooth. In the same entry for 1137 in the Peterborough continuation of the *Anglo-Saxon Chronicle*, the English monk writes (you can listen to this entry online, on the website for this book):

> for æuric rice man his castles makede & agænes him heolden; & fylden þe land ful of castles. Hi suencten suyðe þe uurecce men of þe land mid castelweorces; þa þe castles uuaren maked, þa fylden hi mid deoules & yuele men. Þa namen hi þa men þe hi wenden ðat ani god hefden, bathe be nihtes & be dæies, carlmen & wimmen, & diden heom in prisun & pined heom efter gold & syluer untellendlice pining; for ne uuæren næure nan martyrs swa pined alse hi wæron . . . Mani þusen hi drapen mid hungær. I ne can ne i ne mai tellen alle þe wunder ne alle þe pines ðat hi diden wrecce men on þis land; & ðat lastede þa xix wintre wile Stephne was king, & æure it was uuerse & uuerse.

> for every rich man built his castles and held against him [King Stephen]: and they filled the land full of castles. They greatly worked the wretched men of the land with castle-works; when the castles were made, they filled them with devils and evil men. Then they took the people that they thought had any goods, both by night and by day, working men and women, and put them in prison and tortured them for their gold and silver, unutterable tortures; for there were never any martyrs so tortured as they were. [descriptions of several torture methods] Many thousands they wore out with hunger. I cannot and I will not tell all the wounds and all the pains which they inflicted on wretched men in this land, and that lasted the nineteen winters while Stephen was king; and ever it was worse and worse.
>
> *From the* Anglo-Saxon Chronicle

King Stephen, grandson of William the Conqueror, had taken the throne after the death of Henry I in competition with Matilda, Henry's daughter. His reign was marked by strife and lawlessness and conflict with Matilda, a time called "The Anarchy." The annal for 1137, however, does not deal with high political conflict but instead with the effects of the time on the English population. "Wrecce men" were forced to build castles and "carlmen and wimmen" were tortured for their possessions. Here we see an early text in Middle English which continues the processes of change already begun in Old English. As in the Cædmon passage from the preceding chapter, sentences and word order are much like Modern English except for sometimes putting the object before the main verb ("æuric rice man his castles makede") or the verb before the subject ("fylden hi," "namen hi"). Inflections are limited to the plural ("castles," "deoules"), the genitive ("þa mannes throte," from description of a torture), and a final -e that could mark plural agreement on adjectives ("yuele men") but can also be found with a singular ("rice man"), and perhaps a dative form ("wrecce men" meaning 'to wretched men'). Already we see a number of Anglo-Norman loanwords in the annal, if not in this brief extract, that have become common words in English: *tresor* 'treasure,' *Canceler* 'Chancellor,' *prisun* 'prison,' *iustice* 'justice,' *rentes* 'taxes,' *privilegies* 'privileges,' and *miracles* 'miracles.' These loanwords are all things that the Anglo-Norman speakers had or maintained, and the English speakers used their words to talk about them. Hundreds of French words occur in English texts before 1250 including, as one might expect, a great many related to government and the church: *court, crown, parliament, reign, tax*; *baptism, clergy, communion, prayer, religion, saint, trinity*. A curious effect of this social split was the development of French and English **doublets**, pairs of words for the same thing from each language. Thus, English *swine* were eaten as French *pork*, a *cow* as *beef*, and *sheep* as *mutton*. The production of food was separated from its consumption by the language used to describe it, as were other aspects of production and consumption.

6.3 Norse and English

Doublets also emerged from English and **Norse** but without the social split. The settlement of Vikings in the north and east of England originally occurred in hamlets separate from English settlements – for example, the Five Boroughs of Lincoln, Stamford, Leicester, Nottingham, and Derby created a cluster of strong Norse influence – but trade and intermarriage reduced the distance between the populations. In the later Old English period Norse and English were likely to have been mutually intelligible, which would have been helpful for mixture of the people. After an intensive study, Michael Townend (2002) concluded that there was "a situation of adequate mutual intelligibility between speakers of Norse and English, rather than one involving widespread bilingualism or the use of interpreters." The situation for Norse and English was thus quite different from that between Anglo-Norman French and English. Again, political control in the Danelaw was not the determining factor for the language of the region, but instead the interaction of people talking to each other allowed language patterns to emerge over time.

Because Norse settlement and interaction with the English residents of an area occurred mainly among common people, not nobles, we have little direct evidence from writings to track how the patterns emerged, and yet they did. A typical and familiar case comes in the pronunciation of words spelled <sc->, which in Old English was pronounced [ʃ] but in Norse [sk]. We thus find doublets like *shirt/skirt* or *shrub/scrub*, which were the same word originally but have survived with two pronunciations with somewhat different meanings. While such words were competing in use in Middle English we find pairs like *shred/screde* or *shell/skelle*, of which only the English word has survived into Modern English. Some alternative forms like this exist even today in the North of England, such as Yorkshire *skift, skimmer* where other English speakers would say *shift, shimmer*.

Today we have many Norse words that have simply replaced their English counterparts. We use the originally Norse *sky*, not the English *welkin* (still used much later by Wordsworth in poetry), *egg* and not *ey* (both of these were still in use in Late Middle English), and *cut* and usually not *carve* (the latter just for special purposes like roasts and statues). As for the doublets where the same word survives in two pronunciations with different meanings, we sometimes have English and Norse words for the same thing, originally, that survive with different meanings: *no/nay, craft/skill, hide/skin*. All of these words from Norse belong to everyday life, not to the court or to the church. More examples of everyday Norse loans include *band, birth, bull, dirt, leg, race, root, sister, trust*, and *window*.

Perhaps the most celebrated examples of Norse loans to English are the third person plural pronouns *they/their/them*. Old English used the forms *hie, hiera, him*, which were carried over into early Middle English, but by the end of the Middle English period the Norse loans were broadly established. Some people believe that the third person singular pronoun *she* is also a Norse loan. For one language to borrow another language's pronouns is just not something we expect to happen, just as we do not expect to loan our toothbrushes to strangers. But it happened in English. While various theories have been offered to explain the borrowing of pronouns, including John Fisher's suggestions of the presence of northern workers at **William Caxton**'s printing office (Caxton was England's first printer) at the end of the Middle English period, the pronouns are just another side of a general pattern of borrowing that included a great many common words, as the Norse settlers interacted with their English neighbors in the north and east. While the northerners in the printing office did constitute one contingency, it was not enough to create the whole effect of Norse on English. The Norse influence on English simply emerged over the centuries, no doubt assisted by strong connections between London and the areas north and east of the city. Really, the analogy of one of us loaning somebody else a toothbrush relies too much on personification of language, that a language acts like a person might, when actually languages are not so much objects that have their own existence as they are generalizations about the linguistic behavior of a great many speakers. Emergence over time of preferences for originally Norse variants in the complex system of interactions between speakers is a much better explanation for the development of English than a few workers in Caxton's printing office.

6.4 **Reemergence of English**

In 1204 the French king Philip II Augustus defeated King John of England, so that Normandy was lost for the English crown. King John is perhaps better remembered for his submission to the **Magna Carta**, which limited the absolute power of the English king and led to the establishment of constitutional law. The loss of Normandy, however, is more significant for the English language because it forced the English nobility to choose sides. They could either be loyal to the French king and keep their French estates, or be loyal to the English king and keep their English estates. Many aristocrats had held properties on both sides of the English Channel, and they, including the English kings, often preferred to spend time in France, in Normandy but also in the Bordeaux region in the southwest of the country that had come under English control when Eleanor of Aquitaine, John's mother, had married the English King Henry II. England finally lost its southern French territory only in the fifteenth century, but the loss of Normandy split noble families in the north. While intrigues continued (e.g., Henry III supported rebellious French nobles), some nobles chose their English estates but many families divided their holdings in order to recognize and comply with the new politics. Again, it was not the politics per se that affected the language, but the situations for language interaction that those politics created. When the English manor houses no longer had regular contact and interaction with Normandy, they spent relatively more time with their English subjects.

At the king's court, Henry III still preferred French speakers and appointed many foreigners to positions of power. On the other hand, slowly, beginning with estates far from the king's court, noble families began to use English instead of French as their daily language, and the balance of linguistic interactions among the aristocracy in England shifted, slowly, to favor the emergence of English over Anglo-Norman among this group of speakers.

An early example of writing that accompanied such a shift is the *Ancrene Wisse* (also known as the *Ancrene Riwle*), originally composed in English in the early thirteenth century. It is a manual intended to guide young (noble) women who wanted to retire from daily life and pursue a religious vocation. The beginning of the section on "Love" starts:

> Seinte Pawel witneth thet alle uttre heardschipes, alle flesches pinsunges, ant licomliche swinkes – al is ase nawt ayeines luve, the schireth ant brihteth the heorte. *Exercitio corporis ad modicum valet; pietas autem valet ad omnia.* Thet is, "licomlich bisischipe is to lutel wurth, ah swote ant schir heorte is god to alle thinges. *Si linguis hominum loquar et angelorum, et cetera. Si tradidero corpus meum ita ut ardeam, et cetera. Si distribuero omnes facultates meas in cibos pauperum, caritatem autem non habeam, nichil michi prodest.* "Thah ich cuthe," he seith, "monne ledene ant englene, thah ich dude o mi bodi alle pine ant passiun thet bodi mahte tholien, thah ich yeve povre al thet ich hefde, yef ich nefde luve ther-with, to Godd ant to alle men in him ant for him, al were i-spillet.

> St. Paul witnesses that all outer hardships, and all fleshly pains and bodily labors, all is as naught against love, which purifies and brightens the heart. "*Exercitatio corporis ad modicum valet; pietas autem valet ad omnia.*" That is, "Bodily diligence is worth little; but a sweet and pure heart is good for all things." "*Si tradidero corpus meum ita ut ardeam; si linguis hominum loquar et angelorum; et si distribuero omnes facultates meas in cibos pauperum, caritatem autem non habeam, nihil mihi prodest.*" "Though I know," he said, "the tongues of men and angels, though I did to my body all the pains and passion that a body could suffer, though I gave the poor all that I had, if I gave no love from that to God and to all men in him and for him, all would be lost."
>
> *From the* Ancrene Wisse

The author quotes Paul from the Latin Bible and, since no translations into English were available and since women typically remained untutored in Latin, he provided an English translation. He then offers an **exemplum**, a brief story with a moral attached, to confirm his texts (you can listen to the story online, at the website for this textbook):

Her-to falleth a tale, a wrihe forbisne.

A leafdi wes mid hire fan biset al abuten, hire lond al destruet, ant heo al povre in-with an eorthene castel. A mihti kinges luve wes thah biturnd upon hire swa unimete swithe, thet he for wohlech sende hire his sonden, an efter other, ofte somet monie, sende hire beawbelez bathe feole ant feire, sucurs of liveneth, help of his hehe hird to halden hire castel. Heo underfeng al as on unrecheles, ant swa wes heard i-heortet, thet hire luve ne mahte he neaver beo the neorre. Hwet wult tu mare? He com him-seolf on ende, schawde hire his feire neb, as the thet wes of alle men feherest to bihalden, spec se swithe swoteliche, ant wordes se murie, thet ha mahten deade arearen to live, wrahte feole wundres ant dude muchele meistries bivoren hire eh-sihthe, schawde hire his mihte, talde hire of his kinedom, bead to makien hire cwen of al thet he ahte. Al this ne heold nawt – nes this hoker wunder? For heo nes neaver wurthe for-te beon his thuften . . .

Thes king is Jesu, Godes sune, thet al o thisse wise wohede ure sawle, the deoflen hefden biset. Ant he as noble wohere efter monie messagers ant feole god-deden com to pruvien his luve ant schawde thurh cnihtschipe thet he wes luve-wurthe, as weren sum-hwile cnihtes i-wunet to donne

Hereto falls a tale, a hidden example. There was a lady besieged by her foes, her land all destroyed, and she very poor, within an earthen castle. A mighty king's love was, however, turned upon her so greatly, that he for his courtship sent his messengers, one after another, and often many together, and sent her jewels both many and fair, help for living, help from his noble army to hold her castle. She received them all as someone without feeling, and she was so hard-hearted that he could never get any nearer to her love. What more do you want? He came himself in the end and showed her his fair face, as one who was of all men the most beautiful to behold, spoke very sweetly and such pleasant words that they might have raised the dead from death to life, wrought many miracles, did many wondrous works before her eyes, showed her his power, told her of his kingdom, offered to make her queen of all that he owned. All this availed naught. Was not this disdain a wonder? For she was never worthy to be his servant . . .

This king is Jesus Christ, God's son, that all of these ways wooed our soul that devils had beset. And he, as noble wooer, after many messengers and many good deeds came to prove his love and showed through knightship that he was worthy of love, as were sometimes knights used to doing.

From the Ancrene Wisse

In this era there was no category of writing quite like what we call **literature** today, so it is entirely appropriate that the "tale" here is formed as an exemplum with an interpretation attached to the story. Didactic writing, a branch of philosophy called **ethics**, could have examples from deeds, whether actual historical events or sometimes, as here, events that are **verisimilar**, like what might have happened even if it never actually happened. The church at the time did not approve of outright **fictions**. What modern readers simply accept as stories, medieval readers like the young noblewomen who heard the *Ancrene Wisse* understood in a different way. It was quite normal at the time for a moral to be appended to a story, as we still attach morals to the end of an Aesop's fable. The moral was part of the experience.

Again, as we saw in the Cædmon passage and in the Peterborough extract from the *Anglo-Saxon Chronicle*, sentences and word order are much like modern English, as when the author introduces lists of events in parallel constructions as we might find today: the king sent messengers, baubles, help for living, and help for her defense. We still see inflections for the plural ("fan" with an -*n* plural, "beawbelez," "words"), the genitive ("kinges luve"), and many examples of a final -*e* that could mark different cases ("eorthene castel," "beawbelez bathe feole ant feire," "o thisse wise"). We have an example of the comparative "neorre" 'nearer,' and the superlative "feherest" 'fairest.' There are several French borrowings (in modern forms, *destroy, castle, bauble, succor, noble, messenger, masteries*), yet the passage is certainly continuous with the kind of language in the Peterborough extract, even though it comes from the next century. What is different is the new context for castles and knights. Now, instead of a lawless land, we hear a blend of religion and aristocratic practice so that the Christian message is couched in terms of what knights sometimes used to do – a perfect approach for the daughters of an aristocratic house.

The Early Middle English period saw important changes in the cultural circumstances on the island of Britain. New Norman residents and the older Norse population interacted with the historical English population, with the result that the English language was very different at the end of the Early Middle English period in 1300 from what it was at the beginning, in 1100. The main point throughout all of these changes in vocabulary and inflections is the operation of the complex system of speech, the huge numbers of linguistic interactions between speakers, many of whom spoke different languages. The **external history** of the language – the accumulation of historical events and cultural changes – does not directly affect the **internal history** of the language – the changes in lexicon, pronunciation, and grammar. External history provides a record of changes in the circumstances of daily life for the speakers of English and other languages in Britain. To the extent that such changes – call them **contingencies**, new facts of life – affected interactions between people, different habits in language could emerge over time. It was not the facts of royal succession in the external history that helped to create change in the language directly, but rather differences in the circumstances under which people talked and wrote to each other. Change in English emerges from the interactions of speakers, only indirectly affected by what most external histories of the time record.

6.5 Chapter Summary

In this chapter, two cultural groups interacted with the English: the Norse population from above the old Danelaw, and the Normans, another ethnically northern people who had earlier occupied the Normandy region of what is now France. Both had important influences on English though from different cultural positions: the Anglo-Normans at the top and the Norse integrating with the English at the bottom. The effects can be seen in literary documents across the period, from the end of the *Anglo-Saxon Chronicle* to the early Middle English *Ancrene Wisse*.

Key Terms
Ancrene Wisse
Anglo-Norman
William Caxton
contingency
Domesday Book
doublet
ethics
exemplum
external history
fiction
internal history
literature
Magna Carta
Middle English
Norman
Norse
Tower of London
verisimilar
William the Conqueror

Exercises

6.1 Find images of the Bayeux Tapestry online (Wikipedia has a complete image), and trace the history from Edward the Confessor through the invasion. What do you find most striking about the people and events portrayed on the tapestry? Note the Latin headings for events: can you understand them well enough to follow the action?

6.2 Look up the Domesday Book online (e.g., at www.domesdaybook.co.uk/, or at discovery.nationalarchives.gov.uk/ and search for "domesday book"). How big is it? What are its contents, exactly? Where does the name come from? The point here is not to struggle with the details about the Domesday Book, but instead to understand it as an achievement in bureaucracy.

6.3 For the 1137 entry for the *Anglo-Saxon Chronicle*, go through the language line by line and describe what aspects of the language look backwards to Old English, and what aspects of the language look forward to Middle English. What about word order? How many words do you have to look up because they are too unlike Modern English?

6.4 What do you think of the story part of the *Ancrenne Wisse* example? What do you think of the explanation part? You may be familiar with this two-part structure from Aesop's fables today. How is the story part of the exemplum different from an Aesop's fable? Is the explanation part of the *Ancrenne Wisse* exemplum like the moral of an Aesop's fable?

6.5 Given what you know about the emergence of frequency patterns in a language from Chapter 2, think in more detail about what "change" might really consist of in a language. Is "change" a logical difference, such that one variant of a feature completely replaces another? What kind of change in the frequency profile of variants might count as a "change" in a language? For further information on this point, you may want to consult Chapter 5 of *Language and Complex Systems* (Kretszschmar, 2015).

Audio Samples
Anglo-Saxon Chronicle
Layamon, Brut (circa 1200, West Midland, a story about Arthur and Mordred)
Ancrene Riwle

Further Reading

For good general coverage of Middle English, see Fulk (2012). An introduction that also offers readings is Burrow and Turville-Petre (2005).

Townend (2002) offers the best current account relations between Norse and English speakers during the Old English and Early Middle English period.

Fisher (1995). Fisher's idea that Standard English was jump-started by Caxton's use of people from the North in his London printing office that produced government documents, the Chancery English hypothesis, was first published as an article and later in this book. The argument is less well accepted now than before, but the idea that a mixture of people from different places and a new technology, printing, could change language habits for English speakers remains attractive in the way that it uses external history to explain internal factors. We should now understand that emergence of preferences for Norse variants began long before Caxton, and that the printing office, if anything, helped to influence change as a new contingency for transmission of language.

Allen (1971; 1982). Allen was the champion of the idea that writers and readers in the Middle Ages did not have the same generic categories as modern readers, and in particular that what we now call "literature" was classified by medieval readers as "ethics." For an argument about the importance of verisimilar accounts, see Kretzschmar (1992).

CHAPTER 7

Late Middle English

In this chapter

We look at the Late Middle English period, when English nationalism emerged from earlier Norman dominance of the government, and the nobility began to use more English. The Black Death in the fourteenth century set in motion social changes that altered the conditions for language interactions. These conditions worked with traditional Middle English dialect patterns so that features from many places could mix in growing cities. A letter from the Paston family and a literary example from Chaucer illustrate changes in the language.

7.1 **Return of English**

The fourteenth century is the time when England and English came back into their own in government. Through much of the thirteenth century, English lords struggled against the policy of King Henry III to bring foreigners, Frenchmen, into the English court. Henry's son, Edward I, participated with him to fight against the rebellion of the barons, but Edward, at least, had learned English from his tutors. English kings following Edward I were likewise bilinguals, learning English as an additional language to their native French, until Henry IV (1367–1413) learned English as his first, native language. Indeed, rather than bringing foreigners into the English government, Edward III began the Hundred Years' War (1337–1453) in which the kings of England tried to assert their claim to the French throne. In 1362, Edward III became the first king to speak English in an address to Parliament, and the Official Pleading Act in that year changed the official language for conducting business to English (though records were still kept in Latin). The Late Middle English period is the time when English nationalism was reborn, over two hundred years after the Norman Conquest.

Ironically, the fourteenth century is also the time when a large number of French words came into English. The linguist Otto Jespersen calculated that as many as 40 percent of originally French words in English entered the language between 1250 and 1400. Philip Durkin (2014) notes that new occurrences of French words in English peaked between 1300 and 1500. Perhaps this is not so strange, if we consider that English was in greater and greater use among the noble class and these bilingual (or trilingual, with Latin) English speakers were just carrying over words from their native or habitual French. Thus, originally French (or Latin) words emerged as new options for English speakers, first among the upper class and later among the general population. Complexity science tells us that speakers are not constrained by monolithic linguistic structure, as by a contrast between English and French (or English and Latin); languages do not contact each other, people do. Speakers adapt themselves to the other speakers they interact with, in every situation or interaction. We are all trying to do the best we can, by using all of our linguistic resources, in any situation for speech in which we find ourselves. In the fourteenth century, the rise of bilingualism among upper-class speakers increased the possibility that these speakers would use their language resources, words from both French and English (or also from Latin), as they were trying to speak and write with their fellows. Durkin suggests that it is often difficult to determine exactly where new words from French or Latin came from. A small percentage certainly came from Anglo-French, and another small percentage certainly from continental French, with most of the new English words coming from one of the French sources or from Latin. Words that first occurred in English during this period such as *abolish*, *imaginative*, and *ballad* come from French, but a much larger group of new words might have come from either French or Latin, such as *abound*, *activity*, *analogy*, *application*, *climate*, *economy*, *imaginable*, and *liberality*. Under the circumstance that the new words were most likely introduced by bilingual or trilingual speakers in interaction with each other, it is impossible to cite an exact source language.

Robert Mannyng wrote a history of England early in this process, about 1340, and took care to write in "symple speche" (you can listen to this passage online on the website for this book):

Lordynges that be now here,
if ȝe wille listene & lere [learn] All the story of Inglande
als Robert Mannyng wryten it fand [found]
& on Inglysch has it schewed [shown],
not for þe lerid [learned] bot for þe lewed [unlearned],
ffor þo [those] þat in þis lande wone [live]
þat þe Latyn no Frankys cone [know] . . .
Als þai haf wryten & sayd,
haf I alle in myn Inglis layd,
In symple speche as I couthe,
þat is lightest in mannes mouthe.
I mad noght for no disours [minstrels],
ne for no seggers [sayers, storytellers], no harpours,
Bot for þe luf of simple men
þat strange Inglis can not ken [understand].

At a time of transition in language use, Mannyng noted the difference between what learned and unlearned people might understand. Those who do not know Latin or French may find it hard to understand the "strange" English of those who do know those languages, and who use words from them as if they were English. Professionals like *disours, seggers*, and *harpours* may not be so careful to use English without Latin or French words. It took more time, then, for Latin and French words to filter into the English of the general population after they were first introduced by the upper class.

The greatest contingency of this period was the **Black Death**, which occurred in England mainly in 1348–1349. While estimates vary widely, perhaps half of the population of England died during the eighteen months of the epidemic. Peasants had a much higher death rate than the nobility. This created social and economic disruption because of a shortage of labor and a corresponding increase in wage levels. Somewhat later, the Peasants' Revolt of 1381 did not succeed in changing social conditions, but by 1400 the old feudal system of serfdom that tied peasants to the land had greatly diminished. Thus, in the short term old demographic patterns were shattered by the loss of so many people to disease, and for the long term the traditional feudal social system eventually passed away in favor of rents and payments, as opposed to the duties a serf owed to his lord. The effect on language of the Black Death was to change the circumstances of daily life, so

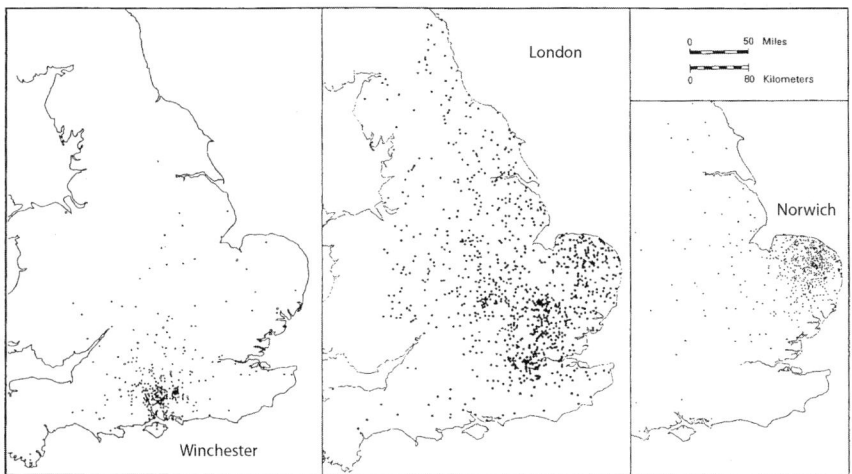

Figure 7.1 Byname migration pattern, Winchester, London, Norwich, circa 1300. Each dot represents the original location of a byname found in the city represented on the map (adapted from Keene, 2000)

that interactions between speakers did not occur just in the former patterns of communication. While the Black Death did not directly cause change in English, it disturbed the pattern of interactions that maintained earlier linguistic habits so that new habits could emerge in the population of speakers. Early Middle English had certainly begun changes away from Old English, as the previous chapter illustrated, and additional changes continued at perhaps even a faster pace in the later fourteenth century and fifteenth century. The contingency of the Black Death created social conditions that were ripe for change in the language.

Change in the traditional social system also made it increasingly possible for people to travel away from their local residences in search of work or opportunity. Derek Keene has shown that fourteenth-century bynames (e.g., Norwich, in the name Julian of Norwich) in regional cities and in London suggest that people migrated from great distances. Figure 7.1 shows the byname migration pattern associated with Winchester, London, and Norwich in 1300. For Winchester and Norwich, regional centers, much of the migration came from nearby with some migration from further away. People had migrated to London from all over the country. Movement across the country, especially to London, only increased later in the period in the aftermath of the Black Death and social change.

At this period, too, London participated in intensive trade with the Low Countries (modern day Belgium and Holland, which were then at the center of European trade), and as much as 10 percent of the London population of 50,000 at the time came from the Low Countries. Within the city the population was mobile, with people changing their residences frequently. However, specialized commercial districts arose, and particular neighborhoods might develop their own habits of speaking as a consequence of the mix of people who lived there. Laura Wright (1996) has documented the "macaronic" mixture of language in London business texts of the time. The complex system of interactions between residents in a neighborhood, city, district, or region, predicts the emergence of particular ways of speaking at every level of scale. Once we know that English people were increasingly on the move in the fourteenth century and thereafter, we can understand how different habits might emerge in different places as a consequence of demographic change.

7.2 Dialect Regions

The traditional pattern of dialect regions in Middle English suggests what habits of speech might have been carried to regional centers and to London in the fourteenth and fifteenth centuries. Figure 7.2 shows the regions, along with some indication of the specific habits that prevailed in different places.

If you compare the Northern, Midland, and Southern areas of this map to the areas shown on Figure 5.4 from the Old English period, you can see that they are quite similar. Old English Northumbria parallels the Middle English Northern dialect area; Old English Mercia the Middle English Midland dialect area; Old English Wessex parallels the Middle English Southern dialect area; and Old English Kent matches the Middle English Kentish dialect area. The old English division between the Danelaw and the West Saxon kingdom parallels the difference between the East Midland (northeast and southeast together) and the West Midland Middle English dialect area. The lines on the map are all **isoglosses**, limits of occurrence for particular variants in the language, based on a study of about 300 texts from the period by Moore, Meech, and Whitehall (1935) (for more information, see the Historical Outlines on the website for this book). So, for example, Line A is the southern limit of where you might expect to find the word *stan* instead of the word *stone*, which comes down to a sound change from Old English to make the vowel in *stone* rounded (see Appendix 1 for discussion of speech sounds). Line B is the southern limit of where you might expect to find *-(e)s* as an inflection on present plural indicative verbs, whereas further south you might find *-(e)n* or *-e* as the present plural indicative inflection. For discussion of the changes that make the other lines, see the Historical Outlines on the website for this book. Some of the lines cross through the dialect areas, as Line B crosses the

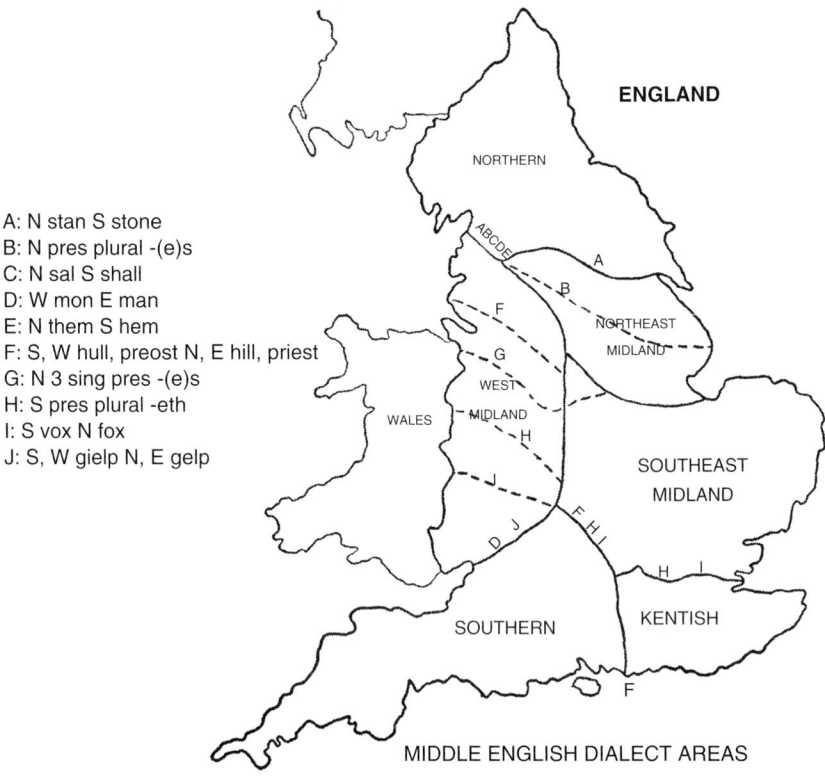

A: N stan S stone
B: N pres plural -(e)s
C: N sal S shall
D: W mon E man
E: N them S hem
F: S, W hull, preost N, E hill, priest
G: N 3 sing pres -(e)s
H: S pres plural -eth
I: S vox N fox
J: S, W gielp N, E gelp

Figure 7.2 Middle English dialect areas (adapted from Moore and Marckwardt, 1965)

northeast Midland and many lines cross the West Midland, but many of the lines bundle together to make the boundaries of the named dialect areas. Drawing isoglosses gives us a convenient way to mark off regions of interest where speech habits may differ.

A more recent method of charting regional patterns in Late Middle English comes from *A Linguistic Atlas of Late Mediaeval English* (McIntosh, Samuels, and Benskin, 1986) and its electronic version (Benskin et al., 2013). The "fit technique" used for this project is based on the idea that Middle English linguistic variation forms a regular continuum, and it makes for a very efficient tool for the analysis and comparison of scribal texts. Maps in the *Atlas* do not use isoglosses, but rather show dots where particular features occurred in the texts included in the project (so-called "**dot maps**," as in Figure 7.3).

Figure 7.3 shows that spellings of *shall*, *should* starting with <x-> were mainly found in East Anglia. These maps make it harder to talk about dialect areas, but they do give specific information about where forms that occurred in manuscripts occurred in particular locations.

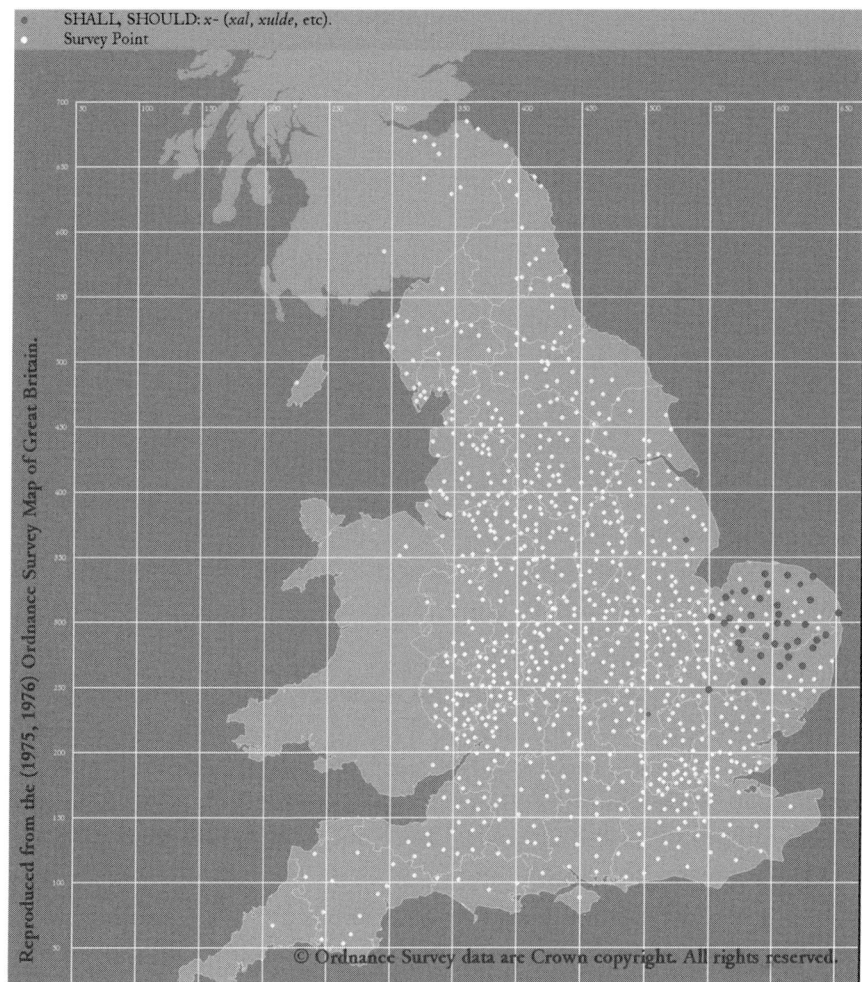

Figure 7.3 Dot map for <x-> spellings of *shall, should*. Dark dots show where <x-> spellings were found (from Benskin et al., 2013)

Of course, when adult speakers moved from region to region, as when many speakers moved to London from across all of England, they took their regional habits with them. This means that in regional centers like Winchester or Norwich or York, and especially in London, people with a variety of habits would interact with each other. As a result of people's interactions, frequency profiles like those described in Chapter 2 would emerge. In each of the Middle English dialect areas, we would expect that there would be a range of possible variants for any linguistic feature, and when those variants were charted by frequency, an A-curve like those described in Chapter 2 would emerge for the range of variants. For example, Figure 7.4 shows the spellings of the word *shall* found in a collection of Eastern texts from the fifteenth century.

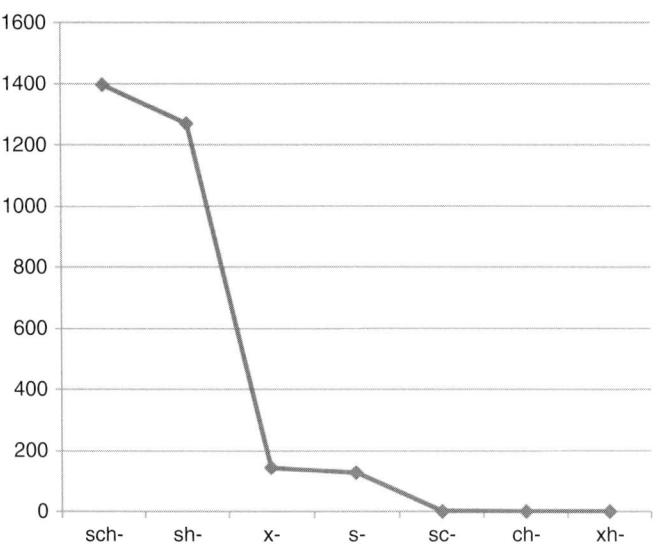

Figure 7.4 Spellings of *shall*, Eastern texts, fifteenth century (adapted from Kretzschmar and Stenroos, 2012)

The spelling *schall* was the most common at the time, followed by the spelling that eventually prevailed, *shall*. Line C in Figure 7.2 indicates that the spelling *sal* was a northern form, and *shall* was used further south, but we see both spellings in the set of Eastern texts in Figure 7.4, just at different frequencies of occurrence. The dot map in Figure 7.3 shows that <x-> spellings of *shall* were only found in East Anglia, but Figure 7.4 shows that such spellings were not the most common spelling there. Isoglosses may be convenient as a generalization, and we do not want to stop talking about dialect areas, but all the same we should realize that people did move around in England then, and still move around now, so in fact we can find many different variants in any one region or place. A single writer could use more than one spelling, as we will see in the letter below. What happened over time to *schall* in the East? The complex system of speech allows for changes to occur, and over time *schall* just became less frequent than *shall*. What is remarkable about these dialect areas and dialect variants is that, while the frequency of many variants will change, the dialect areas themselves, as generalizations over many features, have remained stable over very long periods of time. And many variants, too, have remained stable over time as other variants have changed around them. The complex system of English permits long-term stability while it also allows for changes, some quite slow and some very fast. Complexity science tells us that change is less mechanical or logical than many linguists have thought it to be in the past.

7.3 **English in a Family**

A good example of movement and change in language comes from the **Paston letters**. They were written by members (sometimes by secretaries) of the Paston family, landed gentry in Norfolk, between 1422 and 1509. This letter, from Margaret Paston to her husband John in London, written in 1477, asks for cloth for a new gown because she is pregnant and her old clothes no longer fit:

> To myryth reverent and worscheful husbond, Jon Paston:
>
>   Ryth reverent and worscheful husbond, I recomaunde me to yow, desyryng hertyly to here of yowr wylfare, thankyng yow for the tokyn that ye sent me be Edmunde Perys, preyng yow to wete that my modyr sent to my fadyr to London for a goune cloth of mustyrddevyllers [grey wool cloth] to make of a goune for me; and he tolde my modyr and me wane he was comme home, that he cargeyt [charged] yow to beyit, aftyr that he were come oute of London.
>
>   I pre yow, yf it be not bowt, that ye wyl wechesaf [vouchsafe] to byit, and sendyt home as sone as ye may, for I have no goune to weyre this wyntyr but my blake and my grene a lyer [lyard 'spotted with grey'], and that is so comerus [cumbersome] that I ham wery to weryt.
>
>   As for the gyrdyl that my fadyr be hestyt [promised] me, I spake to hym ther of a lytyl before he zede [went] to London last, and he seyde to me that the faute was in yow, that ze [you] wolde not think ther uppe on to do makyt [have it made]; but I suppose that ys not so; he seydyt but for a skwsacion [excuse]. I pre yow, yf ye dor takyt uppe on you, that ye wyl weche safe to do makyt a yens [before] ye come home, for I hadde never more need ther of than I have now, for I ham waxse so fetys [shapely, meaning 'large'] that I may not be gyrte in no barre or no gyrdyl that I have but of one. Elisabet Peverel hath leye sek xv. or xvj. wekys of the seyetyka [sciatica], but sche sent my modyr word be Kate, that sche xuld come hedyr wane God sent tyme, thoow sche xuld be crod [carried] in a barwe [wheelbarrow] . . .
>
> Your ys, M.P.
>
> From the Paston Letters

We see a number of differences from modern English in this passage, such as putting two words together (*myryth, beyit, byit, sendyt, makyt*), or by taking words we think of as one word apart into two words (*uppe on, a yens* for "against" meaning 'before'). Margaret sometimes spells with an <e> when it is expected (*wete*) or vice versa (*wylfare*). Spellings with <w> and <y> are not what modern readers expect. Spellings with <z> instead of <y> in *yede* and *ye* are striking (though *ze* has reappeared in the 21st century as a gender neutral pronoun for some writers). The formal greeting, "right reverend and worshipful," strikes an odd tone to modern ears, and the use of "ye" and "yow" is the polite form (as opposed to "thee" and "thou"). The closing uses a separate genitive particle, which in modern English would just be "Yours." Margaret uses both the <sch-> and <x-> spellings instead of modern <sh-> in *sche* and *xuld*. All these are changes in the language, variants that had high frequencies then but no longer. Margaret uses two verb forms that are new changes in Late Middle English, on the way to Modern English: the present participle with *-ing* (*desyryng, thankyng, preyng*) instead of the older *-ende*, and the infinitive marked with *-to* (*tobyit, to do*) instead of the older infinitive just with an *-en* ending. As for movement, clearly the Paston men travel back and forth to London regularly, and so create interactions between Londoners and Easterners. And yet otherwise the letter appears to be a familiar exchange between wife and husband. Margaret takes John's side against what her father told her as an excuse, and she seems to joke about her expanding figure and her friend Elisabet, who will be there, even if it takes a wheelbarrow, when the baby comes. This glimpse of life in the Paston family reminds us that, as much as we sometimes want to take the larger view, the English language lives in our homes and letters.

7.4 Chaucer

The most familiar Middle English author is from the end of the fourteenth century, Geoffrey **Chaucer**, who died in 1400. His language has moved significantly towards what we expect from Modern English. Here is the beginning of the General Prologue to **Canterbury Tales**, Chaucer's most famous work (you can listen to this passage online on the website for this book).

> Whan that Aprille with his shoures soote ['gentle, sweet']
> The droghte of March hath perced to the roote,
> And bathed every veyne in swich licour
> Of which vertu engendred is the flour;
> Whan Zephirus eek ['also'] with his sweete breeth
> Inspired hath in every holt and heeth
> The tendre croppes, and the yonge sonne
> Hath in the Ram his halve cours yronne,
> And smale foweles maken melodye,
> That slepen al the nyght with open ye
> (So priketh hem nature in hir corages ['hearts']);

Thanne longen folk to goon on pilgrimages,
And palmeres ['pilgrims'] for to seken straunge strondes
To ferne halwes, kowthe ['known'] in sondry londes;
And specially from every shires ende
Of Engelond to Caunterbury they wende ['go']
The holy blisful martir for to seke,
That hem hath holpen whan that they were seeke.

The online Historical Outlines has a full chapter on Chaucer's English (Chapter 4), including a full phonetic transcription of how Chaucer's lines might have been pronounced at the time. The online Historical Outlines also provides full coverage of Chaucer's inflections, pronouns, and verb conjugations. Inflections and pronouns have largely changed to their modern values, except for the problem of **final -e**. We have now mostly lost the final -e that, for Chaucer, still represented a **reduced form** of many inflections in Old English or in etymological situations where another vowel in Old English has been reduced to -e. Because a final -e was often not pronounced in Chaucer's time, scribes often put an -e where it was neither inflectional nor etymological. Only a few of the words need to be provided with glosses; others may be spelled differently, or take a moment to recognize: "foweles" 'fowls, birds,' "halwes" 'hallows, shrines.' Some French loanwords are used with meanings we no longer recognize readily, like "licour" 'liquid,' while we use the word mainly for alcoholic drinks, or "corages" 'hearts,' while we use the word for a psychological trait, courage. Verbs still have old conjugations, whether the -th ending for third-person singular present, like "hath" 'has' and "priketh" 'pricks,' or the -en ending for third person plural present, like "slepen" 'sleep' and "longen" 'long,' or a strong form that is now weak in Modern English, like "holpen" 'helped.' There is a mixture of pronoun forms: older Southern hem coexists with the incoming Northern form they in this passage. By 1400, then, English was well on its way to something much closer to modern English.

The Late Middle English period saw important changes in the cultural circumstances on the island of Britain. The nobility, and later the wider English population, began to use more words with French and Latin origins. Social changes, too, contributed to conditions that helped to make the English language very different at the end of the period, in 1500, from how it was in 1300. The main point throughout all of the changes in vocabulary and inflections is the operation of the complex system of speech, huge numbers of linguistic interactions between speakers. By the end of the Late Middle English period, English was well on its way to looking like Modern English.

7.5 Chapter Summary

The Late Middle English period was a time of great change in the language. The vocabulary began to be greatly augmented with new words from French and from Latin. Social change following the Black Death disturbed traditional patterns of interaction among speakers, and allowed for more movement of people across the country, all of which created conditions for substantial change in the language. By the time of Chaucer, and even more by the end of the period, the English language was taking on a more modern appearance.

Key Terms
Black Death
Canterbury Tales
Chaucer
dot maps
final *-e*
isogloss
Paston letters
reduced form

Exercises

7.1 Look up the Hundred Years' War (there is a Wikipedia entry among many others), and consider what territory the English king and the French king might have controlled over its course. How do you think this war that was mainly conducted on continental French soil might have affected the English language? Do you think that English soldiers might have brought home any continental French words?

7.2 Look up the Black Death in England online (there is a Wikipedia entry among many others). Was England the only country affected by it? What different estimates can you find for the mortality rate, and which estimates do you think are most credible? Once you know more about the Black Death in general, speculate about how it might have affected local communities and the language in those communities.

7.3 There are four specimens of Middle English dialects in the Historical Outlines available on the website associated with this textbook. Look at each of the four, and try to identify differences between them. NB: you can use the isoglosses on the Middle English dialect map, and the lists of auxiliary characteristics of each dialect area in §107 through §111 of the Historical Outlines.

7.4　Listen to the audio sample of *Gawain and the Green Knight*. Can you identify any features that connect it with the dialect used in the Northwest Midlands? NB: you can use the isoglosses on the Middle English dialect map, and the lists of auxiliary characteristics of each dialect area in §107 through §111 of the Historical Outlines. *Gawain* is a good example of the technique of alliterative poetry, a revival of Old English alliterative poetic style. Describe the alliterative patterns of a group of six lines.

7.5　Look at the online Historical Outlines chapter on the language of Chaucer (Chapter 4), and learn to pronounce the first part of the General Prologue. You can use the phonetic transcription, or try to use the general advice about pronunciation given in the tables.

Audio Samples

Alysoun (a Harley lyric, early fourteenth century)

Dan Michel, Ayenbite of Inwyt (early fourteenth century, Kentish dialect, religious instruction)

Robert Manning, Story of England

Richard Rolle, Bee and Stork (bestiary, mid fourteenth century, Northern dialect)

Chaucer, Prologue, Canterbury Tales

Chaucer, Astrolabe

Gawain and the Green Knight (alliterative romance, late fourteenth century, Northwest Midlands dialect)

Malory, King Arthur (Arthurian romance, mid fifteenth century)

Caxton, Prologue, Eneydos (prologue, late fifteenth century)

Cely letter (letter from a London merchant, late fifteenth century)

Further Reading

Durkin (2014). The Deputy Chief Editor of the *Oxford English Dictionary* has produced this highly readable account of the development of English vocabulary. His earlier book on etymology (Durkin, 2009) is somewhat more technical but still a great source of information on word history.

Benedictow (2004) estimates that mortality was over 60 percent, a high estimate. Lewis (2016) makes a more moderate estimate of 45 percent mortality.

Keene (2000) describes the demographics of the rise of London, a fascinating story of how the population of Britain interacted with its emerging national center. In a pathbreaking study, Wright (1996) documents the mixture of vocabulary from different languages in London English of this period.

Moore, Meech, and Whitehall (1935: 1–60). This early article, as reported in the Historical Outlines online, still offers a clear picture of Middle English dialect areas. The more recent McIntosh, Samuels, and Benskin (1986) was a monumental project whose fit technique has been controversial as a basis for a description of Middle English dialects. For discussion of the technique, see Kretzschmar and Stenroos (2012: 111–122). For a discussion of isoglosses as a way to make dialect maps, see Kretzschmar (2009).

Nevalainen and Raumolin-Brumberg (2016) have been the pioneers in the field of historical sociolinguistics. The *Corpus of Early English Correspondence* offers over 6000 letters that can be mined for linguistic features: www.helsinki.fi/en/researchgroups/varieng/corpus-of-early-english-correspondence.

Chaucer (1987) – The Riverside Chaucer – is a long-running popular collection of the poet's works. Besides *Canterbury Tales*, modern readers will still enjoy *Troilus and Criseyde*, perhaps the best love story ever written in English.

CHAPTER 8

Early Modern English

In this chapter

This chapter describes the emergence of English as a language for all purposes.
Loanwords from French and Latin become more important in the lexicon, amid complaints
over all the new words. Borrowings from Dutch and Spanish are also prevalent, the latter in
conjunction with the spread of English to the New World. At the same time a large change
in pronunciation, the Great Vowel Shift, separated the sound of English from that of
continental languages. Some of the best English poets lived in this period, from Wyatt to
Shakespeare to Milton.

8.1 Emergence of Modern English

During the Middle English period, French remained the language of the
court and the law for much of the time, and Latin was the language of the
church and science. However, the Early Modern period from 1500–1700
saw the transition from English as a language of the common people to
English as a language for all purposes. In order for this to happen, English
acquired words from French and Latin: instead of using the words as parts

of French or Latin sentences, these words became part of English sentences. So, for example, in the language of law all cases were conducted in French until 1362, when all pleadings were supposed to be carried out in English. After that time, many legal arguments were still conducted in French until the end of the Early Modern period. During all of this long and slow transition, French words became used as English words: *justice*, *equity*, *jury*, *judge*, *plaintiff*, *defendant*, *attorney*, *larceny*, *torts*, *bail*, *parole*, and many others. **Loanwords**, or **borrowings**, are words used in one language, like English, that replicate words used in another language, like French. Sounds and grammatical constructions can also be borrowed from one language to another, but words are the feature that receives most discussion. Of course, French lost nothing when English borrowed its words, and English will not be paying French back: the idea of a loan or of borrowing is a metaphor that describes what people do with features in languages.

As we saw in Chapter 1, when people speak or write it can be difficult to match what they do with the idea of a language as a **code**, a list of words and a set of rules for how to put them together. The main point of Chapter 1 was that, in English, *we are not all trying to do the same thing and getting it wrong*. Your perceptions of and your experience with English are just not going to be the same as everybody else's. If we take this idea back to the Early Modern period, we can understand that speakers of English were trying to make their language do things that had historically just been carried out in French or Latin, and so different speakers would have had different ideas about what words to use and still call them "English." Even today, most English speakers know the phrase *déja vu*, French for 'already seen,' something we say when we feel uncannily that some situation is happening to us for the second time. You can find it in English dictionaries (the *Oxford English Dictionary*, described in the next chapter, says that its first appearance in written English is 1903), but the question remains whether it has actually become English or whether people who say it are really using something French. Every English speaker, in the Early Modern period and also today, has had a **repertoire** of words that they are happy to use and call English, but the repertoire is different for different speakers and so there can be disagreement about whether a word is English or not. Compared to English in use today, you can multiply this problem a thousandfold for the Early Modern period. Some linguists will describe the use of words and phrases from one language in another language as **code switching** or **code mixing**, but the important thing is not that speakers are all trying to use the same code and getting it wrong. Speakers are always doing the best they can with what they know. They are not switching or mixing anything, but instead trying to accomplish their communicative intentions with the words they know. Eventually, the complex system of speech allows for words to emerge as common parts of what we say and write to each other, so we can now agree that *déja vu* is English even though it came from French, but during the operation of the complex system that sort of judgment is often far from clear. That is the situation that Early Modern English speakers found themselves in for a great many words.

Early Modern writers noticed what was happening with their vocabulary. Printing had been invented just before 1500, and England's first printer, William Caxton, and his associates created a new market for books in parallel with an increase in literacy. A number of these books addressed educational topics, now in English, and commented on their **vernacular** language as opposed to the Latin that had earlier been used for high cultural activities. Thomas Wilson wrote in 1560 in his *Art of Rhetorique* that

> He that commeth lately out of France, will talke French English and neuer blush at the matter. An other chops in with English Italienated, and applieth the Italian phrase to our English speaking.

As Philip Durkin (2014) reports, Wilson's overall point of view was that "Among all other lessons this should first be learned, that wee neuer affect any straunge ynkehorne termes, but to speake as is commonly receiued," but even Wilson used the words *affect*, *straunge*, *common*, and *receiue* that came originally from French.

8.2 Shakespeare

At the end of the sixteenth century, **Shakespeare** made fun of those who mixed up Latin with their English in *Love's Labor's Lost* (V.i). The pedant Holofernes converses with the curate Nathaniel:

HOLOFERNES: Satis quid sufficit. [Enough is as good as a feast]

NATHANIEL: I praise God for you, sir. Your reasons [discourse] at dinner have been sharp and sententious [meaningful], witty without affection [affectation], audacious without impudency, learned without opinion [dogmatic view], and strange without heresy. I did converse this quondam [former] day with a companion of the king's, who is intituled, nominated, or called, Don Adriano de Armado.

HOLOFERNES: Novi hominem tanquam te [I know the man as well as I know you]. His humor is lofty, his discourse peremptory [decisive], his tongue filed [polished], his eye ambitious, his gait majestical, and his general behavior vain, ridiculous, and thrasonical [boastful]. He is too picked [refined], too spruce, too affected, too odd, as it were, too peregrinate [foreign in manner], as I may call it.

NATHANIEL: A most singular and choice epithet.

While Nathaniel thinks that Holofernes has used a choice bit of description, another character, Moth, a serving boy, thinks that "They have been at a great feast of languages, and stol'n the scraps." Holofernes and Nathaniel are "book-men" and mix their languages, mainly Latin with English, and Shakespeare pillories them throughout the play by having common people comment on their speech, as Moth here, or elsewhere Dull, a constable. Speeches by other characters, here by the courtier Berowne, are not pilloried but still have plenty of borrowed words:

BEROWNE: O, but for my love, day would turn to night!
Of all complexions the culled sovereignty
Do meet, as at a fair, in her fair cheek,
Where several worthies make one dignity,
Where nothing wants that want itself doth seek.
Lend me the flourish of all gentle tongues –
Fie, painted rhetoric! O, she needs it not!

In these seven lines most of the key words are from French or from Latin by way of French: *complexion, cull, sovereignty, fair, dignity, flourish, gentle, paint, rhetoric*. While the magnitude of the use of borrowed words in English came in for comment, and sometimes sarcasm, many loanwords had already become normal.

As we see in the conversation between Holofernes and Nathaniel, not all of the Latinate words they use have survived in use today, and some have survived but with different meanings. Words like *quondam, intituled, thrasonical*, and *peregrinate* need glosses because we no longer use them, and words like *sententious, affection, opinion*, and *peremptory* need glosses because their meanings have changed. *Reasons, filed*, and *picked* may not be Latinate (*reason* comes from French), but their meanings have changed, too. As we shall see from the discussion of C. S. Lewis in Appendix 3, we need to be careful not to lean automatically towards the modern meanings of words when we read an Early Modern author like Shakespeare.

The *Oxford English Dictionary*, discussed in Chapter 9, cites Shakespeare as the first user of a great many new words in English, but that does not mean that Shakespeare invented them all. Shakespeare was a witness to the simmering pot of language of his day, as a great many loanwords came into English. In *Love's Labor's Lost* he makes fun of people for mixing their languages, and by writing down some of what they said he gets credit, instead of the people he listened to, for the first use of new words. It is also true that readers for the *Oxford English Dictionary* spent more time reading and citing words from Shakespeare than they did from other writers, so Shakespeare's popularity has something to do with his getting a reputation as a user of new words. Shakespeare was no doubt brilliant and inventive, but for his use of new words we should consider what was happening around him in the language, as new loanwords emerged in English, rather than give him all the credit by himself.

As counterpoint to Shakespeare's representation of sophisticated language, we can consider a short passage from the diary of Henry Machyn, from June 8, 1557 (you can listen to this passage online in the website for this book):

> The viij day of Juinj cam a goodly prossessyon unto Powlles, and dyd oblassyon [oblation 'religious offering'] at the he [high] auter [alter], sant Clementes parryche with-out Tempylle-bare, with iiijxx baners and stremars, and the whettes [waits 'street musicians'] of the cete [city] playing; and a iijxx copes ['(people in) ceremonial vestments'], and prestes and clarkes, and dyver of the ennes [inns] of the cowrt whent next the prestes; and then cam the parryche with whytt rodes [roods, crosses] in ther handes, and so bake agayne with the whettes playing, and prestes and clarkes syngyng, home-warde.

Machyn, a merchant tailor and undertaker, here describes a procession to St. Paul's church. Priests and clerks and members of the "inns of court" (legal societies) came first, and then members of the parish with white crosses, all accompanied by musicians. The words *procession, oblation,* and *cope,* all from French or Latin, are the kind of loanwords Shakespeare wrote about, but are used here in a diary, not to make fun of anybody. The difficulties here are unfamiliar spelling (e.g., <whent> for *went,* <parryche> for *parish,* <whytt> for *white*) and an unfamiliar discourse pattern (Machyn announces the procession in general in the first section up to the semicolon, and connects a description of the people and musicians to that unit with the word *and*). This entry has none of Shakespeare's poetry (you can listen to Shakespeare's Sonnet 18 online on the website for this textbook) or pillory, but still shows us how new loanwords were integrated into normal speech and writing.

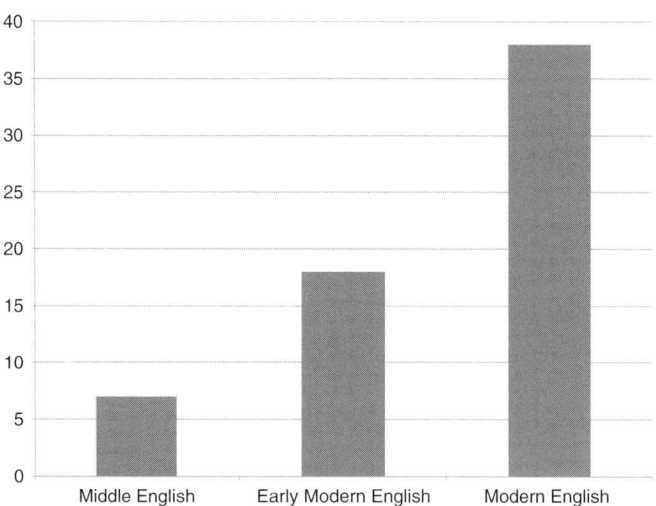

Figure 8.1 Proportion of French/Latin words among the highest-frequency words in English (adapted from Durkin, 2014)

Philip Durkin (2014) has shown us that word history is not just a matter of when loanwords were first used in English, but of how often they were used. Figure 8.1 shows that, while many words may have been first borrowed from French and Latin during the Middle English period, such words had not yet become so commonly used (at least in writing) that they were among the highest-frequency words in English. However, by the Early Modern period, more than twice as many words of French and Latin origin could be found among the high-frequency words, and the proportion would double again for the Modern period. In the complex system of English once French and Latin words entered the language, they could emerge in time as the common way to say things.

Words also entered English from other languages, and that often happened because the Early Modern period is when England and its navy began to engage with the rest of the world. In perhaps the most notable engagement of the period, the English defeated the **Spanish Armada** in 1588 and, besides repelling a Spanish invasion, signaled that England would be a player on the high seas. A decade earlier, Sir **Francis Drake** had sailed all the way around the world, an expedition that was supposed to attack Spanish possessions in the New World. Of course Christopher Columbus had traveled to the Americas in 1492, and the Spanish had explored much of Central America and southern North America in the early sixteenth century. The French, too, explored the New World, notably in what is now eastern Canada. The English were not the first to get to North America, but they established colonies that filled the gap between the Spanish in the south and the French in the north. The **Roanoke** colony was founded in 1586 by Sir Walter Raleigh but later was lost. The **Jamestown** colony began in 1607, Bermuda in 1609, and the **Plymouth** colony in 1620. Many other colonies were started and failed during this time, but by the end of the seventeenth century about 150,000 migrants from all parts of Britain came to North America.

The experience of exploration and colonization offered contact with a number of languages. A large number of loanwords entered English from Spanish in the sixteenth and seventeenth centuries, including *machete*, *mosquito*, *tobacco*, *anchovy*, *plantain*, *alligator*, *cockroach*, *guitar*, *cargo*, and *plaza*. Terms taken from Native Americans were recorded, for example, in Thomas Harriot's *Briefe and True Report of the New Found Land of Virginia* (1588), a report based on the lost Roanoke colony. Some of these words survive today, like *chocolate* and *tomato*, while others, like *openayk* (a kind of potato) and *sacquenummener* (a cranberry) have disappeared. At the end of the seventeenth century, the English took over the Dutch colony in southeastern New York, including New Amsterdam, which became New York. Eventually words like *cookie*, *coleslaw*, *waffle*, and *boss* entered English from this area of contact.

Numerous other words from Dutch came into English in Britain, owing to the active trade between England and the Low Countries during the Early Modern period. Hilary Mantel has written about interactions of this kind in her popular novels about the court of Henry VIII. Words like *uproar*, *snap*, *reef*, and *split* came into English from Dutch in the sixteenth century, and *plunder*, *easel*, *slim*, *smuggler*, *kink*, and *snuff* from the seventeenth century. As Thomas Wilson suggested, words from Italian were also used, as the British fascination with Italy continued (earlier, Chaucer had imitated Boccaccio, for instance). Words that have become common came into English from Italian during the Early Modern period, like *manage*, *per cent*, *post*, *macaroni*, *broccoli*, *opera*, *cameo*, *grotto*, *balcony*, *ghetto*, and *umbrella*. The English were actively engaged in Europe at this time as well as in the New World.

Thomas Wyatt's sonnet "Whoso list to hunt" illustrates this engagement. Wyatt (1503–1542) may have been a lover of Anne Boleyn, the second wife of Henry VIII, and this sonnet may well refer to that liaison. Wyatt had been a diplomat in France, Spain, and Italy for the king, and he brought back the form of the sonnet, here an imitation of Petrarch's Sonnet 190.

> Whoso list to hunt, I know where is an hind,
> But as for me, *hélas*, I may no more.
> The vain travail hath wearied me so sore,

I am of them that farthest cometh behind.
Yet may I by no means my wearied mind
Draw from the deer, but as she fleeth afore
Fainting I follow. I leave off therefore,
Sithens in a net I seek to hold the wind.
Who list her hunt, I put him out of doubt,
As well as I may spend his time in vain.
And graven with diamonds in letters plain
There is written, her fair neck round about:
Noli me tangere, for Caesar's I am,
And wild for to hold, though I seem tame.

We see some words in the sonnet that are plainly from other languages, *hélas* (from French) and *noli me tangere* (from Latin), but several more are actually loanwords that we may not notice. *Vain, travail, faint, diamond, letters, plain*, and *fair* all come from French. The phrase "in a net I seek to hold the wind" is an allusion to Provençal medieval poetry. So, while the sonnet form with its rhyme scheme and division of thought into sections of eight and six lines may be Italian, we also see evidence of Latin, French, and Provençal connections that make the poem truly international in style.

One of the defining features of language development in the Early Modern era was population movement and consequently population mixture. As life became more settled and the margin between life and death became wider during the Renaissance, more people survived and thus many people had to move in order to find work. Keene (2000) reports that most adult Londoners were born outside the city, and that new immigrants to the city may have accounted for two-thirds of the total population. Emigration to North America accounted for as much as 70 percent of English population increase during the seventeenth century, and a majority of those people came to North America through London. In North America, two characteristics of European settlement – introduction of disease and violence towards the survivors – created a pattern of replacement of the native population, rather than integration with it, that would continue long thereafter. Up to 90 percent of the Eastern Native American population was lost owing chiefly to the introduction of European diseases. The colonists, too, suffered high mortality rates of 50 percent or more in the first years at Jamestown and Plymouth, and child mortality was up to 50 percent before the age of twenty, so that the colonies depended on the continuing flood of new immigrants to increase their numbers. Mixed populations of English speakers from different British regions came to every settlement. Even settlements like Plymouth that are often thought to be regionally homogeneous were actually quite mixed, as we know from the Mayflower passenger list and from complaints by the Pilgrims about their non-Pilgrim neighbors. Nobody today preserves in its entirety Shakespeare's English or any other regional British variety from the seventeenth century, because no living language fails to change over time. In the mixed populations in London and North America, the complex system of speech operated so that new habits of speech could emerge in communities with new and changing populations of speakers.

John Winthrop was governor of the Massachusetts Bay Colony early in the seventeenth century. His wife followed him there later, and he wrote to her about what she should bring (you can listen to this passage online on the website for this textbook):

> Be sure to be warme clothed, & to have store of fresh provisions, meale, eggs putt up in salt or grounde mault, butter, ote meale, pease, & fruits, & a large stronge chest or 2: well locked, to keepe these provisions in; & be sure they be bestowed in the shippe where they may be readily come by, (wch the boatswain will see to & the quartermasters, if they be rewarded beforehande,) but for these things my sonne will take care, Be sure to have ready at sea 2: or 3: skillets of severall syzes, a large fryinge panne, a small stewing panne, & a case to boyle a pudding in; store of linnen for use at sea, & sacke [white wine] to bestowe among the saylers: some drinking vessels, & peuter & other vessels: & for phisick [medicine] you shall need no other but a pound of Doctor Wright's Electuarium lenitivum, & his direction to use it, a gallon of scirvy grasse to drink a little 5: or 6: morninges together, wth some saltpeter dissolved in it, & a little grated or sliced nutmeg. Thou must be sure to bringe no more companye than so many as shall have full provision for a yeare & halfe, for though the earth here be very fertile yet there must be tyme and meanes to rayse it; if we have corne [grain] enough we may live plentifully. *Winthrop (1964)*

These directions are quite sensible, and written in a familiar tone. It is interesting to note the directions for management of the sailors ("rewarded beforehande" for good service, and "sacke" for the seamen), and for medicines ("electuarium lenitivum" is a concoction of senna, figs, prunes, licorice, sugar, and other ingredients, good as a laxative). The frequent use of conjunctions, here the <&> symbol, is a common stylistic trait that gives the passage continuity. Spelling at this point is close to modern practice. Winthrop uses *thou* with his wife, the singular form of the second person pronoun, not the more formal plural form *ye*. As with the Paston letter in the last chapter, now a century and a half later, we can see the English language as it lives in our families and letters.

121

8.3 **Features of Early Modern English**

Among the new habits in the language at this time was a change in **rhoticity**, so that some speakers lost the [r] after vowels. In Britain, this **postvocalic *r*** was retained in the west, but lost in London and the east. Because the loss of postvocalic *r* was progressing through the seventeenth century (it was mostly lost in London at the end of the Early Modern English period), some of the new populations in North America lost their postvocalic *r*, such as Boston, New York, and the coastal South, while other American populations retained it. Population mixture allowed for different pronunciations of *r* to emerge in different communities, as the complex system operated in them among local speakers. Another set of changes affected English pronouns. The **wh-relative pronouns** like *who, whom, whose* became popular during this period, and *its* arose as a possessive pronoun. Perhaps the biggest change in pronouns was the shift from separate pronouns for second-person singular, *thou/thee/thy*, and second-person plural, *ye/you/your*. At first the plural pronouns became used as honorifics, as they are in French (*tu/vous*) and German (*du/Sie*), and then the singular forms *thou/thee/thy* became less common and were lost almost completely. Finally, the *ye* subject form was lost, so that *you* was used in both subject and object cases and *your* as the possessive. Notably, Quaker speakers had resisted the honorific forms and continued to use the singular pronouns much longer than other speakers. And in North American speech communities, numerous other second-person plural pronouns arose, such as *y'all* in the American South (some speakers use *y'all* as a singular, though, so the form *all y'all* has emerged as an unambiguous plural form). Again, different communities of speakers could have different features emerge.

Other major changes during this period included a number of ways to use verbs. Most communities saw the loss of *-th* in favor of *-s* for the third-person singular present tense marking. The *-s* was also used for the third-person plural, replacing *-en, -e*, but was subsequently lost in most communities. In Modern English we still see the *-th* ending, but only in religious circumstances. The King James Bible (completed in 1611) has been so popular that its Early Modern language has survived as a special marker of religious discourse (you can listen to passages from the King James Bible online on the website for this textbook). *Thou* and *thee* have also been preserved by the King James Bible, although many modern readers may be confused about their earlier subject versus object usage. These inflectional changes are covered in more detail online in the Historical Outlines text. **Contractions** like *it's* or *didn't* started to become popular during the Early Modern period. The rise of **periphrastic verb** ("helping" or **auxiliary verbs**) also occurred during the Early Modern period. Periphrastic *do* has been retained in Modern English just for questions (*do you want some?*), negatives (*you don't want any*), and emphasis (*I do want some*), while in Early Modern English its use was much broader. For example, Shakespeare has King Henry say, "Worcester, get thee gone; for I do see Danger and disobedience in thine eye." In the same play (*King Henry IV Part 1*), Falstaff says, "For tears do stop the flood-gates of her eyes." **Progressive verbs** that use the suffix *-ing* (*I am walking, I was walking*) also became more popular, as an alternative to the simple present tense (*I walk*) or simple past tense (*I walked*), as illustrated in the Machyn passage. While it is not possible to say for certain that high levels of population mixture *caused* all of these changes in the language, we certainly see that each of these changes progressed at different rates through the different regional communities of speakers in Britain and in North America.

8.4 The Great Vowel Shift

The greatest change of all occurred in English pronunciation, the **Great Vowel Shift (GVS)**, which made the vowels of English differ from those of continental European languages. Between 1400 and 1700, the **long vowels** ([i, eɪ, ɛ, æ, a] in the front, and [ɔ, o, u] in the back) were raised in a process of vowel rotation. **Raising** just means that a vowel was pronounced at a higher articulatory position than it had been before. The term **vowel rotation** suggests that the individual acts of raising tend to raise vowels until they get to the highest position, and then vowels fall along a more centralized track. The process is sometimes called a **chain shift** because the vowels all seemed to move in concert with each other; most have argued that the GVS was a **pull chain** because the vowel [i] at the top of the vowel chart moved and somehow this pulled the others along, and some have argued the opposite, that the GVS was a **push chain** where the low vowels started to rise and pushed the higher vowels along. Neither idea makes much sense, however, because vowels do not exist in the brain in the same way they do on a vowel chart, so pushing or pulling can be no more than a metaphor that describes what we see on a chart better than what we understand of cognitive function.

Figure 8.2 shows the movements in the order in which they are thought to have occurred in the pull chain model.

The first step is that the highest long vowels, [i] in the front and [u] in the back, both become diphthongs [əɪ, əʊ] with the addition of the central vowel [ə]. To use words as examples, the word *bite* was pronounced [bit]

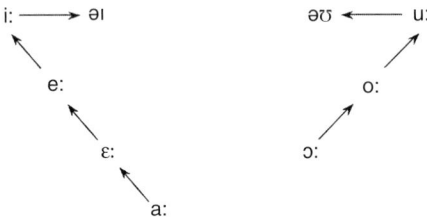

Figure 8.2 Phase 1 of the Great Vowel Shift (author's image)

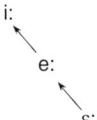

Figure 8.3 Phase 2 of the Great Vowel Shift (author's image)

in Middle English, but after the first step of the GVS the word was pronounced [bəɪt]. The word *cow* in Middle English was pronounced [ku], but after the first step of the GVS the word was pronounced [kəʊ]. Then the next highest vowels in front and back, [e] and [o], rise so that they are pronounced [i] and [u]. Again in words, in Middle English the word *see* was pronounced [se], but after this step of the GVS it was pronounced [si]. And Middle English *food*, pronounced [fod], was then pronounced [fud] after this step of the GVS. Then the vowels below those: in words, Middle English *meat* [mɛt] became [met], and Middle English *boat* [bɔt] became [bot]. Finally, Middle English *mate* [mat] became [mɛt]. These changes were complete by about 1600. Then, as Figure 8.3 shows, there was a second phase of the GVS between 1600 and 1700.

Words that had previously been raised one step, like *meat* and *mate*, were raised one more step in a process called **second raising**, so that *meat* was now pronounced [mit], rhyming with *meet*, and *mate* was now pronounced [met]. A few words did not change, however: *great*, *break*, *steak* still retain their first phase pronunciations as [gret, brek, stek], rather than the pronunciations we might have predicted from second raising [grit, brik, stik]. Later, the original [i] vowels, like *bite* that had changed to [bəɪt], and the original [u] vowels, like *cow* that had changed to [kəʊ], underwent a small further change to [baɪt] and [kau] as many speakers would say them today. The remaining words with the [e] vowel also changed slightly to be pronounced [eɪ], so *mate* [meɪt] and *great* [greɪt].

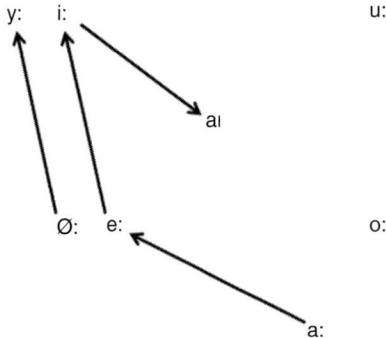

Figure 8.4 Northern Great Vowel Shift (adapted from Smith, 1996)

The GVS is complicated enough when we consider the order in which vowels were raised in two phases, but the truth of vowel change is worse. Different regions of the country had different changes, or different timing of changes, so that the GVS is revealed to be a grand abstraction that applies in many speech communities but not all. For example, Figure 8.4 shows what happened to vowels in Scotland and parts of northern Britain.

The back vowels did not undergo raising, and an additional front vowel in Scottish English was raised. In Scotland in 1700, a *cow* was still a [ku]. In fact, modern dialect survey evidence shows that it is possible to find speakers somewhere in Britain whose pronunciation of particular words today still matches every stage of the GVS. The sound change is just not as neat and regular as the Neogrammarians would have liked. That is how the complex system of speech works, with the emergence of particular habits of pronunciation or word usage in local and regional communities throughout the English-speaking world. Top-level generalizations like the GVS are still useful so long as we know that they are broad abstractions, and that we can expect linguistic life to be much messier on the ground among actual speech communities.

One practical consequence of the GVS was its effect on English spelling. The fact that *meet* and *meat* now sound the same but are spelled differently was caused by the second raising step of the GVS. The same is true of *see* and *sea*. *Been* and *bean* sound the same for many speakers in Britain, but not for speakers in America. The pronunciation of English words also differs from the pronunciation of cognate words in European languages because of the GVS: an English *table* [teɪbəl] sounds different from a French *table* [tɑblə]. This is one reason for the many complaints by learners of English about spelling and pronunciation. As with the problem of what words mean mentioned above, we cannot bring our Modern English sense of pronunciation directly to the Early Modern English period, when the GVS was in progress. If we see words like *meat*, *sea*, and *bean* in Early Modern texts, the authors still may have pronounced them as they were before the second raising, as in rhymes from poems by Alexander Pope like *obey/tea* or *convey/sea*.

Towards the end of the Early Modern period, in 1667, **John Milton** published *Paradise Lost*, another of the great monuments of English literature. Here is a short sample, from the end of Book 2:

> That Satan with less toil, and now with ease
> Wafts on the calmer wave by dubious light
> And like a weather-beaten Vessel holds
> Gladly the Port, though Shrouds and Tackle torn;
> Or in the emptier waste, resembling Air,
> Weighs his spread wings, at leasure to behold
> Farr off th' Empyreal Heav'n, extended wide
> In circuit, undetermind square or round,
> With Opal Towrs and Battlements adorn'd
> Of living Saphire, once his native Seat;
> And fast by hanging in a golden Chain
> This pendant world, in bigness as a Starr
> Of smallest Magnitude close by the Moon.
> Thither full fraught with mischievous revenge,
> Accurst, and in a cursed hour he hies.

Now, at the end of the Early Modern period, we no longer have the difficulty understanding the language that we might have had with Thomas Wyatt at the beginning of the sixteenth century or with Shakespeare almost a hundred years later. We are on the cusp of the modern. Some conventions, like capitalization and spelling, have not yet been established as we have them now. The vocabulary, though, has far fewer unfamiliar words, whether English words we no longer use (only *hie*) or loanwords (only *undetermined*). We today are free to appreciate the epic style of the poetry.

The Early Modern period saw great changes in English that attended great population movements and mixture. Our increasing knowledge of the period, from copious records and printed materials, gives us more evidence than we have had for earlier periods of the language, and that great quantity of evidence also makes the task of historical description more difficult. The more we know about a period, the more we can see all the different speech communities out of which our high-level ideas of

English must be constructed. As we move later in time, the problem, of having too much information to make simple historical descriptions of the language, will only become greater.

8.5 Chapter Summary

In this chapter the English language broke out of its use as the language of common people to become a language suitable for all purposes. In so doing loanwords from many other languages, but especially from French and Latin, entered the language and some of these achieved high frequency. Population mixture was also a factor in change, both in Britain and in new North American colonies across the Atlantic. Changes in pronouns and verb inflections, and especially the Great Vowel Shift, arose as the complex system of speech operated in the mixed populations. By the end of the period, English had become much more recognizable for modern readers.

Key Terms
auxiliary verb
borrowing
chain shift
code
code mixing
code switching
contraction
Francis Drake
Great Vowel Shift (GVS)
Jamestown
loanword
long vowel
John Milton
periphrastic verb
Plymouth
postvocalic *r*
progressive verb
pull chain
push chain
raising
repertoire
rhoticity
Roanoke
second raising

Shakespeare
Spanish Armada
vernacular
vowel rotation
wh- **relative pronoun**
Thomas Wyatt

Exercises

8.1 Select a passage in English of about one hundred words from any written source. Then use the *OED* (or another dictionary) to look up the etymology of all of the content words. You may skip function words like articles, prepositions, pronouns, and auxiliary verbs. Make a list of which words come historically from earlier English or from other languages.

8.2 Select a passage from a Shakespeare play of about one hundred words, and make a list of the words that you do not recognize as being in use in modern English. Look up these words in the *OED* (or another dictionary with historical coverage), and annotate your list of words according to the length of time that each word was used in English.

8.3 People today use *wh-* relative pronouns differently than they were used before. When do you use *who*? When do you use *whom*? When do you use *that* or do not use a pronoun to introduce a relative clause? You may use a usage manual to help you decide.

8.4 Are contractions now natural in both speech and writing? Are there circumstances when you should not use contractions in your writing? You may use a usage manual to help you decide.

8.5 How modern is the English of John Milton? Select a passage from Milton's writings of about one hundred words, either poetry or prose, and make a list of the features that you do not recognize as being in use in modern English. These may be words, spelling, punctuation, or grammatical usages.

Audio Samples

Henry Machyn, Diary (diary of London merchant, mid sixteenth century)
Hugh Latimer, Sermon (sermon, mid sixteenth century)
Shakespeare, Sonnet 18 (late sixteenth century)
Queen Elizabeth, Letter to Burghley (late sixteenth century)

Richard Hooker, Laws of Ecclesiastical Polity (late sixteenth century)
Richard Hakluyt, Discoverie of America (late sixteenth century)
John Smith, Historie of Virginia (early seventeenth century)
William Bradford, Plimoth Plantation (early seventeenth century)
John Winthrop, Letter (early seventeenth century)
Jonathan Edwards, Sinners in the Hands of an Angry God (mid seventeenth century)

Further Reading

Görlach (1991) is a good general account of Early Modern English.

Shakespeare (2013) is a good contemporary edition of Shakespeare's complete works.

Durkin (2014) is a highly readable account by the Deputy Chief Editor of the *Oxford English Dictionary* of the development of English vocabulary. His earlier book (Durkin, 2009) on etymology is somewhat more technical but still a great source of information on word history.

Bailyn's account of the early colonization of North America (Bailyn, 1986) replaces earlier, more romantic, views with a more modern history. Harriot (1951) is a facsimile edition of *A Brief and True Report of the New Found Land of Virginia*.

Mantel (2009; 2012). In her novels, *Wolf Hall* and *Bring Up the Bodies*, Hilary Mantel's descriptions of England and court life in the sixteenth century, through the eyes of Thomas Cromwell, are deservedly popular. The second book describes the relationship of Anne Boleyn and Henry VIII in great detail. The books have also been made into BBC TV series. Can you imagine these TV programs presented with Early Modern pronunciations? Thomas Wyatt was also involved in the politics of the time: he was imprisoned in the Tower of London on suspicion of having committed adultery with Anne Boleyn, and was released owing to the influence of Thomas Cromwell. Wyatt (2015) is a good popular edition of his complete poems.

Labov (1994) is a difficult book, but it provides the best recent defense of traditional ideas about vowel rotation and chain shifts, including modern ones as well as the GVS. An earlier article (Labov, 1981) may be easier to understand. For an opposing view, also on the difficult side for non-specialists, see Stockwell and Minkova (1988: 355–394). This article reports data from the Survey of English Dialects that shows vowels at every stage of the GVS. Smith (1996) reports the Northern Great Vowel Shift, and other local variants.

Milton (2013) is a modern edition of the John Milton's complete works.

CHAPTER 9

Modern English

In this chapter

English extends its reach all over the world during this period, first by ship and later by rail. Colonial varieties of the language emerge in many places, each with its own distinctive set of characteristics. People become increasingly literate as a consequence of more widespread education. The idea of an authoritative variety of English arises, but no language academy is formed either in Britain or America. The rise of industry and science lead to a renewal of word formation from Latin and Greek. At the end of the period, the *Oxford English Dictionary* was created as the best historical dictionary of any language.

9.1 English and Empire

At the height of the **British Empire** near the end of the Modern period (1700–1950), about one-fifth of the world's population and one-fourth of the world's land area were included in it (Figure 9.1). The Roman Empire was not as large or influential as that, as important as it was in its time. The empire was truly global, extending from Australia and New Zealand in the Pacific to India in South Asia, to several African colonies, to North America.

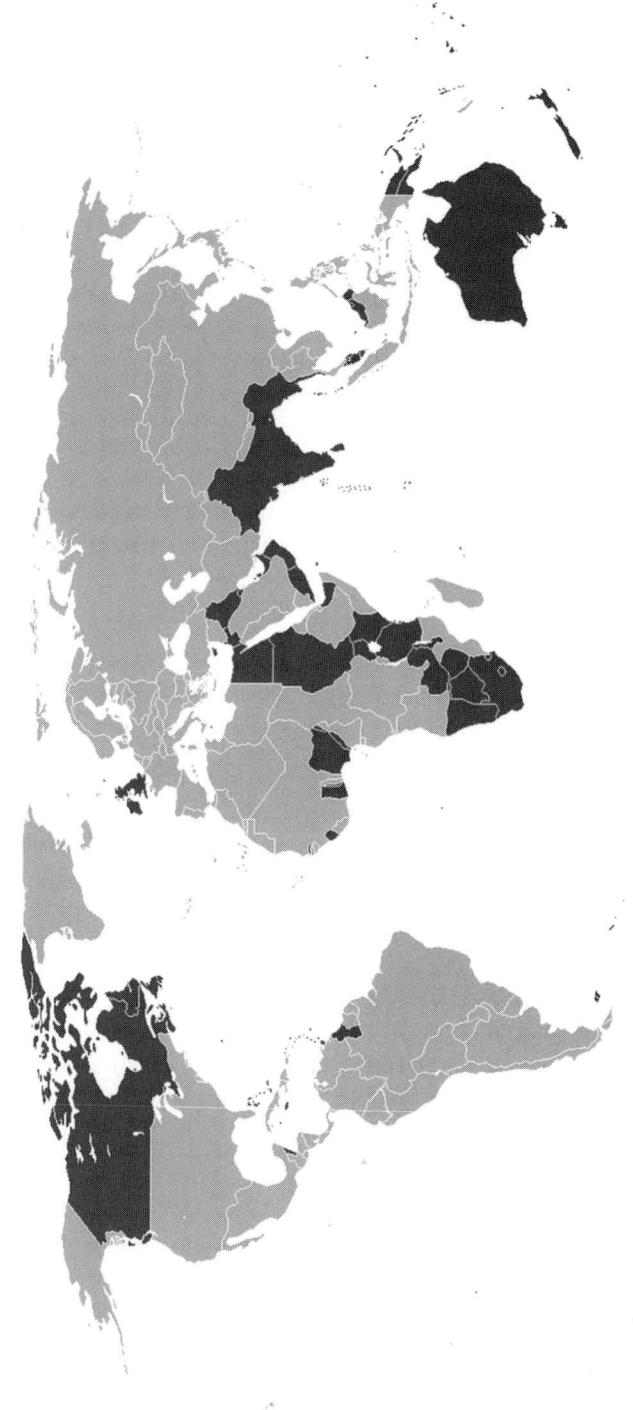

Figure 9.1 British Empire in 1921, the United States no longer a part of it (Wikipedia commons)

Great Britain, as the country was called after the union of England and Scotland in 1707, had at least one colony on every continent. Not only political governance but also dominance in trade constituted British power.

In the eighteenth century North America was the focus for British emigration. What had been coastal frontier outposts in the seventeenth century developed into port cities, and new settlers, and children of colonial families whose lands could no longer support the youngest generation, passed through the coastal ports of entry and headed inland. For the labor market, in addition to single, male indentured servants from London who had supplied the demand in the seventeenth century, about 50,000 English criminals were sent to North America, large numbers of "redemptioners" came from Germany beginning in 1709, and many thousands of Africans came as slaves after 1680. The labor market for such immigrants (but not the slaves, who were legally imported for sale until 1808) served mainly the coastal cities and developed areas. Inland settlement was often accomplished by families, whose pathways west were established by land speculators based in the great port cities. The linguistic consequences of the eighteenth-century pattern of settlement follow from the fact that most new immigrants either stayed in existing settlements as labor, or spent significant time in the vicinity of the coast before moving to lands on the frontier. In either case, the new settlers learned the existing language habits of the existing population centers in the colonies. The patterns of settlement of the second wave after initial colonization thus served to extend inland the emerging linguistic habits of the coastal centers. The great influence of the initial population in an area has been called the **Doctrine of First Effective Settlement** or the **Founder Principle**. Even though the new settlers outnumbered the native-born members of the founding population, the natives were the ones who had an existing functional social system in which local linguistic preferences could emerge and be maintained. New settlers, while they did not lose the linguistic habits of their own upbringing, could not help but acquire the emerging common linguistic features of their new environment, which their children would then acquire natively. New linguistic preferences could in time emerge in inland localities as a product of the people and circumstances in place, but features that had emerged along the coast were broadcast westward with the movement of the population.

At the time of the American Revolution, English in the colonies had already begun to form different habits according to the operation of the complex system. An entry in Amos Farsworth's journal from 1775 provides some clues (you can listen to this passage online on the website for this book):

> Saturday May ye [the] 27. went on hog island And Brought of [off] Six
> hoses [horses] twentyseven hornd Cattel And fore hundred And Eleven

Sheep. about the midel of the afternoon went From hog island to Noddles island and Sot one Hous and Barn on fiar, kild Some hoses [horses] and Cattel Brought of two or thre Cows one horse. I with five men got of the horse And Before we got from Noddels island to hog island we was fird upon by a Privatear Schooner But we Crost the river and about fifteen of us Squated Down in a Ditch on the mash [marsh] and Stood our ground. And thare Came A Company of Regulars on the marsh on the other side of the river And the Schooner: and we had A hot fiar until the Regulars retreeted. But notwithstanding the Bulets flue very thitch yet thare was not A Man of us kild.

Farsworth reports a chaotic day of cattle rustling and an armed encounter. The *ye* form in the date is not the second-person plural pronoun, but instead a common spelling for *the*, which derives from the older use of <þ>, now spelled with a <y> (the origin of modern names beginning with "Ye Olde . . .," meant to add color to an establishment). The passage clearly does not yet show capitalization according to modern practice. Farsworth uses both *hose/horse* and *mash/marsh*, which suggests that his pronunciation was non-rhotic (just as many speakers near Boston still do not use -*r* after vowels). *Sot* reflects the pronunciation of an unusual past tense form of *set*, one still found in American English. Near the beginning of the Modern period not all conventions of spelling and mechanics are yet very common, but some long-lasting features of pronunciation have begun to emerge.

Settlement proceeded generally westward in three large bands as far as the Mississippi River, corresponding to cultural areas known as the **Northern region**, the **Midland region,** and the **Southern region**. Figure 9.2 shows these regions from their origins on the East Coast, with original settlement areas shaded in black. In the North the speech habits that emerged in Upstate New York (which was not the same as the speech of New York City and environs, originally Dutch in settlement, nor the same as the speech of **New England**, which was separated from the **Inland North** by mountains) were carried westward by means of water travel on the Erie Canal and Great Lakes. In the South the land – mountains, piney woods, wiregrass – was not all suited to the pattern of plantation agriculture that dominated along the coast, with Eastern Virginia and Charleston as core areas. Southern settlement thus proceeded more slowly until settlers reached better plantation lands in the plains and Mississippi Basin. Philadelphia was the focal city for settlement in the Midland region, which proceeded west in two broad streams. The National Road was built through Pennsylvania, eventually as far as central Illinois, and settlers could also reach the Ohio River valley at Pittsburgh and then use the waterway to settle further inland. This **North Midland** stream of settlement mixed to some degree with the

Figure 9.2 Settlement of the United States (adapted from Kretzschmar et al., 1993: 159)

speech habits of the Northern region. The more southerly stream of Midland settlement followed the course of the Shenandoah River south through Virginia towards the Cumberland Gap to enter Kentucky and Tennessee. These **South Midland** settlers consisted largely of subsistence farmers, and they occupied whatever land could support them throughout the Appalachian Mountains and the uplands to the west, and they also settled the lowlands where the land was not suitable for plantations. South Midland speakers acquired some speech habits characteristic of the Southern region. These historical patterns of settlement – North, Midland,

and South – created the basic framework of regional American dialects that we still see today. West of the Mississippi River, population density remains much lower than it is in the Eastern United States and broad regional varieties, as opposed to local varieties around population centers, have not formed. The same might be said about Canada, where the west is less densely populated than the east. In the last half of the Modern period, rail lines connected the east and west coast of both the USA and Canada, but these were less important for population movement than they were for business and trade.

At the end of the eighteenth century, the independent United States was formed from the coastal colonies, and more states were created with west-ward population movement. Some British immigrants still came to North America, along with large numbers from other chiefly European countries. The colonial side of the British Empire shifted to the Pacific and Africa. Australia was established in 1788, New Zealand in 1840. Britain took over the earlier Cape Colony in South Africa in 1806, and Kenya was established as a colony in 1920 although the British East Africa company had been in the area since 1888. The British Raj (political control) in India began in 1858, following governance by the British East India Company from 1757. Of these places, colonial settlement from Britain largely took place in Australia, New Zealand, and South Africa, while the rest of Africa and India were useful to Britain mainly for trade. The same is true for many other smaller British colonies, where relatively small numbers of English-speaking Britons lived in order to foster commercial activities. In linguistic terms, the settlement of any of these places was unlike the long-term colonization of North America. Australia was the most like North America, in that the aboriginal population was greatly reduced by European diseases, which made way for British immigrants. The population of Australia only reached about one million by 1860, and ten million by 1960, so that population density for the continent remains quite low. Since Australia is more recently settled than North America and also less densely populated, the complex system of speech there has allowed local variations to emerge that can be combined to form a large-scale national general-ization, but not regional varieties as different as those in America. In that respect, it resembles the American west.

9.2 English Creoles

During the expansion of the British Empire, a number of English-based **Creole** languages were developed (Table 9.1). A creole is a stable native language developed from a mixture of different languages.

Table 9.1 *English-Based Creoles*

Bahamian Creole, The Bahamas
Bajan Creole or Barbadian Creole, Barbados
Belizean Creole, Belize
Bislama, Vanuatu
Gullah language, Sea Islands coastal USA, near South Carolina, Georgia
Guyanese Creole, Guyana
Hawaiian Creole or Pidgin, Hawaii
Jamaican Patois, Jamaica
Krio language, Sierra Leone
Liberian Kreyol language, Liberia
Nigerian Creole English, Nigeria
Pitkern, Pitcairn Islands and Norfolk Islands
Manglish, Malaysia
Singlish, Singapore
Tok Pisin, official language of Papua New Guinea
Torres Strait Creole or Brokan, Torres Strait, and south-west Papua
Trinidadian Creole, Trinidad
Sranan Tongo, Suriname

English creoles appeared worldwide, though the highest concentration of them occurred in the Caribbean. Bajan Creole, from Barbados, was the first of these. While Barbados became an English colony as early as 1627, its way of life changed entirely in the late seventeenth century with the introduction of sugar plantations and the importation of massive numbers of African slaves as labor for them. By the end of the seventeenth century, there were 50,000 slaves and only 15,000 residents of European heritage. A creole typically can develop in a language-contact situation where two different populations speak different languages. One language, in this case English, serves as the **superstrate** or **lexifier** language and provides much of the vocabulary. Another language, often the native language of people with whom English-speaking settlers came to trade, is the **substrate** language which provides the basic grammar. Creoles usually lack an extensive inflectional system, and instead use words and non-word particles to indicate tense and case. Since creole languages are spoken natively by indigenous or African populations, while people of European heritage often continue to use English, creole speakers have low social status. In countries with established creole communities, there is a continuum of possible language types described as **basilectal** (for most creole-like), **mesolectal** (for moderately creole-like), and **acrolectal** (most English-like) varieties. This continuum reflects the frequency of creole features in different communities, and so it is actually a different way to describe the differing A-curves of the complex system. Jamaican Creole (or Patois) is a major source for the Afro-English varieties that are now found in the United Kingdom, as commonwealth citizens have moved to Britain. The (Jamaican) Patois New Testament is in preparation in Britain. The Lord's Prayer looks like this:

Wi Faada we iina evn,	[Our Father who is in heaven,
mek piipl av nof rispek fi yu an yu niem.	hallowed be Your name.
Mek di taim kom wen yu ruul iina evri wie.	Your kingdom come,
Mek we yu waahn apm pan ort apm,	Your will be done,
jos laik ou a wa yu waahn fi apm iina evn apm	on earth, as it is in heaven.
Tide gi wi di fuud we wi niid.	Give us this day our daily bread,
Paadn wi fi aal a di rang we wi du,	and forgive us our debts,
siem laik ou wi paadn dem we du wi rang.	as we forgive our debtors.
An no mek wi fies notn we wi kaaz wi fi sin,	And lead us not into temptation,
bot protek wi fram di wikid wan.	but deliver us from evil.]

From *Di Jamiekan Nyuu Testiment* (2012)

We can see the use of many creole features in this passage. *Mek* (from English *make*) is used to indicate a causative in several lines. *Wi* (from English *we*) is used for both the subject and object forms of the first-person plural pronoun. *We* is the English word *what*. The passage is barely readable for an English speaker, perhaps not intelligible without the translation. Still, it is possible to see that nearly all the words derive from English.

As Salikoko Mufwene (2001) has argued, contrary to much earlier literature, creoles are not a special kind of language (a type that is the same wherever in the world they occur); instead, creoles arise as the result of interactions between speakers who are each using their linguistic resources as best they can to communicate with each other. Mufwene describes a pool of features from which speakers draw, that eventually develops into a set of linguistic habits that we can describe as a creole. Mufwene's argument agrees very well with the idea of complex systems, so that we can understand a creole language as the product of emergence from the interactions of speakers, and the creole continuum as an expression of how creole features are used in different linguistic circumstances.

Edgar Schneider (2007) has discussed the emergence of new varieties of English in former colonies worldwide. His **Dynamic Model** suggests five phases in the evolution of colonial varieties: foundation of the colony, stabilization around the outside norm, nativization, formation of an internal norm, and diversification. Schneider's model is focused on the one new national variety that he expects "ideally" to emerge in the new postcolonial state, and it allows for coexistent systems. What emerges within each community of colonial speakers is the set of top-ranked variants on the A-curves for every element of the language: sounds, words, grammar. The most frequent features from the settlers' language do not automatically become the top-ranked variants in the colonial language, since every set of colonial English speakers comes from a mixed background in Britain. The heart of Schneider's treatment is that each new colonial variety is "an identity-driven discourse construct" in the new speakers' perception. We can understand the developmental phases, then, not as landmarks in the internal linguistic history of a new variety, but as the evolution of the new society's perceptions. Understood in this way, new colonial varieties, like local and social varieties, are emerging all around us every day, as speakers form new groups around the world, and in local neighborhoods, communities of practice, and social settings. It is not a process that happens once and is done. The complex system of speech continues to operate, and new order emerges from it all the time. We can find new varieties wherever we can identify a population of speakers, whether we validate the population with reference to new political realities or just by asking the speakers if they belong to it.

9.3 Ascertainment

While English was expanding far beyond Britain and becoming more diverse, this period saw the beginning of the continuing effort to describe the standard language. The beginning of the Modern period coincided with the **Age of Enlightenment**, in which people expected reason and science to explain the world around us. One expression of the age was the creation of the encyclopedia, a comprehensive reference for all knowledge organized in one place. During the eighteenth century Diderot's *Encyclopédie* was published, soon followed by the *Encyclopædia Brittanica* in Britain. Unlike their modern counterpart Wikipedia, which is an accretion of contributed articles (you, too, can participate in it), the eighteenth-century encyclopedias exemplify **ascertainment**, the idea that knowledge could be organized and shown to be regular. **Modernism** seeks to apply rational, scientific means to reveal the order in the world, or at least to create the appearance of order in rational thought about a more complex reality.

As for the English language, ascertainment meant the description of its fixed and standard grammar. The model was Latin, whose grammar had been described in detail and taught for over a thousand years from books by Donatus (fourth century AD) and Priscian (sixth century AD). Latin was no longer a living language and did not change or have new varieties emerge in it, so it offered a model of a standard language for modern English grammarians to follow. And follow it they did, with eight parts of speech and other characteristics of Latin grammar even though English was a far different language from Latin. Most case endings and inflections in English had been lost by 1700, and words (like *run, house, clock*) could function as different parts of speech in different sentences. **Robert Lowth** (1762) and **Lindley Murray** (1795) wrote famous and long-running grammars in Britain, while **Noah Webster** published his *Grammatical Institute* (1784) in America. Lowth, Murray, and Webster were all prescriptive. Their grammars sought to ascertain the rules of English, to resolve differences in usage, and to point out what they believed to be errors in common usage, thus to improve English by asserting its underlying order and correcting deviations from that regularity. By the nineteenth century, as Richard Bailey (1996) has written, "attitudes toward grammar had hardened into ideology. Using standard forms of the language was a requirement for gentility (and much else)." Belief in a standard English, despite evident variation in every aspect of the language as it is spoken and written in different places and social settings, has become the common consensus belief of English speakers around the world. The same belief in a standard language occurred widely across Europe, to the extent that **language academies** were created to maintain the regularity of the language for Italian (Accademia della Crusca), for French (Académie Française), for Spanish (Real Academia Española), and for many other modern languages. No academy has been created for English, however. Jonathan Swift (1712) was a proponent of a language academy in Britain, and John Adams (1780) argued for a language academy in America, but they never came into existence. Perhaps the best statement why not was the argument of **Samuel Johnson**. Johnson produced the first great English dictionary in 1755, a scholarly record of English words as drawn from the best English authors. In his plan for the dictionary he had written that he wanted to produce "a dictionary by which the pronunciation of our language may be fixed, and its attainment facilitated; by which its purity may be preserved, its use ascertained, and its duration lengthened." However, in the preface to his *Dictionary* when it was published he wrote,

> Those who have been persuaded to think well of my design, desire that it should fix our language, and put a stop to those alterations which time and chance have hitherto been suffered to make in it without opposition. With this consequence I will confess that I flattered myself for a while; but now begin to fear that I have indulged expectation which neither reason nor experience can justify . . . With this hope, however, academies have been instituted, to guard the avenues of their languages, to retain

fugitives, and repulse intruders; but their vigilance and activity have hitherto been vain: sounds are too volatile and subtile for legal restraints; to enchain syllables, and to lash the wind, are equally the undertakings of pride, unwilling to measure its desires by its strength.

Johnson's *Dictionary*, like those that have followed it, have stood as authorities for their readers, even while the lexicographers realize that they are merely witnesses of what people do with the language, not arbiters of what they should do. In his own language, Johnson now uses modern spelling (except for *subtile*) and capitalization, less than a century after Milton's pre-modern usage. His style might be called periodic in that Johnson uses commas and semi-colons liberally to organize the clauses and phrases of his prose. His metaphor of academies guarding the streets of the language is striking, all the more so because *fugitive* (from French, ultimately from Latin) and *intruder* (Latin) are both loanwords. His vocabulary takes full advantage of French and Latin loanwords, familiar to us now as the survivors of the tumult of borrowings in the Early Modern period.

Belief in the idea of a standard language has been spread through the schools as great increases in literacy have characterized the Modern period. In the United States access to public education has been a hallmark of the republic. Noah Webster was chiefly responsible for the institutionalization of an English standard with the great popularity of his **American Spelling Book** throughout the nineteenth century. Initially published in 1783 as part of his *Grammatical Institute*, it discusses the relationship of sound and spelling in English (Figure 9.3). Webster was interested in the creation of a specifically American variety of English, a national language for a new country:

> The author wishes to promote the honor and prosperity of the confederated republics of America . . . This country must in some future time be distinguished by the superiority of her literary improvements, as she is already by the liberality of her civil and ecclesiastical constitutions. Europe is grown old in folly, corruption and tyranny. For America in her infancy to adopt the maxims of the Old World would be to stamp the wrinkles of decrepit old age upon the bloom of youth, and to plant the seeds of decay in a vigorous constitution.

As clearly expressed in this passage, and neatly characterized by Commager (1958), "The driving force in Webster, the compulsion that explains all particular expressions of his ambitions and his energies, was nationalism." The book then provides lists of words whose spelling and pronunciation should be practiced and memorized. Webster was nothing if not a salesman. Webster claimed in 1818 that more than five million

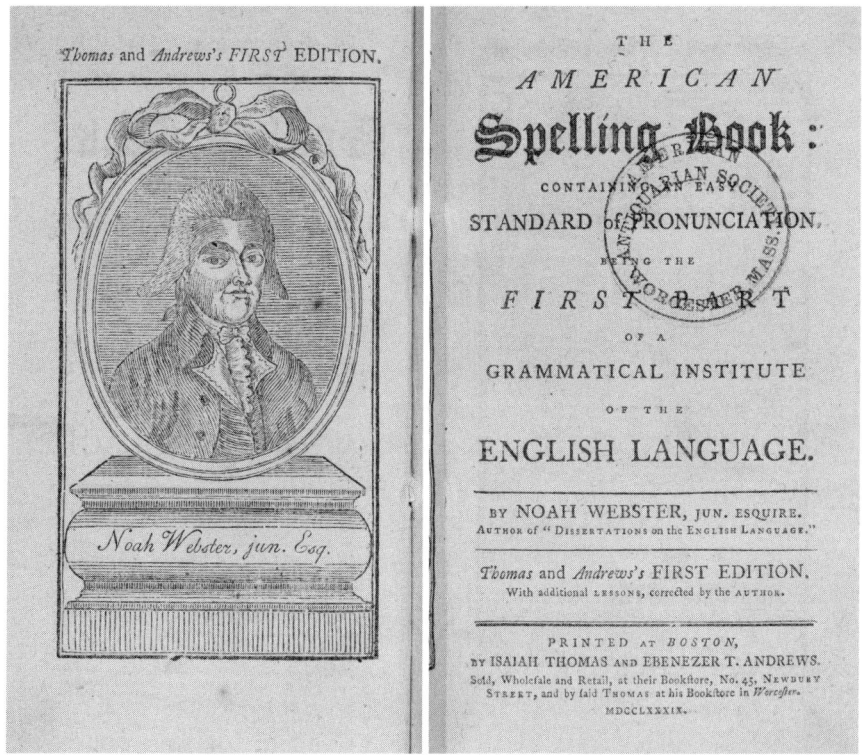

Figure 9.3 Webster's *American Spelling Book* (frontispiece from 1789 edition)

copies had been sold, and over 100 million copies were sold before it was replaced by other books at the end of the nineteenth century. More famous than *The American Spelling Book* but less successful in sales was Webster's *American Dictionary of the English Language* (1825). The success of Webster's promotional efforts created one of the most successful textbooks of all time and made his name, in America at least, synonymous with the dictionary.

While Webster encouraged standardization, he also created most of the modern differences between British and American spelling conventions. Webster's spellings clearly differentiate American English from other world varieties. His successful changes come in four classes:

dropping of final *-k* after *c* in words of more than one syllable (e.g., *music* for *musick*)

uniform use of *-or* for *-our* in words of more than one syllable (e.g., *honor* for *honour*)

uniform use of *-er* for *-re* (e.g., *theater* for *theatre*)

-se for *-ce* in *defense, offense, pretense* but not in *fence.*

141

Other prominent changes include replacement of *-que* with *-k* in words like *cheque/check*, *masque/mask*, and removal of doubled consonants as in *programme/program*, *waggon/wagon*. Many other of Webster's proposed changes have not succeeded, such as simplification of *-ine, -ive, -ite* to *-in, -iv, -it* (e.g., *definite/definit*). Some changes were partially successful such as *f* for older *ph* in *fantasy* but not *phantom*. Some were hit and miss: American English has *draft* for *draught* and *plowman* for *ploughman*, while many other *-augh-* and *-ough-* spellings survive. We still have *island* instead of Webster's *iland*. Some American spelling changes arose after Webster, such as *tho* for *though*, *thru* for *through*, *catalog* for *catalogue*, and *judgment* for *judgement*, promoted by spelling reformers through educational associations and newspapers in the late nineteenth century. Given the relatively small number of characteristic spelling differences like these, and despite the continued emphasis on spelling in American schools and communities, Americans are no better spellers in general than speakers of other varieties of English. Winners of American spelling bees are often the children of immigrants who appear to have taken the lessons of American education more to heart than children from families with longer histories in the country.

Public education took longer to become the norm in Britain but arrived at the same place: inculcation of a belief in a standard language even if the students did not speak it. Mass public education was not required in Britain until the end of the nineteenth century, and the doctrine of correctness began not in the schools but in the (aristocratic) courts. *The Queen's English* and *The King's English* might not be the usage of the queen and king themselves, yet the idealized norm of a standard equates the best speech with the best speakers. In the early twentieth century, the standard in Britain became known as **Received Pronunciation (RP)**, which one author at the time equated with "Good English, Well-bred English, Upper-class English." This form of language was not exclusively aristocratic, since it was said to be spoken by graduates of Oxford and Cambridge, many of whom were not of noble birth although in the nineteenth and earlier twentieth centuries most of the students came from families of means. Since the BBC adopted RP as its standard form of pronunciation for broadcasting, RP also became known as BBC English. When mass public education did become the law of the land in Britain, it taught RP.

The rapid growth of science starting in the nineteenth century provided a steady stream of new English words based on Greek and Latin roots and affixes. Latin had lasted longer in the universities than it had in other domains, and so the mark of an educated person in the nineteenth century was the ability to make classical allusions and sprinkle bits of Latin in prose as if it were a spice. The biological and physical sciences had been studied before the late nineteenth century by individuals within institutional settings, such as Isaac Newton at Cambridge (his *Principia* was composed in Latin). The creation of university departments in the physical and natural sciences began in earnest in Germany at the end of the nineteenth century, spurred by industrial developments like the production of modern colored dyes. New science demanded new words, and Latin and Greek provided the grist for that mill. All of the *-itis* and *-osis* words from medicine, for example, apply Greek suffixes to (mostly) Latin roots to make the names of diseases and conditions. In other fields we see new words like *electron, proton, neutron*; *biology, immunology, psychology* (in its modern sense); *sodium, chlorine, hydrogen, oxygen*; and many others. Many words are compounds from Greek and Latin, like *automobile* (Greek *auto* and Latin *mobile*). Many others apply prefixes like *pre-, post-, sub-*, and *trans-*. Latin may have lost its population of speakers, but Modern scientists used the language for new purposes. Many other words have come into English during the Modern period from all over the world. Since Germany was the center of scientific advancement in the late nineteenth century, hundreds of scientific words came into English from German at that time, many of them ultimately of Latin and Greek origin. The nineteenth century saw another large group of loanwords from Dutch, now from Dutch trading and colonial activities including settlements in South Africa. Many loanwords came from Japan and China in the nineteenth century as trade with Asia advanced. At the same time new English varieties were emerging in colonial settings, words from the world's languages were entering English in its native settings in Britain and America. Some words were new creations, like *Kodak* (1888), *Kleenex* (1925), and *Zipper* (1925), each of these originally a tradename. Science and trade, then, enriched the language in tune with new developments.

Science writing changed from earlier Latin to English in the Modern period. Here is a passage from the Introduction to Charles Darwin's *Origin of Species* (1859):

> In considering the Origin of Species, it is quite conceivable that a naturalist, reflecting on the mutual affinities of organic beings, on their embryological relations, their geographical distribution, geological succession, and other such facts, might come to the conclusion that each species had not been independently created, but had descended, like varieties, from other species. Nevertheless, such a conclusion, even if well founded, would be unsatisfactory, until it could be shown how the innumerable species inhabiting this world have been modified so as to acquire that perfection of structure and co-adaptation which most justly excites our admiration. Naturalists continually refer to external

conditions, such as climate, food, &c., as the only possible cause of variation. In one very limited sense, as we shall hereafter see, this may be true; but it is preposterous to attribute to mere external conditions, the structure, for instance, of the woodpecker, with its feet, tail, beak, and tongue, so admirably adapted to catch insects under the bark of trees. In the case of the misseltoe, which draws its nourishment from certain trees, which has seeds that must be transported by certain birds, and which has flowers with separate sexes absolutely requiring the agency of certain insects to bring pollen from one flower to the other, it is equally preposterous to account for the structure of this parasite, with its relations to several distinct organic beings, by the effects of external conditions, or of habit, or of the volition of the plant itself.

Nineteenth-century writing in English had settled the capitalization issues from the Early Modern period, as in Milton's in *Paradise Lost*. Darwin here capitalizes only "Origin of Species" as the topic for his book. Spelling follows the contemporary standard, except for *&c.*, a dated abbreviation for *et cetera* that now would be abbreviated as *etc.* Use of commas has not yet arrived at contemporary usage, as Darwin, like Samuel Johnson, still inserts a comma between the subject and the predicate when it might clarify the sentence structure, like the comma before *might* in the first sentence here. Darwin's vocabulary is not exactly new, but it does make frequent use of Latinate words that appeared in English in the century or two before his time. *Embryological* and the biological sense of *parasite* are examples of newer Modern scientific words. The entire passage is composed of only five sentences, the shortest containing eighteen words. The last sentence, composed of eighty-three words, makes copious use of dependent clauses and prepositional phrases to create a complex rhetorical statement. Nineteenth-century scientific prose style not only preferred a Latinate vocabulary, but also built complicated patterns in sentences. The contemporary preference for passive voice and shorter sentences in scientific reports had not yet arrived.

9.4 The *Oxford English Dictionary*

A great monument to the English language was built at the end of the Modern period, the *Oxford English Dictionary* (OED). Interested members of the Philological Society in London began a movement in 1857 to supplement existing dictionaries like Samuel Johnson's (still available in revised form), and then to create a new dictionary based on a reading program to recover all the words in English since the year 1000. Volunteer readers combed available texts for citations, and the Early English Text Society was founded in 1864 to provide edited versions of texts from Old and Middle English. Eventually the project was accepted by Oxford University Press, which paid for editorial operations and hired **James A. H. Murray** as chief editor. Simon Winchester (1998; 2003) has told what might have been a rather dry story of the hard work of reading and editing in two colorful and popular books. The first installment of the dictionary was published in 1884, then called the *New English Dictionary on Historical Principles*. The title was changed to the *Oxford English Dictionary* in 1895. The whole run of the alphabet was finished in 1928, and an initial supplement was published in 1933. Murray and his successors as chief editors brought system and science to the creation of the dictionary as nobody had ever done before for any language. Much more could be said about the *OED*, and much has been written about it (see suggestions under Further Reading). You can find out a great deal about the project on the OED website, www.oed.com/About.

The Modern period is best characterized by the worldwide expansion of English, including trade and colonization outside of Britain as well as continuing enhancement of the vocabulary of native English speakers with words brought home from abroad. It is also notable for the rise of science, originally in the Age of Enlightenment and later in the development of modern science in the nineteenth century. Popular attitudes arose about **standardization** of the language, at the same time as English became more diverse than ever as new varieties emerged all over the world. Throughout all of these changes, we must remember that what happened to the English language in the Modern period was not the inevitable endpoint of 1500 years of development and change, as much as the ideology of standardization might make that idea attractive. The Modern period more than ever saw emergence in operation in the complex system of English, from which the state of English in various places – Britain, America, and elsewhere, and in every region and locality within these places – would continue to change and emerge in times to come.

9.5 Chapter Summary

In this chapter the expansion of the British Empire allowed for the emergence of many varieties of English. Settlement patterns created three major dialect regions in the United States. Schneider's Dynamic Model explains similarities in the development of colonial varieties. During the Modern period the idea of standardization of English arose, but no language academy for English was created. Science was responsible for the addition of many words to the language, a great number of them based on Greek and Latin affixes and roots. Finally, at the end of the period, the *OED* provided historical coverage of English unsurpassed among dictionaries for any language.

Key Terms

acrolectal creole
Age of Enlightenment
American Spelling Book
ascertainment
basilectal creole
British Empire
Creole
Doctrine of First Effective Settlement
Dynamic Model
Founder Principle
Inland North
Samuel Johnson
Robert Lowth
mesolectal creole
Midland region
Modernism
language academy
lexifier
James A. H. Murray
Lindley Murray
New England
North Midland
Northern region
Oxford English Dictionary (OED)
Received Pronunciation (RP)
Edgar Schneider
South Midland
Southern region
standardization
substrate
superstrate
Noah Webster

Exercises

9.1 Google "British Empire" and make a list of the modern countries that are now, or have been, part of the British Empire. Do all of them use English as their modern national language?

9.2 Pick one of the American cities covered by Richard Bailey in *Speaking American* (2012) for the Modern period: 1700 – Charleston, 1750 – Philadelphia, 1800 – New Orleans, 1850 – New York, or 1900 – Chicago. Briefly discuss the cultural conditions at the time as they might have affected the emergence of language habits there.

9.3 Google "British East India Company" and look up its history. How did it combine trading interests with colonial governance? Why did the British government take over its role in India in 1858?

9.4 Look at a section of Johnson's *Dictionary* (johnsonsdictionaryonline.com): choose a letter, and then a range of words. In the section you choose, what authors does Johnson use to illustrate word usage? Do you find any definitions that surprise you (like, perhaps, the one for *net* or for *oats*)?

9.5 Go online and look at some entries in the *Oxford English Dictionary* (many universities have a site license that will give you access at www.oed.com). How do the entries differ from those in Samuel Johnson's *Dictionary* (see Exercise 9.4)? How are they different from those in a modern one-volume desktop dictionary?

Audio Samples

Amos Farsworth, Journal

Thomas Jefferson, Essay on Anglo-Saxon (early nineteenth century)

Further Reading

Detailed information about the early settlement of the United States and about its eastern communities can be found in Kretzschmar (1993). Survey research in the Linguistic Atlas movement required good information about history in order to try to explain dialect patterns, and so this volume is a good place to start for study of the contingencies of settlement that led to the emergence of language patterns in America.

Mufwene (2001) explains his theory of creole formation, and how the social situation of creole speakers can affect how a creole language is understood. The Jamaican Patois New Testament is published as Di Jamiekan Nyuu Testiment (2012). A good general textbook on creoles is Holm (2000).

Schneider's Dynamic Model (Schneider, 2007) is the best current description of the common points of development for colonial varieties. He has also published a short textbook on the subject (Schneider, 2011). The most recent book by another famous World Englishes scholar is Kachru (2017). The late Braj Kachru's model of concentric circles of English, the inner circle, the outer circle, and the expanding circle, is well known.

Commager's account of Webster (Commager, 1958) remains influential. For a more developmental view of Standard American English, see Kretzschmar (2010).

Bailey (1996) is a colorful account of writing, words, grammar, and other aspects of the language, which brings life to the times. His posthumously published work (Bailey, 2012) chooses a city for each fifty-year period in the history of English in America to provide the same kind of lively, detail-filled history of American English.

Winchester (1998). The writer is not a lexicographer himself, and perhaps that qualified him to find all the interesting and human bits in the story of the *OED*. A more personal view is available in Murray (1977). More scholary histories of the *OED* have been published by Mugglestone (2000), Mugglestone (2005), Brewer (2007), and Ogilvie (2012).

 CHAPTER **10**

Contemporary English

In this chapter

The Contemporary period builds on the foundations laid down in the earlier periods but is itself culturally distinct, characterized by new social and cultural patterns in the Information Age. Residential patterns have changed since the Second World War with increasing mobility of the population. Many people move between regions within their countries, or even move between countries. This period is often called the Information Age, from the rise of telecommunication and later computing. Still, the circumstances for emergence in English continue to operate. A big new issue for English is the number of people worldwide who may use the language occasionally but still speak other languages at home.

10.1 English As We Live Today

The circumstances of everyday life for many English speakers have changed substantially since the Second World War. Transportation systems have grown enormously, including the construction of the Interstate highway system in America following the example of the German Autobahn, construction of elaborate freeway systems in and around urban areas worldwide, and the great expansion of air travel. Improved transportation offers new opportunities to those people who are willing to leave their local communities in search of better jobs, resulting in greater **mobility**. In America, about 20 percent of the population now moves to a new residence each year. Most people move within the same locality; over 60 percent of the American people still live in the state of their birth. The large number of people who stay near home helps to account for the continuing existence of the large regional dialect patterns, in the United Kingdom as well as in North America, that arose during the Modern period or before. Only 3 percent of the American population moves out of state each year, and people with a college or higher degree are about twice as likely to move to a different region as those with less education. These statistics indicate that blue-collar Americans can and do move long distances, but because of economically stratified housing patterns they are likely to find new neighbors who are long-time residents of their new state and locality. White-collar Americans are far more likely to move as part of a national job marketplace in the professions, and they are likely to live in neighborhoods with a smaller proportion of people who were born in the same state. These circumstances have led to maintenance and growth of regional and local urban speech habits among blue-collar Americans, while white-collar Americans are more and more likely not to participate as fully in the regional and urban varieties of their communities.

10.2 Urbanization and Networks

This pattern has also been followed in many other countries, as the **urbanization** that began in the Modern period as a consequence of industrialization has greatly increased since the Second World War. Only about 20 percent of the population still lives in rural areas in North America and the United Kingdom, only about 15 percent in New Zealand, and about 10 percent in Australia. New urbanization in the Contemporary period has created new housing patterns, which has affected how people talk to each other.

In the traditional European pattern, before the Contemporary period, people used to live in a great many hamlets or villages, which were a day's journey away from a smaller number of larger towns, which were in turn located within traveling distance of a small number of cities (Figure 10.1).

This pattern emerged from the complex system of markets. When most people lived in small groups in rural areas, people tended to know and talk to each other. Leicester, for instance, was at the center of a set of five different smaller towns (Sheepshed, Market Bosworth, Hinckley,

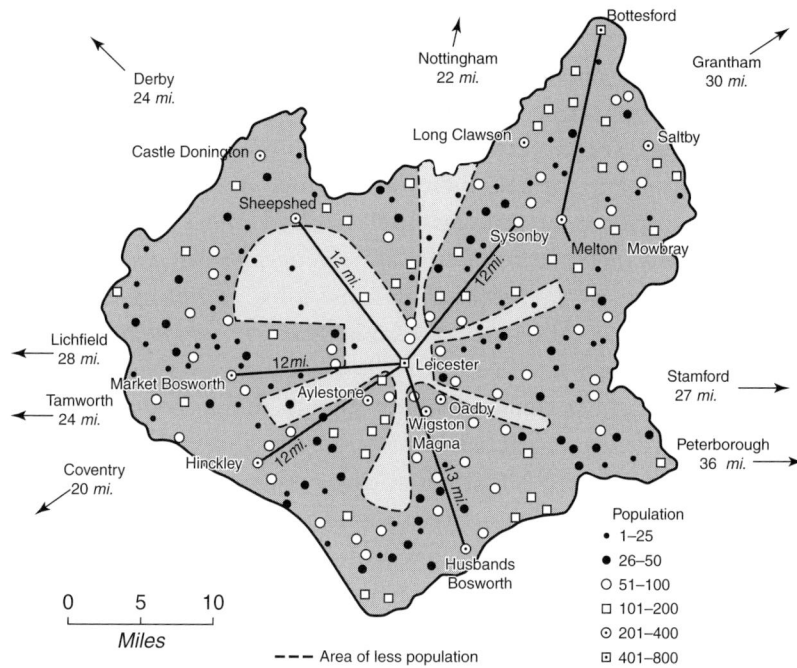

Figure 10.1 Leicester locality, circa 1086 (adapted from Russell 1972: 32)

Husbands Bosworth, and Sysonby) that were each about 12 miles away. Each of the smaller towns, in turn, was surrounded by numerous smaller places. The nearest town of the same size as Leicester was Bottesford, about twenty miles to the northwest. In a demographic pattern like this one, people would talk more to their neighbors in very small places, and could meet and talk to others who lived further away when they went to one of the small market towns or to Leicester itself. The network of communities thus existed at different scales, from tiny villages up through a central market town.

The pattern in English colonies established in the Modern period might be a little different – individual farms or residences might be some distance apart – but the scale of villages, towns, and cities remained, and most people still knew and talked to each other in small groups. Late in the Modern period the pattern began to change: 1920 was the first American census in which over half of the population lived in urban areas. The new urban pattern includes the city itself, and **suburbs** in which many people live and from which they travel to work in the city. The new residential pattern limited how many neighbors knew and talked to each other, especially in wealthier suburbs where the houses occupy more land and residents have the resources to live independently. Proximity of residence in the Contemporary period is only part of the picture for linguistic interaction.

151

As time goes on in the Contemporary period, some of these suburbs develop their own jobs and become **edge cities**, urban places in their own right that are part of a large metropolitan area based on a large city.

Now, when people talk to their neighbors less in bedroom communities or edge cities, **social networks** and **communities of practice** have become very important for linguistic interaction. A social network (a linguistic term, not the same thing as how the term comes up in popular usage) is composed of those people in some geographical area who are linked to each other by, say, doing the same jobs, attending the same schools or churches, or going to the same pubs. A social network is **multiplex** if people tend to have more than one tie (say the same job, church, and pub), and is **dense** if many people share the same links; density and multiplexity create **strong ties**. Dense and multiplex social networks tend to maintain characteristic varieties of English. On the other hand, **weak ties** involve participation in networks that are neither dense nor multiplex, such as someone who does not share a job or church with very many neighbors. Weak ties tend to spread new or different linguistic features. So, for instance, if someone lives in a neighborhood with a dense and multiplex social network but happens to have a job across the city, that person can take characteristics shared in their strong-tie social network to new interactions at work. American blue-collar urban communities tend to have strong social networks that maintain their varieties, while American white-collar communities tend to be dominated by weak ties. Social networks can have different sizes, but many studies of social networks have found core groups of ten or twenty people, often with one or two people who are the best connected at the center of them.

Communities of practice are groups of people who are all engaged in the same activity. They need not be in the same geographical place. For example, those people who enjoy and perform hip-hop music are members of a community of practice. American hip-hop has several regional centers, including Atlanta, New York, and Los Angeles. Hip-hop artists tend to move between these centers in order to work on different projects, so that an Atlanta artist may perform in a New York or Los Angeles production. As one might expect in a complex system, there are characteristics of hip-hop that belong more to Atlanta than to other places, or more to Los Angeles than to other places, but still there is a national hip-hop community of practice – indeed, an international hip-hop community of practice since hip-hop has gone global. Communities of practice may be composed of just a handful of people, or like hip-hop, they may have thousands of members. They may well have central members who are best connected to other members of the group. The important thing to remember about communities of practice, as with social networks, is that membership in the group means more linguistic interaction within the group, which in turn leads to the emergence of some language characteristics that occur with higher frequency within the group. Regarding the hip-hop community, its violent language and use of the word *bitch* have come in for comment by non-hip-hoppers, but within the community these characteristics are understood to have their own meaning appropriate to hip-hop.

New population patterns, networks, and communities of practice have created new social differences in English. Before the Second World War, professionals and the cultural elite were not so likely to move out of region, and they participated in regional speech patterns. Their education and cultural experience merely shaped what they learned in their communities, made them less likely, for instance, to use words like *ain't*, or to say *seen* and *come* as the past-tense forms of *to see* and *to come*. They still knew and used the special pronunciation and vocabulary of the region. Now, however, especially among younger speakers, the avoidance of speech habits that belong to any regional or local urban voice has come to be a mark of education. Highly educated speakers commonly limit their use of regional or social features when they talk in formal situations. A great many educated speakers still know and use regional and local features when they talk in informal settings, as when they are among family or local friends, but many educated speakers grow up in weak-tie communities where they have little opportunity to acquire regional or social speech habits. In Britain, these speakers tend to use RP, or perhaps **Estuary English** in the southeast; in North America speakers simply avoid usages associated with particular social groups. Most of these speakers assume that what they are doing is speaking Standard English (but see the following chapter). Individual speakers, whether educated or not, now have the choice of associating themselves through their speech habits with speakers of increasingly rare rural regional varieties, with speakers of growing local urban varieties, or with speakers who limit their use of regional or social habits. People will choose to talk like the people they want to be like – this happens as the result of interaction, and is the most basic property to support emergence – and their choices may change from one conversation to another in different networks and communities of practices, even within the same geographical community.

Some geographical varieties do continue to emerge. The large regional patterns established earlier in the United Kingdom and the United States remain as a basic framework for local emergence. The

Table 10.1 *African Diaspora in English-Speaking Places*

Location	Percentage of African-heritage population	Number of African-heritage population
United States	14%	43 million
Caribbean	73%	23 million
United Kingdom	3%	2 million
Canada	3%	1 million
Belize	31%	100,000

Wikipedia, under the words "African diaspora"

plantation Southern variety of American English survives now mainly among older speakers and among African Americans, after the loss of cotton culture to the boll weevil and the Dust Bowl in the early twentieth century. Many Southerners migrated North causing depopulation, and pine trees replaced cotton as a staple crop. Some Northern workers migrated South away from the Rust Belt towards new factories in the South in the second half of the twentieth century. These disruptions owing to the commercial climate promoted change, as the migrating population mixed with the settled population. William Labov (1981) and Labov, Boberg, and Ash (2006) have documented changes in progress in pronunciation, similar in form to the Great Vowel Shift, within the American North (**Northern Cities Shift**) and South (the **Southern Shift**), but these changes have not disturbed the large regional pattern. A similar set of sound changes may be affecting London.

African Americans, especially, migrated to urban centers, where they were mostly relegated to segregated housing, which helped to preserve their plantation Southern way of speech. The African diaspora has established large populations of people of African ethnicity, both black and black-mixed people, in many countries (see Table 10.1). Among English-speaking places, the United States has the highest population of African-heritage residents, forty-three million (outside of Africa itself, Brazil has the highest population of African-heritage residents worldwide, fifty-six million).

While the bulk of these populations originally arose through the slave trade, in the Contemporary period voluntary migration has added to them, or created them in the United Kingdom and Canada. Also during the Contemporary period, the social status of citizens of African heritage has begun to improve. John Rickford (2007) documents the situation of "spoken soul" in the United States, where speech patterns have emerged among a growing African-American middle class different from those found in urban segregated communities.

When African American English first became a target for linguistic analysis following from race riots in American cities in the 1960s, it was studied as a monolithic variety, called African American Vernacular English (AAVE). Some linguists (like Rickford) preferred the **Creole Hypothesis** that African-American English had emerged as a contact language like creoles in the Caribbean. Others preferred the **Anglicist Hypothesis** that the features of AAVE could be traced to features of English speakers who were the owners or overseers of slaves. There is no debate that Gullah, a variety of English spoken in the Sea Islands near South Carolina and Georgia, is a creole but the scholarly tide has shifted away from the Creole Hypothesis as more evidence has been gathered. A more recent view suggests that African Americans have acquired features from the English around them, say in different communities in North Carolina, and that urban African American English is emerging in its own directions in different cities around the country. As we expect in the complex system of language, speakers of African heritage interact with other speakers in localities everywhere they live, and so different habits can emerge in cities and the country, and in poor and middle-class communities.

10.3 The Information Age

A new source of community interaction in the Contemporary period comes through telecommunication in the **Information Age**. While television was invented in the Modern period, production of civilian radio and television equipment was stalled during the Second World War, and so the widespread commercialization of television occurred after the war; the first color TV broadcast was in 1954. The rest, as they say, is history: television became and remains a universal telecommunications medium in all developed countries, now often by digital cable instead of broadcast means. TV has been uniquely qualified to spread commercial information, especially on channels with advertising. The English language has been affected in that trade names can be established and spread quickly on TV. Some commercial names were invented when national manufacturing and distribution networks were created to replace homespun production of goods. The names *green beans* and *cottage cheese* replaced a great many local names for the same items, as the canned and frozen versions of the former and refrigerated versions of the latter in the dairy case became commonplace in grocery stores. In the television era, every holiday season brings a new toy or gadget advertised heavily on TV, and everybody must learn the names of top toys and gadgets to satisfy their children and families (Rubik's Cube in 1980, Care Bears in 1985, Teenage Mutant Ninja Turtles in 1990, Pogs in 1995, the Razor Scooter in 2000, Xbox 360 in 2005, iPad in 2010, Apple Watch in 2015, and who can guess what to come). TV, however, has not changed the basic operation of the complex system of language. English speakers still form communities where different linguistic features can emerge at the top of the frequency profile after massive interaction between speakers and writers, not through passive absorption from TV shows and commercials. TV cannot participate in dense and multiplex networks to establish and maintain aspects of an English variety, but it can act like a weak link to help transmit features like commercial terms.

New words and usages have emerged in the contemporary period through normal means. The word *like* is a good example. It has become very frequent, especially among younger speakers, as a **quotative** (as in *I was, like, do you want to go to a movie? And he was, like, sure, which one?*) or as a **discourse particle** (as in *They have, like, no money*). The quotative usage displaced earlier *goes/went* (as in *He goes, sure, which one?*), and both of those are alternatives for *said* (as in *He said, sure, which one?*). The usage as a discourse particle alternates with many other possible forms, of which the most common is the (non-)word *um* as it is spelled in North America or *erm* as it is spelled in the United Kingdom.

Words recently added to the *Oxford English Dictionary* include *auto tune* 'adjust pitch automatically with software,' *half-ass* 'insufficient,' *koozie* 'canned-drink sleeve,' *twerk* 'dance move,' and *Yooper* 'person from the Upper Peninsula of Michigan.' In Australia, the phrase *no worries* is a tag comment, like *cheers* in the United Kingdom (nobody now seems to say *g'day*, an Australianism made famous in the 1980 *Crocodile Dundee* movies). Also in Australia, speakers tend to shorten words and add a [i] sound at the end, as in *footy* 'several kinds of football,' *barbie* 'barbeque,' and *brekky* 'breakfast.' The complex system of English easily allows for new words and usages to enter the language at low frequencies, and some of those will rise in frequency and emerge as familiar, common parts of the language. People often say that nothing is certain but death and taxes, but to those two we can certainly add change in the language.

Linguistic interaction does occur in another aspect of the Information Age, **social media** like Facebook or Twitter or Reddit. In the early days of **CMC** (computer mediated communication), new forms emerged like the **emoticons** :), ;), and :(and numerous **acronyms** or abbreviations, like *LOL* 'laugh out loud,' *what r u doing* 'what are you doing,' or *CUL8R* 'see you later.' Some of these forms became popular when texting on the first cellphones required multiple keystrokes on the numbers of a keypad to render letters of the alphabet. Some of them, like *LOL* or *WTF*, have crossed over into common use in written and spoken English (pronounced as [ˈɛlouˈɛl, ˈdəbljutiˈɛf]). Users tend to feel free not to observe the usual conventions of English punctuation and spelling in CMC, apparently viewing it to be less like writing and more like speech, which has never required strict observance of conventional grammatical rules. Other rules apply, however, such as the conventional use of @ 'an individual' or # 'hashtag, used with topics' in Twitter. Words can come to have special meanings in social media, such as the special meanings of *friend/unfriend* or *like* on Facebook. CMC environments can be considered to be communities of practice, where we can expect particular usages to emerge as very common. In the history of CMC, people commonly interacted on electronic bulletin boards or in electronic chat rooms focused on particular topics, which meets the definition for a community of practice. Users of Twitter – 650 million as of 2015, nearly 300 million of them active users – make up one large-scale community of practice in the complex system of language, and within that large group a great many smaller groups certainly exist. Reddit is not as old and not yet quite as large, with 250 million users using a huge variety of subReddits devoted to different topics. Facebook is much larger with 1.3 billion users as of 2015, and all of them are organized into smaller friendship groups in which users average 130 friends. Not all of these friend relationships amount to the strong ties of a multiplex social network, but it is certainly true that many Facebook users make their accounts very personal by including pictures and talking about their "status," and Facebook has become an important means for families and friends to stay in touch with one another. While remote linguistic interaction on Facebook or other CMC modes is certainly more limited than face-to-face interaction can be, it has a real effect on the complex system of English.

10.4 **World Englishes**

Postcolonial Englishes continue to emerge and develop in the Contemporary period. A good example is the state of Hawaii, which became an American territory late in the Modern period and became the fiftieth American state (thus the long-running TV show, *Hawaii 5-0*) in

1959. A set of isolated volcanic islands in the middle of the Pacific Ocean, Hawaii was originally settled by Polynesians who arrived by canoe. It was "colonized" by American businessmen in the sugarcane industry, who deposed the Hawaiian queen and lobbied to become an American territory. Only about 3 percent of the Hawaiian population today comes from ethnically direct descendants of the original Polynesians; "new Hawaiians" are a mixed stock with contributions from the Chinese, Japanese, Portuguese, Philippine, and other workers who came or were brought to the islands as labor. English speakers in Hawaii today seamlessly integrate some aspects of the former Hawaiian language. All speakers pronounce place and personal names in the manner of Hawaiian, which had five vowels and seven consonants, and which articulated consecutive vowels with an intermediate stop. So, *Hawaii* is pronounced [hə'waɪʔi], not with the off-island pronunciation that does not have the stop [hə'waɪi]. Locals do not pronounce the name of a local road, *Likelike Highway*, as [laɪklaɪk haɪweɪ] but use the Hawaiian-influenced pronunciation [likelike haɪweɪ]. Some words, too, have carried over. *Aloha* is not just a greeting but a kind of Hawaiian welcoming philosophy, and people often say *mahalo* instead of *thank you*. In consequence of its mixed population Hawaii developed a **pidgin** language (a language with simplified grammar used among workers with different language backgrounds) called Hawaiian Pidgin, and some words from it are used freely in Hawaiian English. Instead of giving someone a *dirty look*, a Hawaiian is likely to give them *the stink eye*. Visitors may be asked to take off their *slippers* 'shoes,' often pronounced [slɪpəz]. These differences and others like them make Hawaiian English its own postcolonial variety, even though its speakers believe that they remain in the mainstream of English. Similar differences can be found in many postcolonial settings around the world, where residents retain something of their precolonial language(s) while they still participate in worldwide English.

The largest number of users of English does not speak it as a native language, or even speak it very well at all. Following the Second World War, English has become a **lingua franca**, a language used for trade or other communication between people who do not speak the same language. Airline pilots worldwide, for instance, are supposed to use English to communicate with the airport tower. English is used as a first or native language, or **L1**, in a few countries like the United States, the United Kingdom, and Canada. In many other countries, especially in the European Union, English is taught as a second language, or **L2**, in elementary schools so that a very high percentage of the population, especially younger speakers, can speak English moderately well. In other countries around the world English is not universally taught, but some bits of English occur widely for trade, a status known as **use** of English, sometimes called **L3**. Figure 10.2 shows the percentage of L1 and L2 English speakers by country for most of the world, but even in places like China or India (both below 20 percent), a very large number of people may not speak English but still use some part of the language in their daily lives, from isolated words up to set phrases or sentences.

The list of places with the most English speakers (as of 2015) may be surprising (Table 10.2). Countries where English is spoken as a native language by a very large number of people only occupy places 1, 5, 9, 13, and 15 out of the top twenty. Many of the rest of the top twenty countries have a relatively small percentage of English speakers out of a large overall population, which makes for a large number of English speakers. India, Pakistan, and Nigeria each has more English speakers than the United Kingdom, and together they have more than the United States. Because countries in the European Union actively teach English to schoolchildren, Germany, France, Italy, the Netherlands, and Poland have relatively high percentages and high numbers of English speakers. English is truly a world language when we consider it as a lingua franca, even more so when we include all of those people, perhaps two billion of them, who just use parts of the language occasionally.

The politics of English as a world language make for lively discussion. Many people are afraid of cultural hegemony with language as its symbol. That is, they are afraid that participation in the world economy will lead to the loss of the distinctive traditional culture of their region. Language, most often English, becomes a proxy for the economic and political issues that are the real causes of change. The English language has never by itself endangered anybody's culture – but traditional cultures worldwide are certainly in danger of change owing to the improved transportation and information options of the Contemporary period, which reduce the isolation of each culture worldwide from every other culture. Many of the word's seven billion people have chosen to adopt contemporary ideas and products from outside of their regions, whether brought to them as material goods or found by the people themselves through modern telecommunication and computers. New ideas and change do create conflict, and very often either the issues for discussion or the discussion itself will be expressed in English.

The world has seen an accelerating pace of change since the Second World War, both in the residential patterns of countries in which English is a native language, and in countries where English is an L2 or L3. The new tools of the information age make it difficult for anyone worldwide to

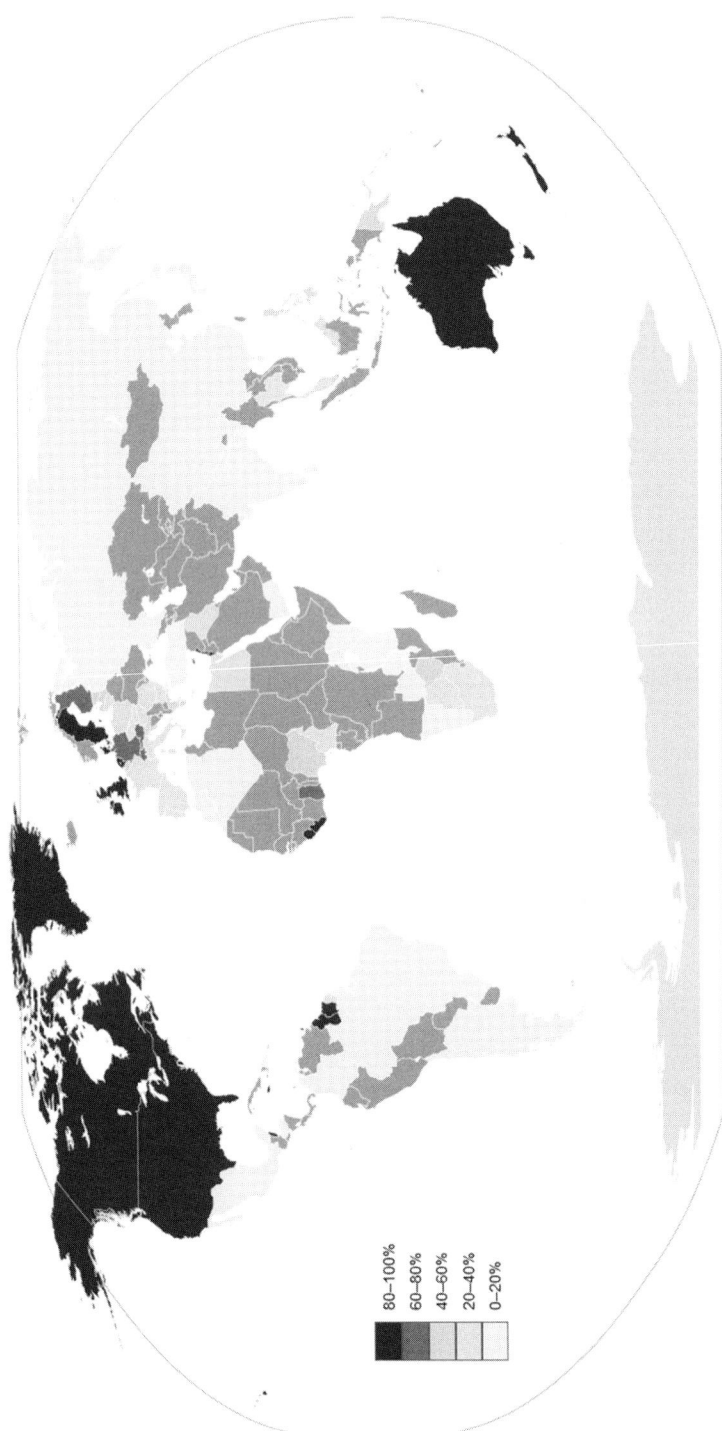

Figure 10.2 Percentage of English speakers worldwide (Wikipedia commons)

80–100%
60–80%
40–60%
20–40%
0–20%

Table 10.2 *Ranked List of Countries by Number of English Speakers*

Rank	Country	Percentage of English speakers	Number of English Speakers
1	United States	94%	298 million
2	India	10%	125 million
3	Pakistan	49%	92 million
4	Nigeria	53%	82 million
5	United Kingdom	98%	64 million
6	Philippines	57%	57 million
7	Germany	64%	51 million
8	Bangladesh	18%	29 million
9	Canada	86%	28 million
10	Egypt	35%	28 million
11	France	39%	25 million
12	Italy	34%	20 million
13	Australia	97%	17 million
14	Thailand	27%	17 million
15	South Africa	31%	16 million
16	Netherlands	90%	15 million
17	Nepal	46%	14 million
18	Poland	33%	13 million
19	Turkey	17%	12 million
20	Iraq	35%	11 million

Wikipedia, under the words "List of countries by English-speaking population"

gnore the fact of change. What remains constant, whether in new social networks or communities of practice, including social media, is the operation of the complex system of speech that self-organizes English into varieties with their own characteristics in an unlimited number of communities, large and small, all across the world. As sociolinguist Peter Trudgill has said (Hughes and Trudgill, 1983), "A world where everyone spoke the same language [or variety] would be a very dull and stagnant place." We can embrace contemporary change, whether or not we like the new things that happen. We cannot stop it.

10.5 **Chapter Summary**

In this chapter we have seen how changes in the residential patterns in English communities have led to changes in how people interact with each other linguistically. Far from slowing down the rate of change in

English or making English more similar in different places, cultural change makes it easier for spoken English to become more different in different places. Social media and other aspects of our Information Age have not changed the underlying complex system of English, but they have made it easier to transmit commercial names and have created new communities of practice. Most English speakers would be surprised that a majority of English speakers worldwide do not speak English natively, and many do not so much speak English as use it. Use of English as a lingua franca puts it in the middle of political discussions about cultural change.

Key Terms
acronym
Anglicist Hypothesis
CMC (computer mediated communication)
community of practice
Creole Hypothesis
dense
discourse particle
edge city
emoticon
Estuary English
Information Age
L1
L2
L3
lingua franca
mobility
multiplex
Northern Cities Shift
pidgin
postcolonial English
quotative
social media
social network
Southern Shift
strong tie
suburb
urbanization
use
weak tie

Exercises

10.1 Think of a large city near you, and try to collect words or usages that seem to be more common in that city than in other places around the country. Does the variety of your city have a special name? Hint: place names and proper names are part of what can distinguish the language of one place from another.

10.2 Think of a large city near you, and consider the local places that are a part of its metropolitan area. Can you identify suburbs? Edge cities that appear to have their own job base? For these suburbs and edge cities, can you say that any particular kind of people live in each one? Perhaps people have particular jobs or income levels, or have other characteristics that make them prefer to live in the community they inhabit.

10.3 What new usages besides *like* do you think are emerging around you? Many localities or networks or communities of practice will have their own frequent usages. Make a list of five words or usages that seem to be more common in a network or community of practice in which you participate. If you go online to corpus.byu.edu, you will find a corpus called Global Web-Based English (GloWbE) that offers collections of texts from twenty countries where English is spoken.

10.4 Do you use acronyms or abbreviations when you use different kinds of CMC? Is the language of texting different from Facebook or Twitter? If you are on Facebook, how many friends do you have, and do you think that they are connected to you by strong ties (as might be found in a dense and multiplex network) or by weak ties?

10.5 If you go online to corpus.byu.edu, you will find a corpus called Global Web-Based English (GloWbE) that offers collections of texts from twenty countries where English is spoken. Enter the corpus, type a word into the "Search String" box, and click Search. What does it mean that the numbers for some of the countries (as shown by their abbreviated names) are highlighted in a darker color? Try several words, and make notes about which words seem to be more common in which countries. Are there any words that do not have any highlighted countries?

Further Reading

Milroy (1987). Lesley Milroy, and her husband James Milroy, pioneered the use of social network analysis for linguistics in their work in Belfast. They are able to show that three different neighborhoods in Belfast have distinctly different linguistic characteristics, and that women from the neighborhoods who had jobs in the city could help transmit characteristics. This work has been widely influential. The idea of maintenance of language varieties in dense and multiplex social networks is best discussed in (James) Milroy (1992).

Eckert (2000). In another widely influential work, Eckert pioneered the study of communities of practice. Her initial study is based on participant observation of students in a high school, some of whom were "jocks" who supported school activities, and others of whom were "burnouts" who resisted what the school was trying to give them. For a description of hip-hop language in America, see Wilson (2007) and Alim (2006). Labov's description of North American sound changes in progress can be found first in print in Labov (1981: 267–309). For a full description of the changes, see Labov, Boberg, and Ash (2006).

African American English has been a celebrated topic for over fifty years among American linguists. Rickford and Rickford (2007) is an excellent introduction to the subject. Mufwene (2001) offers a sensitive analysis of how varieties like African American English can grow and change. Wolfram and Thomas (2008) documents African American English as it reflects local language in North Carolina communities. The study of African American English has always carried with it an interest in social justice, as in Labov (1972).

Tagliamonte and Denis (2008: 3–34). Tagliamonte has been among the foremost analysts of language in CMC. This article is the third most popular in the history of the journal *American Speech*, which is a highly ranked academic journal but usually very readable nonetheless. Another article in *American Speech* considers the status of *like*: D'Arcy (2007: 386–419).

Kachru (1992); Kachru and Kachru (2009). The late Braj Kachru was one of the leading scholars to study English as a world language. For a more popular treatment, see Crystal (2003). For English as a lingua franca, see Seidlhofer (2011).

CHAPTER 11

Standard English

In this chapter

Standard English is not the same as varieties of English that have emerged from the complex system of the language. It is an institutional construct, to the extent that schools convey the idea of a standard and attempt to teach prescriptions about the language. Usage manuals do not agree about what issues to cover. Differences between Standard English in Britain, in North America, and in other places reveal that many standards are in use. Some kinds of standardization of language, like standard spelling, can be useful for the purposes of electronic communication, and such standardization might make it easier to communicate across time and distance. What is more important is the idea of standards, and how that idea plays a role in social relations.

11.1 Codification?

We have already seen a number of references to Standard English. In Chapter 5 you saw that some modern writers about Old English refer to a West Saxon "standard," and there were some institutional efforts to standardize Old English late in the Old English period. However, the appearance of greater regularity in later Old English comes from the fact that most of our surviving manuscripts come from the Wessex region, while the variation that existed in other regions survives in just a few texts. Chapters 6 and 7 discuss the idea that Standard English was jump started by Caxton's use of people from the North in his London printing office. That argument is less well accepted now, and we should understand that the printing office, if anything, helped to influence change as a new contingency for transmission of language. In Chapter 9 the idea of Standard English was described from its real origins in the Modern period. In Richard Bailey's words (1996), by the nineteenth century "attitudes toward grammar had hardened into ideology. Using standard forms of the language was a requirement for gentility (and much else)." Indeed, literacy as taught in the growing schools was associated with both morality and government, as in the motto inscribed over Angell Hall on the University of Michigan campus (completed 1924, it repeats the motto from the 1871 University Hall it replaced): "Religion, morality and knowledge being necessary to good government and the happiness of mankind, schools and the means of education shall forever be encouraged." The idea of Standard English thus means much more than codification of English into a set of rules: it represents social order, moral uprightness, rationality, even nationalism. No wonder Standard English is a staple of language arts teaching in primary and secondary schools worldwide.

Codification of a standard language might be thought to consist of writing down what people say or write, in order to make a grammar or a dictionary. Unfortunately, nothing could be further from the truth for language as people actually use it. As we have seen, words and usages emerge as more or less frequent alternatives among a wide range of variants in any variety, and different words and usages may emerge in all of the different varieties from different communities of speakers, large and small, regional and social. The English language is inherently multi dimensional in this way, with all the different frequencies of use for features in different communities. Writing down what people say whether as rules in a grammar or lists of features, is a difficult job, and making just one list of rules or features, a standard list, will be in conflict with what people actually say and write in many different places. Today English speakers continue to be dominated by a dichotomy between "Standard English," that proper English that we get in school from the earliest grades, and "nonstandard" English, what we actually say or write. Standard English is a creation of people who write school grammars and reference books, and who apply their own impressions of standard to their works. Standard English is not a variety of a language that has emerged among any population according to the processes of complex systems.

11.2 **Usage Guides**

A Dictionary of Modern English Usage, the 1926 **usage guide** prepared by **Henry Fowler,** may be the most famous representation of Standard English. It is still in print in a 2015 fourth edition, though with substantial rewriting. The book was not based on extensive research (unlike the *Oxford English Dictionary* described in Chapter 9). Fowler was an Oxford-educated former schoolteacher, a freelance journalist who brought his own personality and opinions to the work. In this way he qualifies as a language **maven,** a label that indicates a trusted expert, but when applied to English language experts the word suggests someone who has the chutzpah to identify the *correct* bits of language and complain about the wrong ones. As Stephen Pinker wrote about mavens, their "rules conform neither to logic nor to tradition, and if they were ever followed they would force writers into fuzzy, clumsy, incomprehensible prose, in which certain thoughts are not expressible at all." Language mavens are only experts in a highly restricted sense.

William Safire, the longtime writer of the popular *On Language* column in the *New York Times*, was another self-professed maven, a word which he thought conveyed a hint of self-criticism. Safire knew that he was not himself a trained expert in the English language – he did not finish college and was a political speech writer and columnist – and often invited academic experts to answer questions. But that did not stop him from being an outspoken defender of what he believed to be correct English. The author of a contemporary usage guide, Bryan Garner, also a prescriptivist, spent much of his career writing about legal texts. We have no shortage of contemporary language mavens, and people tend to believe them because of the association of Standard English with cherished principles in society. In the United Kingdom there remains a healthy complaint tradition of people who write to newspapers to complain about what they think are incorrect usages, and they differ from language mavens only in that they do not take on the role of an expert. The existence of mavens and the complaint tradition in the United Kingdom comes from the dichotomy that English speakers worldwide, and speakers of many other languages, too, have been taught to believe implicitly that using a language has a correct way (the standard) and a wrong way (anything else, even if it is our normal way of speaking and writing).

When usage guides are considered as a whole, they contain many thousands of different **prescriptions** but only a small fraction of them are repeated in a majority of the manuals. In one count by Don Chapman, 3,500 prescriptions were proposed in the usage guides of the last century, but most of them have not been repeated at all in another usage manual (7,800 one-offs), fewer than a quarter have been retained in recent usage manuals (2,800), and fewer than a tenth are present in even half the usage manuals (1,100). This much uncertainty and disagreement about how to represent Standard English creates a problem for teaching language arts in the schools. As William Labov (1972) has put it, "For many generations, American school teachers have devoted themselves to correcting a small number of nonstandard English rules to their standard equivalents, under the impression that they were teaching logic." Teachers and language mavens who proscribe usages often supply a rationale like "two negatives make a positive" that sound logical (here like the application of signs in multiplication), but in fact such statements have no basis in either usage or logic. Negatives are most often additive in English, not alternative like signs in multiplication. Even the simplest English rules in school grammars, like using the appropriate case or agreement in number, sometimes fail. Nobody still says *it is I* even though the subject case of the first person pronoun is grammatically correct; everybody says *it's me*. The difference between *who* and *whom* is most often not observed in actual speech and writing, although teachers may mark it. Agreement in number is violated in sentences like *everyone has their own book*, but that is what people say and frequently write, especially when they are trying to avoid using a gender-specific pronoun like *his* or *her*. It is easy to make a rule in a usage guide or grammar, but knowing which rules to follow or which ones to enforce is a more difficult problem.

An English language academy could do no better than the language mavens. No grammar, whether prescriptive or descriptive, could ever capture all of the grammatical constructions in any variety, because the A-curve distribution of variants tells us that there will be many times as many constructions that hardly ever occur than there are common constructions that we are likely to notice, with new constructions arising all the time. We understand the constructions in the long tail of the A-curve, in part because some of them happen to be more frequent in different regional and social domains or in different text types, but largely because the same variants tend to be in use everywhere even if they occur at low frequencies and so we may have heard them before. The very idea of Standard English as a rigid set of rules excludes any effective management of the differential frequencies of feature variants and constructions in the language as it is used. That said, we have a longstanding commitment to the idea of a Standard, and that commitment is not going away. The important thing is to understand where the idea of a Standard has come from (as in Chapter 9), and to come up with an idea of how a Standard relates to what people normally say and write. It is not a case of a correct way versus a wrong way, but instead an issue of what language is appropriate in any kind of situation for language use.

Table 11.1 *Variants for "Fifteen Minutes before the Hour"*

quarter to	480
quarter till	392
quarter of	353
(x) forty-five	50
fifteen (minutes) till	21
fifteen (minutes) to	14
lacks (quarter/fifteen)	4
three quarters past	3
quarter before	1

From www.lap.uga.edu

Let us look at a grammatical A-curve, one for what to call the time when it is fifteen minutes before the hour, based on the evidence of the American Eastern States survey introduced in Chapter 2. One might think that there was a standard way to tell the time, but perhaps not. Table 11.1 shows a list of what people said, grouping the answers into major categories that leave out superficial variations like which hour it was (e.g., leaving out the "seven" in "quarter to seven").

People chose either the word *quarter* or the word *fifteen* in most of the answers, or else gave a digital answer with *forty-five* (this for data gathered in the mid twentieth century, before digital clocks!). Then people used one of four different prepositions (*to, till, of, before*) most of the time, except for four people who used the verb *lacks* and three people who chose *three quarters past*. Figure 11.1 shows the A-curve for the various combinations.

Which should be the standard form? Three prepositions (*to, till, of*) occur in the majority of the responses. All of the responses, even those without *to, till, of*, are easily understandable. None of these forms is stigmatized as the usage of uneducated or otherwise "nonstandard" people, although any of the less-frequently occurring forms might have been singled out in this way if a maven had noticed the variation in usage. Language features that we call "standard" do not emerge from the interactions of speakers. They have to be chosen by someone who takes that responsibility upon themselves. In Britain, North America, and elsewhere, we do appoint academies or allow mavens to choose the Standard way to say and write things, even if that choice is not our most common way of speaking and writing.

Standard American English grammar and lexicon are different from Standard British English (RP) and standard postcolonial varieties. Typical lexical and grammatical differences are quite familiar, such as American/

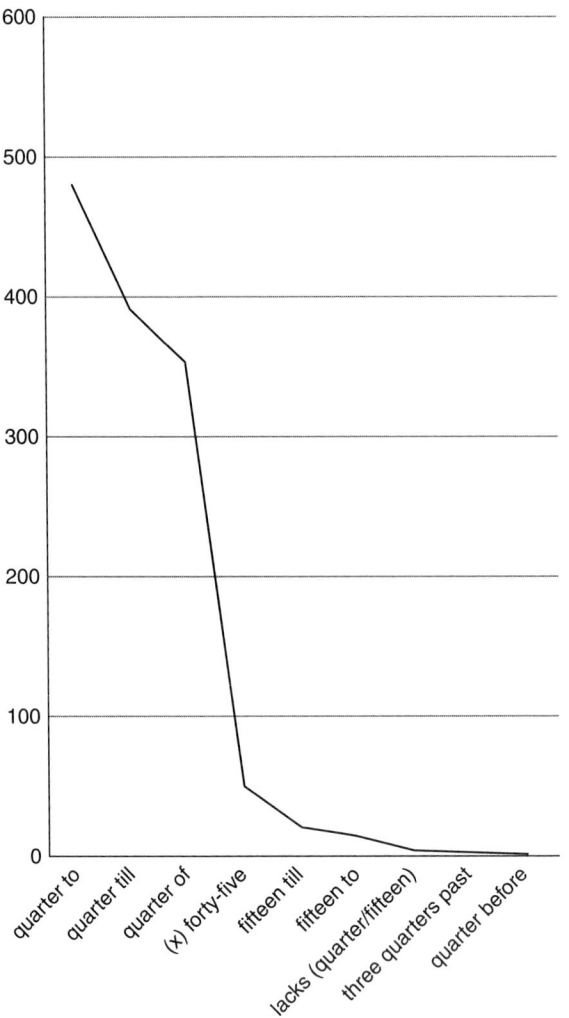

Figure 11.1 A-curve for what to call the time when it is fifteen minutes before the hour (adapted from www.lap.uga.edu)

British *trunk/boot, windshield/windscreen, truck/lorry, elevator/lift, apart-ment/flat, toilet/loo, Mind your head/Caution, government is/government are, in the hospital/in hospital.* Most differences are more subtle. For exam-ple, Americans and Britons both have the words *post* and *mail* but use them differently. Corpus analysis, the search for usage tendencies in large bodies of writing drawn from American, British, and other world sources, is the best way to discover and understand these subtle differences (see Appendix 3). Even homely coordinating conjunctions like *and* occur at statistically significantly different rates in corpus analysis of British English and American English. Every word in the language and every grammatical construction are likely to be used somewhat differently in the Standard English of different world varieties of the language, because every word and every construction will be used at somewhat different rates and with somewhat different collocations.

Thus, we cannot very well make a list of differences, even though our impression from all the subtle differences is that Standard English is certainly not the same in the United Kingdom, North America, and their postcolonial counterparts. The actual difference between the Standard English of different countries is in the frequency profile of the A-curve for variants that emerges in every country: most of the same pronunciations, words, and usages are used in every country, and the differences between countries occur in the different rates that different variants are used. Particular variants will be higher on the A-curve in any country while other variants are lower, and the whole collection of higher and lower variants in the frequency profile is what creates the Standard in a country. For example, Figure 11.2 shows the rates at which *quarter to, quarter of*, and *quarter till* are used in twenty English-speaking countries worldwide (from the GloWbE corpus; see Appendix 3). The numbers in the figure refer to the actual number of times the phrase was found in the corpus for each country, and the shading shows the rate of occurrence (how many times the phrase was found, divided by the number of words in the corpus), the higher the rate the darker the shading. *Quarter till* does not occur very often (even though it was the second most common form in the Eastern States survey), with a token only in Ireland (IE). We see many examples of *quarter to*, at different rates for different times; the highest rates are the dark boxes under Ireland (IE), Australia (AU), New Zealand (NZ), India (IN), Hong Kong (HK), and South Africa (ZA). *Quarter of* has an intermediate frequency overall, with dark boxes under the USA (US), Ireland (IE), Australia (AU), and New Zealand (NZ). Is *quarter to* more standard than *quarter of*? Are these phrases more or less standard for different times of day? Figure 11.2 shows that there is substantial variation, that telling time is not standard, and that people talk about it a little differently wherever you go.

The difficulty of determining what a standard should be has also been a problem in English spelling. The idea of fixing spelling began in the Early Modern period, but as we have seen in earlier chapters, spelling remained quite variable long after that. As we saw in Chapter 9, Webster advocated new spellings in America that have made British and American spelling different. Even today, spelling can be variable in informal communication like personal letters and CMC. However, formal communication, especially in printing, now generally has standardized spelling with a much smaller percentage of variation. The long process of standardization has

First table — rates of occurrence of *quarter to*:

#	CONTEXT	ALL	US	CA	GB	IE	AU	NZ	IN	LK	PK	BD	SG	MY	PH	HK	ZA	NG	GH	KE	TZ	JM
1	[QUARTER] [TO] [THREE]	40	13	4	8	4	1	1	3					1	1	2						1
2	[QUARTER] [TO] [ONE]	31	3	3	8	2	4	6	1					1	1	1				1		1
3	[QUARTER] [TO] [TEN]	26	3		11	4	2	1	2						2						1	
4	[QUARTER] [TO] [FIVE]	26	3		7	1	4	2				1			1	3	2			1		1
5	[QUARTER] [TO] [NINE]	21	5	1	5	6			1						1		1				1	
6	[QUARTER] [TO] [FOUR]	21	4	2	7	3	1					2					2					
7	[QUARTER] [TO] [SEVEN]	21	1	2	4	1	2	4	1	2					1			1		1	1	1
8	[QUARTER] [TO] [EIGHT]	20	4	1	5		1	2	1	2	1							1		2		
9	[QUARTER] [TO] [SIX]	17	1		3	2	1	1					1		2			1				
10	[QUARTER] [TO] [ELEVEN]	17	4		6		2			2			1			1		1		1		
11	[QUARTER] [TO] [TWELVE]	15	1		2	2	4	1	1							1	4	1		1	1	
12	[QUARTER] [TO] [TWO]	13	3		2	2	1		1												1	
	TOTAL	268	45	13	67	27	23	18	16	6	1	4	2	2	8	7	10	3	0	7	4	5

Second table — rates of occurrence of *quarter of*:

#	CONTEXT	ALL	US	CA	GB	IE	AU	NZ	IN	LK	PK	BD	SG	MY	PH	HK	ZA	NG	GH	KE	TZ	JM
1	[QUARTER] [OF] [ONE]	57	19	1	11	5	3	4	2		2	1	2	2	1	1	1		2		2	
2	[QUARTER] [OF] [NINE]	9			1		8															
3	[QUARTER] [OF] [EIGHT]	7			2			5														
4	[QUARTER] [OF] [THREE]	4		1	2									1								
5	[QUARTER] [OF] [TWELVE]	1																				1
6	[QUARTER] [OF] [SEVEN]	1												1								
7	[QUARTER] [OF] [FOUR]	1	1																			
	TOTAL	80	20	2	16	5	16	4	2	0	2	1	2	2	1	1	1	0	2	0	2	1

Third table — rates of occurrence of *quarter till*:

#	CONTEXT	ALL	US	CA	GB	IE	AU	NZ	IN	LK	PK	BD	SG	MY	PH	HK	ZA	NG	GH	KE	TZ	JM
1	[QUARTER] [TILL] [FIVE]	1			1																	

Figure 11.2 Rates of occurrence of *quarter to*, *quarter of*, and *quarter till* (from GloWbE corpus, corpus.byu.edu/glowbe)

meant that English spelling preserves different spellings for homophones like *meat/meet* and *sea/see*, which spell words differently according to their pronunciation before the Great Vowel Shift (as mentioned in Chapter 8). The unpredictability of the complex system has preserved the similar spellings for words that are no longer homophones, like *bean/been* (still a homophone in British English) and *great/greet*. We do not always use the same spelling for the same sound, as for the [ʃ] in *shade* and *station*. Still, increasingly from the nineteenth century on, in formal writing the same word is most often spelled with the same string of letters. This does have the positive benefit of making it easier to search for words online and in electronic databases – shopping is more reliable! The relative success of standardization of spelling may also make it easier to under-stand documents from distant times or places, although, as we have seen, a word may preserve its spelling over time without preserving the same meaning. Relative standardization of spelling will have mixed results in the future.

11.3 Who Speaks Standard English?

Change in the urban demographic pattern since the Second World War contributes to the idea of Standard English. Weak ties in social networks tend to promote the transmission of features from group to group, not the maintenance of strongly marked features within a community. At the same time, the most highly educated segment of the population became more mobile nationally, owing to improved transportation. Now, the youngest generation in Roswell, GA, an edge city near Atlanta, has a greatly dimin-ished traditional Southern accent compared to their parents and grand-parents. This development corresponded to tremendous population growth including many outsiders in Roswell, so that many people might say that younger people in Roswell were speaking Standard English. Still, the younger generation does not use some uniform, leveled, default Standard American English. The youngest generation in Roswell uses fea-tures that their parents and grandparents had used at low frequencies, often now emerging as high frequency alternatives. Loss of the characteristics of a traditional English variety does not mean that the community has shifted to Standard English. The contingencies of technical and demographic change keep the complex system of speech in motion, and allow for the emergence of new features, a new way of talking in Roswell.

The highly educated have less access to local and regional speech, and among themselves often tend to suppress whatever such features they have. The term **General American** has sometimes been used as a proxy for the

English of highly educated Americans, because the label gives the impression that there is something "general," or common, or popular, about it. Similar terms, General Canadian and Standard Canadian English, offer the same impression. Actually, just the reverse is true. Highly educated speakers remain a minority of the population (at this writing, 39 percent of Americans have completed a postsecondary degree, and 47 percent of Canadians, but only 27 percent of Britons), and rather than sharing characteristics of speech as the term "general" implies, their speech actually tends to be more mixed in its characteristics than the more strongly differentiated regional and social varieties of the less-mobile working-class and middle-class speakers. In Roswell, of nine younger speakers studied, all of them except one do use at least some Southern features at different rates. So, the natural speech of highly educated speakers retains some characteristics of regional speech, typically those that have not attracted notice as regional characteristics, different characteristics in different regions. The mobility of educated speakers adds to the inconsistency, because educated speakers in any given location are likely to exhibit regional characteristics brought from many regions. There is nothing general about this mixture of characteristics.

People who believe themselves to be using Standard English actually employ their home varieties, but try to suppress those variants that they have noticed as being different from what other people say, or that they have been taught to consider unacceptable. Speakers of home varieties with relatively more variants that have been noticed and proscribed, and speakers who have less exposure to or interest in education, will of course appear to be more nonstandard in their speech. It all comes down to **perception**, what people notice. In one study, speakers from the state of Michigan were found to have great linguistic self-confidence, a belief that they speak "correct" English. At the same time, people from other places in America often notice the Michiganders' accent (many of them have one of the ongoing changes in American pronunciation), and consider that they sound anything but standard. The same is true in the United Kingdom of those who have an Estuary English accent, people who believe themselves to be using Standard English but actually have pronunciations quite different from RP. Variability that does not rise to the level of perception, especially the perception of the speakers themselves, can pass for Standard English. Finally, mobility among the more educated has also helped to create the impression that highly educated speech should not sound regional. News readers may think that suppression of noticeable variants somehow gives them objectivity by avoiding local or social connections, but it is actually just a symptom (not a cause) of greater mobility and changed housing patterns. The lack of regional variation on network news programs in

America – different regional voices may now be heard on the BBC – is thus just another manifestation of perceptions. None of these problems with perception, of course, gets in the way of our social consensus that there is in fact a Standard. People perceive their own language in relation to their understanding that there is a Standard, and their confidence that they are speakers who approximate it.

Demographic change and mobility show us that the language used as Standard English parallels the language of other regional and social cultures, characterized by a mixture of feature variants that come from the experience of speakers in their particular regional and social circumstances. What distinguishes such speakers, then, is their choice, based on their perceptions, to believe in and try to enact the ideal of Standard English. Allegiance to Standard English can be called a **voluntary association** with like-minded people, one allowed by the modern possibility for self-selection by many contemporary English speakers, not only of where and how to live, but for Standard English, how to communicate. Standard English, then, is an ideology (as are the standard versions of other languages), but it is more than that. It is a lifestyle choice compounded with other preferences and behaviors for how to live one's life, such as belief in the value of higher education and attendant aspects of culture. There is nothing any more wrong with believing in the use of the Standard than being a Democrat or a Republican, Labour or Conservative, a Man United or a Man City fan, a lover of classical music or of rock music or hip-hop (and an upholder of the Standard could be any of these, too), or being an advocate of any other lifestyle choice in association with like-minded people. Indeed, college communities are a good example of **voluntary regions** because people who prefer the same kinds of lifestyle choices as those who try to enact Standard English tend to congregate in them. Given our social consensus on a belief in Standard English, individual speakers can choose how their lives relate to it.

11.4 **Language and the Law**

Other typical associations may be more problematic. Standard English in the United States often has an association with the English Only movement, for example, which takes the use of Standard English to be a matter of patriotism. A belief in Standard English has traditionally been associated with conservative educational practices, of the "readin', writin', and 'rithmetic" style of regimented instruction. Standard English is often associated with moral behavior, and with intelligence since an ability to manipulate Standard English is included in educational and intelligence testing. At this writing, thirty-two American states have passed laws making English the official language of the state. These laws typically do not define English, much less declare what is Standard. The laws also do not prohibit people from speaking another language. They do, however, in the words of the law in the state of Kansas, say: "The official language is designated as the language of any official public document or record and any official public meeting." This statement parallels the Official Pleading Act of 1362 (mentioned in Chapter 7), when English first became the language of law in England, but goes further by requiring that documents be maintained in English. In 1362, England was in the midst of breaking away from its French connections and changing the language of Parliament was part of that process; in the twenty-first century, perhaps state legislatures believe that they are protecting their societies from incursions by immigrants who speak other languages. In a larger view, these associations of English and Standard English with political points of view are really accidental, not essential. There is nothing about Standard English, per se, as an ideology and lifestyle choice, which commits those who value it to take any political positions, but then again, there is nothing about Standard, per se, to prevent it from being associated with political or social causes. Some of the special uses of language to support political positions are described in Appendix 3.

Standard English is also associated with the law courts. In the opinion of the judge in the famous 1979 Ann Arbor decision on language variation in the schools, C. W. Joiner equated the school "standard" with the language of "the commercial world, the arts, science, and professions." Judge Joiner distinguished between "black English" and "standard English," and clearly thought that "black English" deviated from the "standard English" that he believed to be in use in school and in educated realms of society. For Judge Joiner, "standard English" constituted the normal language of his own community of educated people, to which students in the school should aspire even if their own ("deviant") home and community language differed from it. Former American Supreme Court justice Antonin Scalia similarly advocated the **plain language rule** (also known as the **plain meaning rule** in English law) for the interpretation of statutes and of the constitution. He has written (Scalia and Garner, 2012) that "words, like other conventional symbols, do convey meaning, an objective meaning, regardless of what their author 'intends' them to mean." Justice Scalia did admit that we need to consider when and where words were used in order to establish their conventional meaning, but his position remains a strong endorsement of what is conventional and thus standard. The idea of plain language undervalues the multidimensional nature of language in favor of the power of convention. Justice Scalia was right to question whether, especially in law, one can substitute an author's intention for what a law actually says, but his assumption that what a law says can be plainly interpreted in Standard English is open to question. The language of the law has historically been notorious for convolutions designed to make sure that only one meaning can be derived from, say, a contract, which suggests that plain language may be more difficult to interpret than is generally assumed. Still, the idea that plain language should have a plain meaning, as a result of our belief in Standard English, obtains still in the law and elsewhere in life around us.

One outcome of the popular ideology of Standard English has been justification of all sorts of discrimination and cultural bias. Discrimination in employment on grounds of language may be a proxy for discrimination on other grounds such as ethnicity or national origin (e.g., "somebody who talks like *that* can't be a librarian"). It may be shocking to some that use of nonstandard language for portrayals of marginal or threatening characters is a common characteristic of Walt Disney children's movies. Given the historical American obsession with spelling (now shared in other countries as well), poor spelling may be grounds for someone's argument to be thrown out without consideration of its merits.

When Standard English is associated with everything good in society, perceived faults in the use of Standard English can make people appear to be less than the best. Our shared belief in Standard English can be used by some people as a cover for prejudices they hold on other grounds. However, because of our social consensus on a belief in Standard English, this kind of discrimination may be less a matter of individuals with racist views, and more an essential misunderstanding of how language actually works in our societies. We all come to know what we expect to hear in linguistic interactions in a range of familiar situations, and when other speakers do not do what we expect, we think that they are rude (if they know better), or uninformed (if they really do not understand), or, to put the case more generally, that speakers who do not conform to the regularities of speech that belong to a particular situation of language use are not competent to participate in the interaction. If we understand language in use more accurately, we can try to assist speakers who are not competent to participate in particular situation by translating what they actually say into the language required by the situation, or by teaching them to do so themselves – which is what Judge Joiner advocated.

Where, then, does the idea of Standard English really come from? The idea that there is a standard form of a language starts as an **observational artifact,** something that we just perceive to be there. Such use of perception to create objects is normal for people; we all learn to see things around us, like the sky or a beach, even though they are actually composed of a great many components that we perceive together and choose to consider to be one object. This is certainly true of language, which has a large number of possible alternatives for any linguistic feature. However, because frequency profiles emerge from the complex system of language, we usually say or write one of just a few things for any feature, in any situation like the social networks or communities of practice in which we are involved. Variants of features that are massively more common have a strong perceptual advantage because of the ever-present A-curve distributional pattern, and they come to be perceived as "grammatical" or "acceptable." **Grammaticality** is something that we notice after the fact of usage, given our perception of the frequency profile of variants. The idea of Standard English thus arises from the same source, the perceptual advantage of top-ranked variants in the frequency profile. This is how Standard English can be different in different countries. Language mavens compete to tell us which variants, typically their own, we ought to consider to be standard, and they do so without necessarily paying attention to which variants are actually top-ranked in their communities.

Standard English is not a fact because it is an underlying linguistic system, but because of the *belief* of language users in the real existence of the languages out of all the welter of component words and features, based on their perception of the A-curves for every feature. That is, people share cognitive tools for processing their experience with speech, and the A-curve distribution of variants helps to create our cognitive picture of the language we use. We then come to believe that the variants with which we are most familiar constitute the normal form of our language, in any situation in which we use it. Even though the A-curve distribution of linguistic tokens is not something that our grammars have taken into account, it is the A-curve distribution from the complex system of language that allows us to perceive and believe in the existence of grammar, and following that a standard grammar. Grammar is thus a social phenomenon, something that emerges from the usage of a community of speakers. The idea of grammar requires the emergence of familiar variants, at all levels of scale, from huge numbers of interactions between speakers who use variants in the complex system of speech. Standard English is just one step further in the social process, an attempt by some speakers, the language mavens, to tell the rest of us what the best set of variants might be.

Even if Standard English is something that cannot be defined very well in objective grammars or lists, and even if it is something more subject to perception and belief than we might have believed, we still must cope with its presence as a fact of life in English-speaking communities. The idea of Standard English is completely embedded in our school systems, in our legal systems, and in the minds of English speakers worldwide. Standard English is a social fact, if not clearly a linguistic fact. Academic linguists have made little headway when they have tried to tell people that the language actually works in ways other than how people believe it does according to the idea of a standard. The most that those of us who know about the history of the language can do is to understand what lies behind Standard English, and bring that knowledge to public discussions where language is an issue. Once we understand that English is emerging all around us every day, in different countries worldwide, and in different places and social circumstances in every country, then we can try to avoid using the idea of a Standard for unfair or unjust purposes.

11.5 Chapter Summary

In this chapter Standard English was shown to be a much more difficult thing to define than most of us would believe. Usage guides do not share their prescriptions, and language mavens compete to say what prescriptions we should prefer. The idea of Standard English has been promoted by demographic change, but it actually comes down to the perception of speakers and their choice of believing in a language standard. The embedding of Standard English in schools and courts means that we have to cope with it, even when we understand how it has arisen from the nature of the complex system of language.

Key Terms
codification
Henry Fowler
General American
grammaticality
maven
observational artifact
perception
plain language rule
plain meaning rule
prescription
William Safire
usage guide
voluntary association
voluntary region

Exercises

11.1 Collect a set of at least three usage guides (several are listed under Further Reading). Start with the entry for *hopefully* and then, for each of the guides, make a list of the twenty entries in order that come next. How many are the same? How many are different? Do they give the same advice about the entries they have in common?

11.2 Collect a set of at least three one-volume desktop dictionaries. Look in the Front Matter for each dictionary for its discussion of Usage Labels or Usage Notes. Do all of your dictionaries take the same approach to usage? How do they mark entries in the dictionary as having some special usage status?

11.3 Google the word "Ebonics," and find out about the controversy in the late 1990s regarding the Oakland school board and its attempt at special treatment of Standard English. In your view, what were the main issues of the controversy? Why do you think this became such a celebrated case?

11.4 Google the 1988 Kingman Report on the teaching of English language in the United Kingdom. In your view, does the report's discussion of Standard English (Chapter 2, paragraphs 31–38) provide an adequate description? What about the goals stated in Chapter 5 (beginning on page 52)?

11.5 The completion test for the end of primary school in an American state demands that students be able to "Eliminate fragments and run-ons," "Analyze sentences for misplaced and dangling modifiers," "Analyze sentences containing usage errors, such as subject–verb agreement, use of non-standard English, double negatives," "Determine correct spelling of grade-level words in the context of a sentence," and "Determine correct usage of parts of speech in sentences, such as verbs (tenses, phrases, forms), prepositions, nouns, conjunctions, adverbs, interjections, adjectives." Given what you now know about Standard English, what do you think this test is really testing? Is it of the same order as a test in mathematics. If so, why? If not, why not? What do you think of this test as a matter of educational policy for the state?

Further Reading

Milroy and Milroy (2012). The Milroys offer the best account of the role of Standard English, especially as it appears in the United Kingdom. Another source for popular views of English is Cameron (2012). Curzan (2014) discusses the process of standardization. Wright (2000) has a collection of articles about the earlier history of standardization.

There are many usage guides available. Here are references to some of them: Butterfield (2015); Peters (2004); Garner (2009); Lester and Beason (2012). Chapman (2009) contains the tabulations of usage prescriptions he presented at the annual SHEL conference.

Information about the Roswell project can be found in Kretzschmar (2016: 159–176).

Scalia and Garner (2012). Here Scalia and Garner (the author cited in the chapter for his usage guide) defend textualism as an approach to legal interpretation. They assert a large number of what they call "canons" designed to reduce the ambiguity of legal interpretation. The book carries over the flavor of Garner's usage guide, in that it is prescriptive in its assumption of standards of correctness. Tiersma and Solan (2012). The authors are two of the great names in forensic linguistics, the application of linguistics to legal issues.

Baron (1990) discusses the English-Only movement.

Websites that advocate English as an official language include www.usenglish.org and proenglish.org.

Lippi-Green (2011). This celebrated account of discrimination based on Standard English ideology is the one with a chapter on Walt Disney movies.

CHAPTER 12

The Future of English

In this chapter

The Star Trek syndrome offers a poor prediction of the future of English. Instead, we can predict that the complex system of language will continue to operate in different populations of speakers. Continuing change creates challenges in our schools, and in communities worldwide where English is used as a lingua franca. Knowing how change works, however, gives us access to the English of the past and the English of the future.

12.1 Star Trek Syndrome

The long-running Star Trek series on television and in the movies offers prediction of what English might look like in the future (Figure 12.1). provides a convenient portal to the twenty-third and twenty-fourth centuries, and while language-contact situations still do occur despite the use of machine-based universal translator, Galactic Standard English seems t have taken hold. Ensign Chekov has a Russian accent in the original T series and the newest movies. As late as the twenty-third century (in th original Star Trek series), remnants of an American Southern accent st remained in the speech of Dr. McCoy, but these seem to have disappeared the Next Generation, and appear less certain in the newest movies. Sco

Figure 12.1 Lifestyle pictures / Alamy Stock Photo

and Irish accents seem to have become an occupational dialect for engineers like Mr. Scott, or Miles O'Brien in the Next Generation. And astoundingly, what should have been French from the Next Generation's Captain Picard somehow turned into the captain's RP, which perhaps indicates the long-term success of the language-teaching sections of the Oxford or Cambridge university presses. The world of Star Trek's twenty-fourth century will not have much variation to offer.

This prediction of standardization, call it the **Star Trek syndrome**, is certainly wrong. If English goes to the stars, there will be even more room for emergence of different features in different groups of people, whether groups defined by geography (planets?) or communities of practice (uniform colors representing occupations?), or other means. The constant lesson of the history of the English language is that the complex system of language continues to operate, and new varieties keep emerging all the time. The rise of Standard English in the Modern period and the continuing belief in Standard English of educated people in the Contemporary period cannot hide the high level of variation that we actually observe in all periods. The Star Trek syndrome, like plain meaning, substitutes the perception of its believers for the facts of the language. It might be better for Star Trek fans to consider that the universal translator is always turned on, and that is why everybody is speaking Galactic Standard.

183

12.2 **What to Expect**

What should we expect instead? In both the United Kingdom and North America, old settlement patterns have created long-lasting cultural regions, which have come to be a part of how we think about ourselves and our fellow citizens. The North and the South have been different cultural regions in the United Kingdom for over a thousand years, and have been different cultural regions in the United States for over 200 years. The people in the areas change over time, but there are continuing interactions within the cultural regions, more within regions than between regions, so the regions have remained stable over the passage of long periods of time. Continuing linguistic interactions in the complex system within these regions mean that a better prediction is to expect that English will change regionally. There have been some major cultural shifts during all that time, such as the loss of the plantation system in the Southern United States with a subsequent African American diaspora, but these are exceptions that prove the rule. So far, mobility has been low enough that great regional patterns remain. The real change between earlier varieties and contemporary varieties is a reversal of the roles played by the more educated social elite and blue-collar speakers. In earlier periods the density of contact between different parts of the population allowed commercial elites to have an influence in the maintenance of local varieties. Today, modern local varieties are maintained by middle- and working-class speakers, and it is the elites who tend to have weak ties and thus less participation in local varieties because of their greater mobility.

When elite speakers used to use the same regional speech as everybody else, the psychology of language in the school was different: local language was not stigmatized but preferred. Today, the belief in Standard English has changed that. Deviation of local norms from school standards is not necessarily a sign of the failure of local schools. It just reflects a change in the composition of those who set local norms, from an elite population that has now changed to be most characterized today by higher education, to middle- and working-class population for whom elementary school and high school are still sufficient to offer them opportunities in local business and factories. Speakers from these social classes may in fact be able to shift their use of optional features towards "school" language, but strong community solidarity makes such speech exceptional for them.

Now, success in school often means leaving the local community, for example to go away to college, and not everybody wants to do that. A larger proportion of the population has a college degree today than the proportion before the Second World War, but the larger current proportion still does not constitute a majority of the population. A decision not to enter into the national marketplace of the highly educated is not necessarily an admission of failure, but a choice to enact one's preference for the common purposes of the local community. If we think that everybody wants to be highly educated, national language standards and standardized tests are perfectly acceptable. However, if we think that people should have choices, we may in future decide to recognize local speech and local issues for students who want to stay home. This has already begun for schools in the United Kingdom. We can predict a continuing division between the highly educated population who believe that they speak the Standard English that the schools are teaching, and local populations who understand what the schools want from them but prefer their home language. Both of these populations share a belief in Standard English, they just make different decisions about what they want to do with it.

For particular words and usages, we can predict continuing change. Words will continue to change in meaning in the future as they have in the past (see Appendix 3), and words can mean different things in different situations of use, whether in different places or in different contexts. To say that a text means what it says will continue to be a debatable proposition, because the same text can mean different things depending on where, when, in what circumstances, and by whom it was written. The complaint tradition will also continue, by those who continue to think that any change from what they believe to be Standard English must be something worse, not something better. Some changes, like quotative *like*, will appear to be striking deviations; others, like the verb *google*, will accompany new objects or processes that need new names and so will cause fewer complaints. Most changes, however, will be more subtle. The frequency profiles of collocations, so important for the construction of meaning in English, are already different in different populations of speakers, and they can change over time as new high-frequency variants emerge and the former top-ranked variants decline in their numbers (again, see Appendix 3). In hindsight we can recognize great changes over long periods of time, like the change from English as a synthetic language to an analytic language, or the Great Vowel Shift, but from day to day and from year to year, we will find it difficult to notice such change. We will just observe that people in one group use English differently from people in another group, as different features have emerged as most common in them in the complex system of language.

Worldwide, we can predict that English will not replace all of the world's languages. Neither will Chinese, as predicted by some futurists. People will continue to use local languages, and will use English (or Chinese) as an L2 or as a lingua franca, or they will use parts of English (or Chinese) for trade purposes without becoming fluent in the language. Cultural change

185

worldwide will continue, and complaints that English is driving out local culture will come with it, but those complaints about the English language will continue to be misplaced. It is not English as a language that drives cultural change, but instead the choices of people worldwide about the lifestyle they wish to live. We have seen the great expansion of English worldwide owing to the success of the British Empire, and the continuing influence of English in the Contemporary period in what has been called the American century. Whether the American success in the world will last longer than the British Empire, nobody can say. While it lasts, however, we can predict that English will remain the principal lingua franca throughout the world.

12.3 Will Change Be the End of English?

Will English as a language fall apart because of this continuing change in the language? In a word, no. The Indo-European language developed many daughter languages as its speakers prospered and moved to occupy more territory. Once they moved, their language changed in different ways in different places because their new communities had much less contact with their original communities than speakers had with each other in local interactions. In the contemporary world and into the future, we have new contingencies of life – easy long-distance transportation and telecommunication – that will continue to connect English speakers worldwide.

A good example of this fact comes from the new quotative *like* feature discussed in Chapter 10. New research shows that quotative *like* has expanded in four distant cities all at the same time (Figure 12.2).

Measurement of the usage of people born in different decades is called **apparent-time research**, a substitute for not having actual evidence going back into the past. The darkest line in Figure 12.2 shows the growth of quotative *like* in Toronto, Victoria (a city in western Canada), Christchurch (New Zealand), and Perth (Australia), among people born in the decades indicated at the bottom of each chart. It has surpassed *say* as the quotative marker in all the cities except Christchurch, and even there it is much more frequent among younger people than it is among older people. Other words used as quotatives, like *think, go,* and a zero form (no word used to introduce a quotation), behave somewhat differently in each city. However, the large decline of *say* and the large increase of *like* on the A-curve for each place shows us that modern transportation and communication can indeed allow changes in the language to occur on a broad basis across the world, not just in local places.

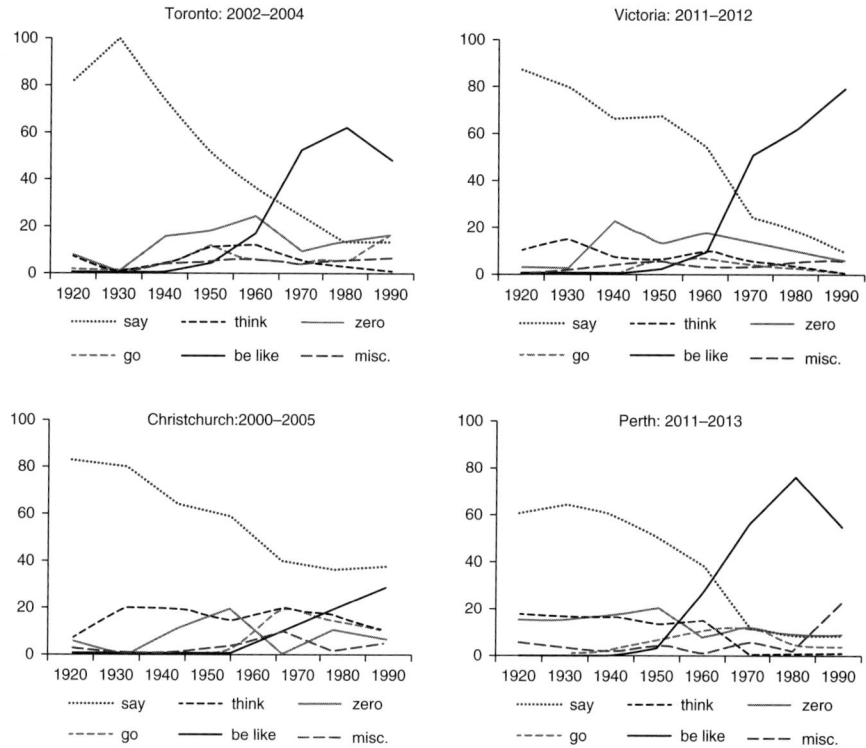

Figure 12.2 Quotative *like* in four cities (adapted from Tagliamonte, D'Arcy, and Rodríguez Louro, 2016)

We can make one A-curve to cover the variants in all four of the cities (Figure 12.3).Figure 12.3 shows that, while the frequencies of each of the quotative words have changed between people born in the 1950s and people born in the 1990s, the A-curve is still present for both the older and the younger speakers. Change in the language has not meant that the complex system has changed, only that the order of words on the A-curves has changed. This A-curve for all four cities is not identical with the A-curve for any single city – Perth turns out to be closest – but that is what we expect from the complex system: a different A-curve can emerge for each local place, and putting the evidence together at a higher level also produces an A-curve, one that may not match any of them made at lower levels. Of course, this process of observation could be repeated for every feature of English, all pronunciations and grammatical usages as well as the choice of word used as a quotative. English can be one language, and yet have different varieties wherever you go. Because of the new contingencies of transportation and communication, English is unlikely to break up into a range of unintelligible

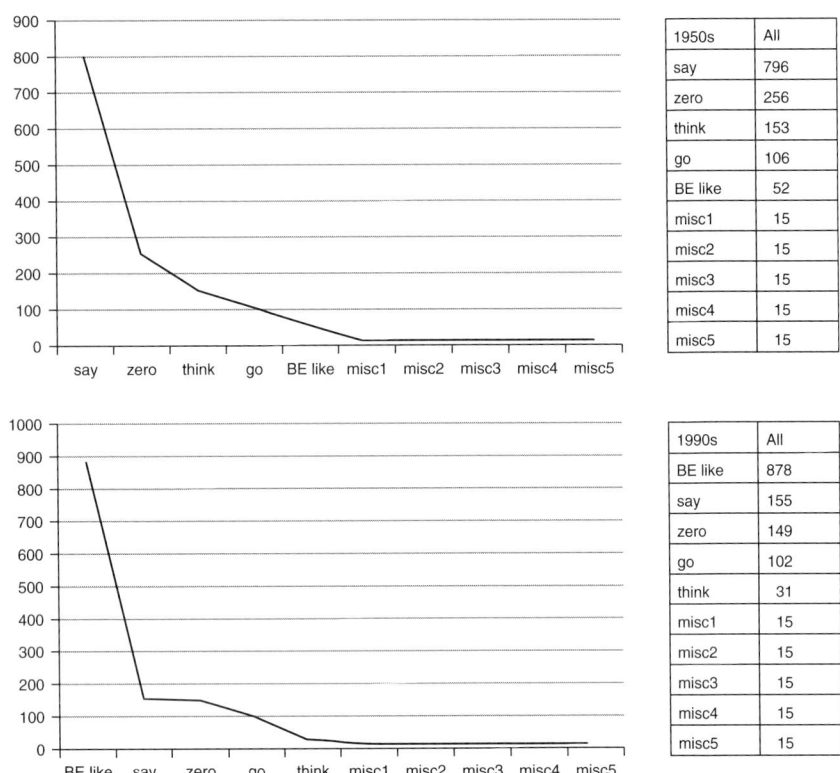

1950s	All
say	796
zero	256
think	153
go	106
BE like	52
misc1	15
misc2	15
misc3	15
misc4	15
misc5	15

1990s	All
BE like	878
say	155
zero	149
go	102
think	31
misc1	15
misc2	15
misc3	15
misc4	15
misc5	15

Figure 12.3 A-curve for quotative variants in four cities (adapted from Tagliamonte, D'Arcy, and Rodríguez Louro, 2016)

languages. English will be a little different wherever it is spoken, and a little different for different groups of people in each of those places.

The future of English is encouraging. It will be spoken by some as a native language, and by many more as a second language or lingua franca. There is no reason at all to think that the English language is in decline. As great a writer as Chaucer was, or as Shakespeare was, we cannot complain that the language has changed after their time. A knowledge of the history of English gives us access to our full tradition of writing in English. And a knowledge of the history of English gives us confidence that we will be able to cope with any change that occurs as time goes on. It will be entertaining to watch it.

12.4 **Chapter Summary**

English will not become more standardized as time goes on. Speakers will continue to vary in their use of English in regional and social communities, and in communities of practice. While Standard English remains entrenched in the schools, we may choose to grant additional recognition of local varieties. The English language does not cause other languages to become endangered, but cultural change worldwide may continue to encourage the use of English as a lingua franca.

Exercises

12.1 The future of English is a lively topic online. Google "future of English" and describe the different ways that bloggers, news outlets, and authors imagine the future of the language.

12.2 Apparent-time research measures the speech of people born at different times. Clearly, people born in the 1950s and people born in the 1990s are both alive at the same time. What does this mean with respect to the A-curve you could draw for any language feature for a population at one moment in time? Do you think older people stop learning new things in language as they get older?

12.3 If there is a division between communities of English speakers based on education, so that highly educated speakers have different language habits from speakers less committed to education, what do you think the schools should do about it? Would it be better for schools to make more use of community (non-standard) language, so that students might feel more comfortable there and get a better education?

12.4 Many American states require a History of the English Language course before certification for anybody who wants to teach English in public elementary or secondary schools. Now that you have read this book, argue the specific grounds on which such a requirement should be either retained or abolished. You may wish to argue pro or con, but do pick one side – no fence sitting! You may wish to consider both intellectual and practical reasons for your argument.

12.5 If you were producing a futuristic movie like Star Trek, how could you avoid the Star Trek syndrome and indicate that people from different places (parts of the galaxy!) did actually talk differently? Authors who use literary dialect often use subtle indications of differences in people's language, not full-blown rewriting that their readers would not understand. What sorts of subtle clues could you use, in pronunciation or vocabulary or grammar?

Keywords
apparent-time research
Star Trek syndrome

Further Reading
Information about quotative *like* comes from Tagliamonte, D'Arcy, and Rodríguez Louro (2016).

While the complex system of speech does not permit us to predict particular future changes in a language, the idea of making such predictions is explored in Kortmann (2001: 97–114) and Sanchez-Stockhammer (2015).

For compendia of information about the English language, including many topics covered in this book, see Crystal (1995); or, for a volume arranged like a dictionary, see McArthur (1992).

There are many other textbooks about the history of the English language. Prominent traditional texts are Baugh and Cable (2012); Pyles and Algeo (2004); Algeo (2009); Millward (1989); Milward and Hayes (2011); Barber (1993); and Barber, Beal, and Shaw (2009). These books tend to be much longer than this book, each with its own flavor and specialties in coverage.

Terms and Concepts for Studying the English Language: Expression of Words with Sounds

In this chapter

When we express ourselves in English, we think first of the words we use. A word is a particular kind of linguistic unit, built from speech sounds when we talk and represented with the alphabet in writing. English has an inventory of words, and also an inventory of speech sounds, that make the language what it is, in contrast to other languages that have different inventories of words and sounds. Normal writing with the letters of the alphabet is not exact enough for a good description of speech sounds, and this chapter discusses more scientific ways of representing the sounds of speech.

A1.1 **Regularities in Language**

As suggested in Chapter 1, most people deal with language and language varieties according to their perceptions of difference, and they are often not very good at imitating or describing particular linguistic features that help to form their perceptions. Linguists believe that every language has a set of regularities, a **grammar**, by which speakers of the language can judge which pronunciations or words or expressions are a normal part of the language. English speakers, for instance, know that *dog* is an English word, and they would reject *chien* as an English word. French speakers would accept *chien* and reject *dog*. When they arrange words into a phrase, English speakers would accept *the green slipper* but not *the slipper green*; French speakers would accept *le soulier vert* but probably not *le vert soulier*. Confusion by English speakers between the French words *vert* 'green' and *verre* 'glass' is probably responsible for turning Cinderella's perfectly reasonable *green* slipper in French into the famous English *glass* slipper. Such confusions are likely to occur when the speaker of one language has to try to cope with another language. Linguists, therefore, often rely on a **native speaker** of a language, somebody who has learned a language at home during the normal period of childhood language acquisition, as the source of the most authentic judgments about what belongs to the grammar of a language and what does not. As the chapters of this book show, however, different native speakers of English will give different answers, something of a problem for making a grammar of English. Native speakers also do not grow up with any very precise set of terms and concepts to describe their language. In this chapter we will develop a decent set of terms and concepts for us to use in describing the emergence of English.

A1.2 Words

When asked to talk about how languages work, most people would say that languages are made up of **words**. That is not wrong, just not very precise. For instance, if someone writes "I am going to ride the route," they have written seven words; if an American speaker says the same sentence out loud, it most likely will sound something like "I'm gonna ride the route" – is this only five words, or still seven? In British English, the late author Terry Pratchett frequently used the word *wossname*, just one word that really stands in for three in "What's its/his name," or perhaps even the four words in "What is its/his name." An American might say "whatchamacallit," today most likely from the five words "what do you call it" but with an extra "ma" thrown in the middle (historically, the word probably comes from "what you may call it," which explains the extra "ma" but which people are unlikely to say anymore). In order to talk about words, to tell what words are and how they work together, we need a set of more precise terms and concepts.

Words are composed of two essential parts: their **expression**, the physical sounds or appearance in writing that we can recognize, and their **content**, the meaning(s) that we attach to them. Ferdinand de Saussure (1986) famously talked about the *signifiant* and the *signifié*, in English the *signifier* and the *signified*, as two elements of the **linguistic sign**. Words and linguistic signs are not exactly the same thing, but for the purposes of this book common words can serve well as examples of linguistic signs. For instance, the English word *tree* has a particular sound when spoken, and when written it is composed by a particular sequence of **letters** of our Roman alphabet. The English word *tree* can also be represented by fingerspelling gestures in American Sign Language (ASL) or another sign language for the deaf (or by its own gestured sign – but that would be sign language itself, a different language and not a representation of English), by a pattern of bumps on a flat surface in Braille for the blind, by a sequence of electronic codes in a computer, or by still other modes of expression. Linguists generally consider the spoken form of English to be the primary mode of expression, and other modes like spelling to be derivative forms (in ASL and other sign languages, however, signs are the primary form). Writing has gained such social prestige that it sometimes seems that we ought to speak as the language is written, instead of write the language as it is spoken, but that is actually a recent cultural development in the history of the language.

We can distinguish the spoken sound of *tree* from the sound of other words, even when some of the component sounds in the word are the same: *tree* does not sound the same as *try, tray, true, free,* or *Brie*. It also does not sound the same as other words that may include the sound of *tree* but also have additional sounds, like *treat, treatise, gantry*. The expression of a word must have just the right "sound shape," just the right combination of sounds (or just the right sequence or pattern in other modes), not too much or too little, for us to recognize it as itself. So, *wossname* and *whatchamacallit*, like *gonna*, are words in and of themselves because they have their own sound shapes. These words are related to multiword phrases, yes, but we recognize them for themselves, and so do many dictionaries, though not so many yet for *wossname*.

As for content, the meaning of a word or sign is something that speakers of a language give to it, not something that naturally belongs to the sounds. There is nothing about the sound shape of *tree* that naturally connects the sounds to the woody plant. Languages besides English have different words for *tree* that can serve just as well, like French *arbre* or German *Baum*. Even words that are supposed to sound like the noises they represent (in the rhetorical trope known as **onomatopoeia**), like *ring* or *splash*, are not the same in different languages. Dogs *bark* and cats *purr* in English, but German dogs *bellen* and cats *schnurren*, while French dogs *aboient* (related to English *bay*) and cats *ronronnent*. The content of words and linguistic signs is arbitrary, in the sense that any meaning might be associated with any sound shape. Indeed, very frequently more than one meaning can be associated with a sound shape: both dogs and trees have *bark* in English. When one word has multiple meanings, we call it **polysemic**. Some words have just one meaning, like many words from science and technology, but thousands of the most common words in English are polysemic and some of them have a long list of different possible meanings.

Semantics is the name most often applied to discussions of word meaning. The word *semantics* can have a bad reputation among non-linguists, as when some argument is said to be "just a matter of semantics." Truth is, it is extraordinarily difficult to pin down exactly what words mean because the same word (1) can indeed mean different things to different people, (2) can mean different things in different situations of use, and (3) is likely to change its meanings or to develop new ones. As Benjamin Whorf (Carroll, 1956) has famously argued, what words mean depends on when and where they are used. This explains the long list of possible meanings for many of the words in the dictionary – and as long as the list may be, it cannot ever be complete because new meanings for words are constantly arising as new people use them in new situations for new purposes. Dictionaries can only be witnesses for the way that speakers of a language use words; the essence of the job for makers of dictionaries is to collect words and meanings as best they can, and to describe how people have used them up to the time when the dictionary is printed or made public online. Dictionary makers cannot control how speakers choose to associate meanings with words. That is good for business, since dictionary publishers need to keep making new dictionaries so that their readers will know about new words and the new meanings of previously existing words. The complexities of modern culture ensure that English generates new words and new meanings at a tremendous rate every year, and its speakers adapt their language to their needs. The important thing to know about semantics is that the meaning of words is not fixed, whether in time or in place of use, and so speakers (and those of us interested in how they talk) must always be aware of how word meanings must be negotiated, not merely assumed, in every conversation.

A1.3 Speech Sounds

In order to describe the expression of words in more detail, we need to be able to make sense out of the sounds of speech. Although spelling does not give us any clue, most Americans have heard the word *route* pronounced so that it rhymes with *boot*, and have also heard it pronounced so that it rhymes with *bout*. Similarly, many people in Britain would normally pronounce a word like *car* without articulating the -*r* sound that we spell at the end, and many fewer would normally articulate the -*r* (the proportion of how many people articulate the -*r* is reversed in America). In order to deal with differences in pronunciation that spelling with the letters of the Roman alphabet does not represent (or actually hides – *lead* can rhyme with both *seed* and *said*), we need a set of terms and symbols for the exact description of speech sounds, **phonetics**. The most widely used set of **phonetic symbols** comes from the International Phonetic Alphabet (or **IPA**). Each of the phonetic symbols represents a recognizable speech sound, a **phonetic segment**. Table A1.1 shows the subset of IPA symbols that are used in this book to describe English speech sounds; some of the vowel sounds are shown with the different symbols commonly used to represent British and American English. There are many more symbols in the IPA than just those in the table, because it is sometimes necessary to describe speech sounds in much more detail than this book ever does, and because the IPA is designed to be able to represent all of the speech sounds that exist in the world's languages, some of which English does not commonly employ. In Table A1.1, English words are set next to each phonetic symbol as a guide, but since English speakers do not all pronounce the same word in the same way, the words can be only a rough guide to the sounds represented by the symbols. As shown in Table A1.1, linguists conventionally represent phonetic symbols inside of **square brackets** [ ]. Some letters that we use for spelling have the same graphic shape as some phonetic symbols, so it is important to make sure that phonetic symbols are kept separate from letters by use of the square brackets. If we need to be sure we are talking about spelling, we can use **angle brackets < >**, so that <pit> is 'a deep place' while [pit] is, in the author's case, his brother. While letters often do represent the same sound, they do not always do so (e.g., the spellings *son* and *sun* for the same pronunciation [sʌn], or the same spelling *read* for both [rid] and [rɛd]); phonetic symbols always represent the same sound. The table has an entry for each vowel and consonant that English speakers often use for telling words apart.

The list in Table A1.1 has the advantage of being the same set of symbols used in two of the leading English pronunciation dictionaries, the *Oxford Dictionary of Pronunciation for Current English* (Upton, Kretzschmar, and Konopka, 2001), which is also the basis for pronunciations given in the online 3rd edition of the *Oxford English Dictionary*, and the *Routledge Dictionary of Pronunciation for Current English* (Upton and Kretzschmar, 2017), which offers updates on the Oxford pronunciations. The special phonetic symbols on the chart can all be found in "Unicode" (the coding system by which computers handle letters, numbers, and symbols), and Unicode fonts can be found on most computers such as the "Arial Unicode MS" font provided with Microsoft Windows.

Many stressed vowels are realized as a **diphthong** – two adjacent vowel sounds in the same syllable – when people actually articulate them, such as [eɪ] (as in *pate*) and [Am ou, Br əu] (as in *Poe*) indicated opposite as common English pronunciations. It is possible to have more than two adjacent vowel sounds in the same syllable (e.g., triphthong for three, tetraphthong for four), and very often a vowel sound that we consider to occur alone in a syllable (a **monophthong**) actually has another vowel sound there, too, when people articulate it. If you sometimes think you have heard [piit] and [puu] for *Pete* and *Pooh*, you probably have. However, on the vowel chart linguists usually reserve the term diphthong for Am [aɪ, au, oʊ, ɔɪ] and Br [ʌɪ, au, əʊ, ɔɪ]. Gradations of sounds slightly different from all of the basic phonetic symbols in IPA can be represented with **diacritics**, but these diacritical marks are not represented on the table. On vowel charts in other books (often British ones) you may well see *pate* shown with [e] and *Poe* shown with [o]. Length markings are traditionally used with vowels in Britain, as for [u:] in *Pooh*, but generally not in America. Watch out for the pronunciation keys in American dictionaries! They typically do not use the IPA, and the traditional terms for "long" and "short" vowels found in American dictionaries are not related to the actual length of sounds. So, for example the pronunciation for the word *pate* might be written as <pāt> and called a "long *a*," when in fact there is nothing long about that vowel. Similarly the pronunciation for the word *pat* might be written as <păt> and called a "short *a*," when there is nothing short about that vowel.

Vowel sounds are characterized by a relatively open passage for air through the mouth, and different vowel sounds come from holding the mouth and tongue in different positions. So, at one end of the scale, doctors want their patients to say the [a] sound because among all the vowel sounds the position of the mouth is the most open and the tongue is most relaxed, so the doctor has the easiest time seeing into the

Table A1.1 *IPA Symbols for English Sounds Vowels*

		Front:			Central:		Back:		
High:	i	*Pete*	[pit]			u	*Pooh*	[pu]	
	ɪ	*pit*	[pɪt]			ʊ	*put*	[pʊt]	
Mid:	eɪ	*pate*	[peɪt]			Am ou, Br əu	*Poe*	[pou, pəu]	
	ɛ	*pet*	[pɛt]			Br ʌ	*putt*	[pʌt]	
				Am ə	*putt* [pət]				
Low:	Am æ, Br a	*pat*	[pæt, pat]			ɔ	*paw*	[pɔ]	
				Am ɑ	*pot* [pɑt]	Br ɒ	*pot*	[pɒt]	

In this table and the tables which follow, "Am" indicates a symbol used for American English; "Br" indicates a symbol used for British English.

Unstressed Central: alone, sofa [əloun, soufə]

(schwa [ə] is usually used in unstressed environments, but it is also used as a stressed vowel in Am)

Diphthongs:

Am aɪ, Br ʌɪ	*pike*	[paɪk, pʌɪk]
au	*pout*	[paut]
ɔɪ	*poison*	[pɔɪzn]

Consonants

Stops:			Affricates:		
b	*by*	[baɪ]	ǰ, ʤ	*giant*	[ǰaɪənt, ʤaɪənt]
p	*pie*	[paɪ]	č, ʧ	*chide*	[čaɪd, ʧaɪd]
d	*die*	[daɪ]			
t	*tie*	[taɪ]	Nasals:		
g	*guy*	[gaɪ]	m	*my*	[maɪ]
k	*kite*	[kaɪt]	n	*nigh*	[naɪ]
			ŋ	*sing*	[sɪŋ]

patient's throat. On the other hand, photographers want their subjects to say words with the [i] sound, like *cheese*, because among all the vowel sounds the position of the mouth is most closed – so the photographer can avoid getting tongues and throats in the picture. Linguists talk about vowels as relatively **high, mid,** or **low,** as Table A1.1 is labeled, according to whether the mouth position is relatively **closed** (high) or **open** (low) or in between (mid). Linguists also talk about vowels as relatively **front, central,** or **back,** again as Table A1.1 is labeled, according to

Consonants (cont.)

	Fricatives:			Others:	
v	*vie*	[vaɪ]	l	*lie*	[laɪ]
f	*fie*	[faɪ]	r	*rye*	[raɪ]
ð	*thy*	[ðaɪ]	w	*wine*	[waɪn]
θ	*thigh*	[θaɪ]	j	*yipe*	[jaɪp]
z	*Zion*	[zaɪən]			
s	*sigh*	[saɪ]			
ž, ʒ	*vision*	[vɪžən, vɪʒən]			
š, ʃ	*shy*	[šaɪ, ʃaɪ]			
h	*high*	[haɪ]			

whether the tongue position is relatively relaxed (back) or thrust further forward in the mouth (front), or in between (central).

Consonant sounds are characterized by some sort of constriction in the passage of air through the mouth. Again as labeled in Table A1.1, the air may briefly be blocked at some point (**stop** or **plosive** consonants, as in [b, t] sounds), or made to pass through a narrowed passage that causes turbulence in the air flow (**fricative** consonants, as in [f, s] sounds). The stoppage or narrowing occurs at different locations in the mouth, created by subtle movements of the tongue or lips. Affricates are consonants in which a stop and a fricative occur in close combination, i.e., a stoppage of the air flow is immediately followed by narrow opening that causes turbulence, as in [ʤ, tʃ] sounds. For **nasal** consonants, there is a stoppage of the air flow through the mouth, but the speaker allows the air to escape through the nose instead, as in [m, n] sounds – which explains why people with a bad head cold have trouble pronouncing some words as they normally do. Linguists also describe consonants by whether the **larynx**, or voice box, is creating sound while the consonant is articulated (a **voiced** consonant, as in the [v] sound), or whether the larynx is not in use during articulation (an **unvoiced** consonant, as in the [f] sound). All vowel sounds are voiced. It is important to note that consonants often have voiced and unvoiced pairs with the same place of articulation: [b/p, d/t, g/k, v/f, ð/θ, z/s].

Although a range of IPA symbols to describe consonants and vowels has just now been set out, the fact is that speech sounds are much more complicated than the IPA can describe. There are a great many factors, some that every speaker is aware of like pitch or intonation or breathiness or rate of speech, and some that speakers do not remark upon but still actively use in their speech (like various harmonic effects, or "formants," in the physical acoustics of speech sounds), that are not included in what the IPA considers. **Acoustic phonetics** is the study of speech sounds that traces the physical qualities of speech sounds and plots them on charts. The entire IPA symbol set is a useful generalization that captures some but not all of the qualities of speech sounds; the subset of the IPA used here is an even greater generalization, but still useful for the purposes of the book. As one might

197

say, you don't need a scalpel if all you want to do is cut butter. We can describe English speech sounds in useful ways with our relatively limited set of phonetic symbols.

While we sometimes want to describe speech sounds exactly, in phonetic terms, we also sometimes want to describe speech sounds according to the way that we use them to tell words apart. One of the ways that we know which sounds we need symbols for is to look at words that have a difference of only one sound in their sound shapes, like *tree* [tri] and *true* [tru]. Linguists call words like *tree* and *true* a **minimal pair** because of the single distinctive difference: [i, u]. Both of these happen to be high vowels, but since we tell these two words apart (and other pairs like them) in English just on the basis of the single difference between these two sounds, we know that we must have different symbols for each sound. When linguists talk about the capacity of sounds to be used for telling words apart, i.e., about distinctive differences between sounds, they use the term **phoneme**, and they put IPA symbols between **slanted lines** (sometimes called **virgules**), like /i, u/, to represent sounds taken to be phonemes for a given language or variety. Each speech sound that we recognize as a phoneme can also be called a **segmental phoneme**. Thus, the IPA symbols [i, u] represent phonetic sounds when found in square brackets, and /i, u/ inside of slanted lines represent the claim that these sounds are phonemes, sounds used for telling words apart in a given language or variety, as they do in English. Because the idea of a phoneme is based on a distinctive difference, slightly different sounds, each called an **allophone**, might occur and still make the distinction. So, in the word *pot*, the phoneme /p/ is pronounced with a small breath of air ("aspiration"), while in the word *spot* the phoneme /p/ is pronounced without the aspiration. It is still the phoneme /p/ in both cases even though we could represent the phonetic segment involved a little differently in the two cases, e. g., by using a diacritical mark for aspiration with the [p] in *pot* (of course in this book we are not using diacritics) and not use it for the [p] in *spot*. A phoneme, therefore, actually represents the range of sounds, the range of allophones, that can be used when a segmental phoneme is used as a minimal pair. So, *pot/lot* is a minimal pair, and *spot/slot* is a minimal pair, even though different allophones occur for the /p/ in each pair. It is useful to be able to talk about phonemes (or phonemic segments) as a level of abstraction higher than the exact description of speech sounds as phonetic segments.

The notion of the phoneme is useful for talking about the whole system of sounds used in a language or variety, all of the distinctive vowels, or all of the distinctive consonants. What counts as "distinctive" varies between languages and varieties. So, for example, [l, r] are distinctive and thus serve as the phonemes /l, r/ in English, but the two sounds are not distinctive in Japanese; this of course gives rise to imitations or bad jokes by English speakers in which *fried rice*, [fraɪd raɪs] in English, is pronounced [flaɪd laɪs] in Japanese, as if it were spelled *flied lice*. Within American English, some speakers do not use the sounds [ɑ, ɔ] to tell words apart, and some speakers do, so that for some American English speakers the words *Don* and *dawn*, or *hock* and *hawk*, rhyme with each other (i.e., their vowel sounds are not distinctive), and other American English speakers consider each of these to be a minimal pair. This means that there are at least two different sound systems within American English – actually there are many more than that. Similarly, many speakers of British English do not pronounce the [r] after vowels as in *bar, barn*, while others (usually from the North or West) do pronounce it. All British speakers normally pronounce an [r] *between* vowels as in words like *barrow*. British English also has multiple sound systems among its speakers.

We can still make a generalization that English has one sound system even though we know that not all speakers of English share it, which is useful, say, when we want to differentiate world varieties of English. Indeed, since the different speakers of any variety will not always keep the same pairs of vowels and consonants distinct from each other, and even individual speakers are not entirely consistent in how they pronounce vowels and consonants, any claim for a sound system, whether for an individual person or a group of people, will be a generalization. It is fine to make generalizations about sound systems if we need to do so to for particular purposes, and is it also just fine to talk about phonetic sounds rather than phonemes if that is what works best for our needs. We just have to keep straight whether we are talking about phonetic speech sounds or phonemic systems at any given time.

A1.4 Chapter Summary

This chapter described what words are, and how the same word can mean different things. The chapter also covered speech sounds in some detail, in particular by offering the IPA as a way of representing speech sounds. Vowels and consonants have their own sets of terms to describe them, which are related to the manner or articulation of each sound. While we sometimes want to describe speech sounds exactly, in phonetic terms, we also sometimes want to describe speech sounds according to the way that we use them to tell words apart, in phonemic terms. Different inventories of speech sounds commonly occur in different languages, and different inventories even occur for different communities of speakers within the same language. Still, we can make useful generalizations about the speech sounds used overall by the speakers of a language.

Key Terms
acoustic phonetics
affricate consonant

allophone
angle brackets < >
back vowel
central vowel
closed vowel
consonant
content
diacritics
diphthong
expression
fricative consonant
front vowel
grammar
high vowel
IPA (International Phonetic Alphabet)
larynx
letter
linguistic sign
low vowel
mid vowel
minimal pair
monophthong
nasal consonant
native speaker
onomatopoeia
open vowel
phoneme
phonetics
phonetic segment
phonetic symbol
plosive consonant
polysemic
segmental phoneme
semantics
slanted lines / /
square brackets [ ]
stop consonant
unvoiced consonant
virgules / /
voiced consonant
vowel
word

Exercises

A1.1 Look up the words *gonna, whatchamacallit,* and *wossname* in at least three dictionaries to see if you can find them there. While you are at it, look up the common contractions *isn't, didn't,* and *ain't.* You may look in paper dictionaries (if so, use a "desk" dictionary or a one-volume larger diction-ary, not one of the small ones often sold next to the romance novels), or use online dictionaries. Keep a record of what you find in which dictionaries. Do all the dictionaries have the same content? Do the dictionaries say anything about the usage of these words?

A1.2 Find three paper dictionaries, either "desk" dictionaries or one-volume larger dictionaries. In each dictionary, start at the entry for the word *dictionary* and make a list of the headwords for the next 30 entries. Are your three lists all the same? How many of the entries are in all three dictionaries? How many entries are in only one dictionary?

A1.3 Go online to www.oed.com (if your institution has a subscription) or use a paper copy of the *Oxford English Dictionary.* Look at the word *brave,* or the word *nice,* or the word *silly.* How many meanings does this word have? How are the different meanings related in time? Earlier and later? Are different meanings used in the language at the same time?

A1.4 Transcribe the following words with the appropriate phonetic symbols (different speakers may have different transcriptions for some words):

Heal	High
Hill	Howl
Hale	Hoist
Hell	Hole
Hal	Hull
Hall	Who'll

A1.5 Make a list of minimal pairs that show the difference between the voiced and unvoiced pairs of consonants, like *vast* and *fast.*

Further Reading

Saussure (1986). Ferdinand de Saussure launched modern linguistics at the turn of the twentieth century. Later theories advanced upon his notion of speech sounds, for instance, but his work is still well worth reading to discover basic decisions that form the foundation of the field. This translation by Roy Harris has become the standard English version of this classic text. Always highly readable by both beginning and advanced students of linguistics and literary theory, Saussure's ideas are made clearer by Harris's annotations and his clear treatment of the three key terms *langue, langage*, and *parole*.

For a selection of Whorf's writings, see Carroll (1956). Carroll's valuable introduction offers a balanced appraisal of Whorf's well-accepted notions about language and some of his ideas that have never, for cause, achieved much of an audience. The essays presented also offer a balance of the classic and the erratic. Notably worth reading are Whorf's essays on Hopi, and "The Relation of Habitual Thought and Behavior to Language."

Oxford English Dictionary, www.oed.com. The *OED*, as most people call it, is the premier historical dictionary of any language. It does not have all the words in the English language – no dictionary could do that – but it has the best historical treatment of what English words have meant over the centuries.

Upton, Kretzschmar, and Konopka (2001). This is the reference-book form of the database that serves as the pronunciation resource for the *OED*. There are other well-known pronunciation dictionaries for British English, but nothing else quite so fully realized for American English. The newest edition of this resource is Upton and Kretzschmar (2017), which contains updates in transcription practices and thousands of additional words.

Ladefoged and Johnson (2014). This is the most recent edition of one of the world's most popular textbooks in phonetics. Until his death not long ago, Peter Ladefoged was one of the principal figures in the study of speech sounds. The Sounds of Speech app available from the University of Iowa at soundsofspeech.uiowa.edu is a useful electronic tool for both the sound and articulation of consonants and vowels in American English, all transcribed in IPA.

Terms and Concepts for Studying the English Language: Beyond Expression to Content

In this chapter

This chapter talks about how to put linguistic units together. While individual units, like words, can have meaning, most of the information content we want to share with others through language is conveyed by our ability to put units together, in order to make compound or inflected words, in order to make sentences, and in order to make the larger patterns of discourse. Both sentences and discourse follow regularities in how to put words and sentences together, so that the speaker and the receiver in a linguistic exchange can both judge what to expect.

A2.1 **Hierarchy in Language**

Linguists often talk about a **hierarchy** of concepts for adequate description of how languages work. The need to do so appears quite clearly when we want to move from discussion of the expression of a "word" to its content. Words like *treehouse* or *bluebird* have a meaning for content, but they are clearly composed of other words (and thus they are called **compound words**); the separate component words of the compound have their own separate meanings for content when they are not used as part of the compound. The meaning of compound words is more than the sum of their parts: a *bluebird* is not just any *bird* that happens to be the color *blue*, but instead a particular species of bird that happens to be blue. Thus, the word *bluebird* does not mean the same thing as the word *bluejay*, even though both are birds and both are blue. Similarly, we know what a *tree* is, and we know what a *house* is, but we cannot predict that *treehouse* in English usually refers to 'a small structure built in the branches of a tree and used for children's play.' After we know the meaning of *treehouse*, we can readily see how it is reasonable to put *tree* and *house* together to refer to what we mean by *treehouse* – but only after, not before.

The component parts, *tree* and *house*, *blue* and *bird*, contribute something to the content of the compound words *treehouse* and *bluebird*, and so we need a concept to describe something that plays this role between expression and content. Linguists use the term **morpheme** to refer to the association of a sound shape with a particular meaning. Some morphemes are **free** to stand on their own as separate words, and some are **bound**, in that they must be used in combination with other morphemes. In *treehouse* and *bluebird* two morphemes that can be free have been put together into a compound. Adding morphemes to make new words, like making *unhappy* from the bound morpheme *un* and the free morpheme *happy*, is known as **derivational morphology**. **Inflectional morphemes**, on the other hand, must be bound to a free morpheme: the *-s* that makes a word plural must be bound to a free morpheme, as in *trees*, which does not make an entirely new word, just a variant form of the free morpheme. Inflectional morphemes carry a sort of grammatical meaning, like the plural meaning that *-s* can provide. The *-s* can also make a verb agree with its subject, as in *he walks*, or (expressed in writing with an apostrophe) it can indicate possession, as in *the boy's treehouse*. In each case, the addition of an *-s* to *tree*, *walk*, and *boy* contributes something to the morpheme to which it is bound. It is worth pointing out that the sound shape of the *-s* is different depending on the sounds of the morpheme to which it is attached: *-s* is pronounced [z] when attached to *tree* or *boy* (whether the *-s* marks the plural or the possessive) and pronounced [s] when attached to *walk* (whether the *-s* marks verb agreement, the plural, or the possessive). These differences, called **allomorphs**, occur because of the sounds that come before the *-s*. The [z] sound is used after voiced consonants and vowels, and the [s] sound is used after unvoiced consonants. So, because it is the **environment** in which the *-s* occurs (whether it comes after a voiced sound or an unvoiced sound) that determines the difference, linguists are willing to consider the different pronunciations of *-s* to be the same morpheme.

We would not normally consider *trees* to be a different word from *tree*; we often say that we have added an **inflection** (*-s*) to the **root** or **base** form of the word (*tree*). The concept of the morpheme just gives us a more precise way to talk about **word formation**, the composition and content of words. We can distinguish between compound words, and words assembled in derivational morphology, and inflected forms. We can talk about **loanwords**, when an entire word is borrowed from another language, like *cookie* from Dutch or *taco* from Spanish. The history and nature of English culture gives English a great many loan words. Sometimes, however, words are not borrowed as whole units, but are composed from morphemes that come originally from another language. The word *refrigerator*, for example, is composed of morphemes originally from Latin, even though the Romans never had such a device for keeping things cold. Many modern technical and medical words are built from morphemes originally used in Latin and Greek. Our ability to recognize morphemes that have been in English for a long time and also those that come from other languages and become English when borrowed, and our ability to distinguish base and inflectional morphemes, allow us to begin to bridge the gap between expression and content.

A2.2 **Words in Patterns**

This is not the place for an extended discussion of **syntax**, the patterns in which English speakers normally assemble sentences. Let us rely on the efficiency of our former school language-arts teachers to have provided us with some vocabulary, such as **noun** (think person, place, or thing) and **verb** (think action or state); **subject** and **predicate** (think the major parts of a sentence); and **present** and **past tense** (think time), that we can share. Table A2.1 offers lists of functional elements in sentences and clauses, as they are arranged into sequential patterns with different constituents. The term **phrase** indicates a combination of words, and the term **clause** indicates a combination of elements, each of which can consist of one or more words, into one of a set of typical patterns. The terms **NP (noun phrase)** and **VP (verb phrase)** are often applied to sentences to help us distinguish the organization of these functional elements more clearly. The NP can consist of a single noun as its **head,** but it can also have optional elements: a **determiner** like *the* or *a/an*, and **modification** like an adjective either before or after the noun. **Prepositional phrases** (like *on the boat*) are common modification elements, that is, a combination of words that begins with a preposition and includes at least one word, usually a noun, that serves as the object of the preposition; prepositional phrases usually come after the noun they modify. Verb phrases must have a main verb as head, and they, too, have optional elements. **Auxiliary verbs** occur before the head in the VP, like *was* in the verb phrase *was not taken at the time*. **Negation,** like the *not* in *was not taken at the time*, also occurs before the head. Modification in the VP is movable: the prepositional phrase *at the time* in the VP *was not taken at the time* occurs at the end, but it could also be moved to any position in the VP and can even be moved to occur before the subject, as *at the time attendance was not taken*.

Verb valency refers to the common sequences which are found frequently with particular verbs. The intransitive (think of a sequence with no object, like *the boat sails*), transitive (think of a sequence with an object, like *the crew sails the boat*), and linking (think of a state, like *the crew is on the boat*) are the most common, while the double-object pattern (think of a sequence with two objects, like *Americans elected a businessman president*) is less common but not rare. Many verbs can be used with more than one kind of clause pattern. Clauses may be **finite,** in which case we usually call them **independent** (or **main**) if they can be used as full sentences, or **dependent** if they must be associated with an independent

Table A2.1 *Sentence Patterns*

Phrases			
Noun Phrase (NP)			
Determiner	Modification	Head	Modification
Optional	Optional	Required	Optional
The	*old*	*man*	*on the boat*
Verb Phrase (VP)			
Auxiliary	Negation	Head	Modification
Optional	Optional	Required	Optional, Movable
was	*not*	*taken*	*at the time*

Phrase Notes: Particular words may be more likely with a particular option. Modification is usually adjective or prepositional phrase with nouns, and adverb or prepositional phrase with verbs.

Clause Patterns			
Intransitive verb valency			
Subject (NP)	Predicate (VP)		
The boat	*sails*		
Transitive verb valency			
Subject (NP)	Predicate (VP)	Indirect Object Optional	Object
The crew	*sails*		*the boat*
The crew	*gave*	*him*	*the boat*
Linking verb valency			
Subject (NP)	Predicate (VP)	Complement (NP or Adj)	
The crew	*is*	*on the boat*	
Double-object verb valency			
Subject (NP)	Predicate (VP)	Object	Complement (NP or Adj)
Americans	*elected*	*a businessman*	*president*

Clause Notes: Modification occurs as part of NP or VP. Non-finite clauses (infinitive, participial) have a clause pattern without the subject, and may serve as head or modification.

clause within a sentence (often because they begin with a subordinating conjunction, like *because, so, since, until*). Clauses can also be **non-finite** if they employ **infinitives** or **participles** for their predicates and do not have a subject (like *to sail a boat, sailing a boat*). Again, the terms and ways of talking about sentences require more detailed treatment than is possible here, and there is no one best set of terms or way of talking about them. Besides functional elements, sentences and clauses can also be described according to their informational content: **given** information usually precedes the **new** information, and the **topic** for what a sentence is about usually precedes the **comment** being made about it, and if the given/new information or the topic/comment is not in this order we can suspect that special emphasis is being given to one of the kinds of information. The term **grammar** is often used to refer to the patterns of syntax; however, the term *grammar* can also refer to the whole structural system of a language, including pronunciation and lexicon and discourse as well as syntax. Unlike the impression that many of us may have taken home from school, habits of use for syntactic patterns differ by speaker and by situation of use, just as the expression and content of words do. The syntax and discourse patterns of English are no more fixed for all people or for all time than are the meanings of words.

   It may be useful to think about syntax, and the words from which sentences are built, in comparison with putting together a bicycle. In former days it was a custom among parents to buy a bicycle as a present for a child by mail order; it would arrive in a box, "some assembly required," and many a birthday or holiday eve was spent in the struggle to make the parts in the box into a functional bike. One important part of the directions for assembly was the parts list. We can think of the dictionary as a parts list for a language and, just as for the bicycle parts list, we can hope that the dictionary provides a good description of parts, the possible words and meanings of the language. Most parents, however, would also need directions about how the parts fit together to make the bicycle work, and that is what a good description of syntax can do for a language. Many bicycle parts look like they might fit together, but forcing them together will not let the child ride. And different bicycles have similar but not identical parts, so that while sometimes it is possible to share parts between different bicycles (e.g., to substitute different wheels or gears), there will often be unpredictable results from the attempt. We can think of a good formal description of the syntax of a language as the best fit for the available parts of the language.

A2.3 **Patterns beyond Sentences**

Our school English teachers have also given us terms for patterns at the level of **discourse**, patterns beyond the level of the sentence, for which many of us have been taught terms related to different larger forms, like introduction, body, and conclusion for **paragraphs** in an essay. Our former school language-arts teachers, however, have not given us as many terms to talk about units of organization in language larger than a sentence as they have terms at the sentence level. We know something about paragraphs, and we know something about writing an essay (think of the typical five-paragraph structure) or writing a poem (think of a sonnet or haiku). While a poem may have formal rules, like the fourteen lines in a rhyme scheme for a sonnet, or three lines without rhyme for a haiku, paragraphs and essays are usually described more generally, say as having a beginning, a middle, and an end. Language-arts teachers usually place more emphasis on how to use evidence in paragraphs in order to make a point, and on how to build a rhetorical structure in an essay. The terms *introduction, body*, and *conclusion* can be used for the parts of either paragraphs or essays. Paragraphs and essays do have functional requirements, but these demands are not usually discussed with an array of specific terms as we have for syntax. Nonetheless, we can still recognize that paragraphs and essays do have characteristic patterns that we can call discourse.

Another way to talk about discourse requires us to identify recognizable situations for use of language, either written or spoken. We can call these **text types**, whether they are written down as actual texts or they are types of spoken conversations. Some text types are very large, like "writing" considered as a text type as opposed to "speech." Other text types are small, such as "letter," and even the smaller types can be further classified, as in the sequence "letter," "business letter," "job application letter," and even "job application letter for which the applicant does not have all of the qualifications." Each text type can be recognized because it has characteristics that allow it to be distinguished for itself. These characteristics are not rules, in the sense of something that is either there or not, but rather probabilistic: we are more likely to use some particular words and phrases in a particular text type. So, in a letter to someone in your family, like your grandmother, you will generally be more familiar in your choice of words than you would tend to be in a job application. There are no sharp boundaries for text types, which exist along a continuum of possible types in multiple dimensions. There is a whole range of kinds of letters that you can write to your grandmother – thank-you notes, requests for recipes, notes to accompany pictures – and each one of these has specific characteristics in addition to the informality of writing a letter within the family. The same is true of conversations. Have you ever thought you were having a conversation of one kind, say about the events of the day, and then realized that the conversation was actually about something else, like criticism of your bad behavior? The continuum of text types, whether spoken or written, can sometimes produce very subtle exchanges in language, and sometimes lead to misunderstandings when one person does not understand a conversation or piece of writing in the same way as another person. The distinctions we draw between texts are essentially arbitrary: we all just have to be able to recognize a piece of writing or a conversation as its own kind of thing, and trust that our partner in the exchange recognizes it as the same thing.

Some analysts, "formalists," have tried to establish formal terms for text types, in the same way that language-arts teachers have a set of formal terms for syntax. For instance, André Jolles named nine "simple forms" as the basic set of text types that we use for all purposes: legend, saga, myth, riddle, proverb, example, report, tale, and joke. These are supposed to be low-level discourse "natural" structures, from which larger discourses can be built or expanded. Selection of some set of elemental forms responds to "formalism" in aesthetic theory, which seeks universal properties of discourse. It would be useful if we could make these simple forms work, but the continuum of text types makes that difficult. We sometimes talk about **genre** as a literary or aesthetic category, but the selection and definition of some set of genres, like novel versus short story or prose versus poem, can only ever be an approximate description of what we do with the continuum of text types. Moreover, text types undergo continual change over time in response to "ecological" conditions of authors, readers, and society: Jacques Derrida (1980) says that "at the very moment that a genre or a literature is broached, at that very moment, degenerescence has begun, the end begins." Text types are always a moving target.

One of the principal methods of discourse study focuses on the relationship between the author and the recipient of some conversation or piece of writing, **critical discourse analysis (CDA)**. People enacting CDA often talk about the power relations between the author and the recipient, such as an older person as author and a younger person as recipient, or a richer person as author and a less-well-off person as recipient. Young people cannot talk to older people in the same way that their elders talk to them. Poorer people may feel that they cannot talk to their well-off neighbors (their "betters," to use an old-fashioned term) in the same way that they talk among themselves. These sorts of problems commonly occur in English literature (think Jane Austen), and they also occur in our daily lives even though we may not think of them in this way. Asymmetry in power relations is a fertile source of discussion about discourse.

In fact, there is a whole range of things someone needs to know in order to use language well in a community. We can call this **communicative competence**. A good example is how close you should stand to someone when you are having a conversation. Native English speakers frequently think that the right distance is about an arm's length. Speakers from other cultures, say from Spain or Poland, may feel more comfortable with a much smaller distance. Cultural attitudes towards politeness, sometimes called "face" (as in the phrase about a *face-saving* action), are another important factor in communicative competence. The kind of assumptions that we generally make when we have a conversation are set forth in **Grice's maxims** (Grice, 1975), which refer to quality, quantity, relevance, and manner. That is, we all assume in a conversation that someone will be telling us the truth, and will give us enough information but not too much, and information that is relevant, all in a manner that is unambiguous and orderly. So, when we use a language like English, it is not just the words we need to know, and not just the syntax, and not just the text types corresponding to different situations of use, we also need to know where and when and with whom we are using the language, and we rely on the good will of the parties in any linguistic exchange. That is a lot to keep in mind, and it explains why language is not such a perfect system as it is sometimes made out to be.

Since, as we have seen, the parts of the language, its words and meanings, are different from time to time and from place to place, we can expect that the syntax and discourse patterns will also be different from time to time and from place to place. Different varieties of a language, like British English and American English, have different parts, and so they must have a different "best fit," and the same is true of the different regional or social varieties within British English and within American English. It is sometimes possible to exchange parts between these varieties, just as sometimes one can exchange the handlebars or the pedals between different kinds of bicycles. But sometimes not. And sometimes the use of different parts from different varieties, or somewhat different arrangement of the parts from the same variety, will work but will lead to an odd ride.

A2.4 Chapter Summary

This chapter has described how to put linguistic units together to create the meaning we need to share with language. We sometimes use inflections or create compound words, we make phrases and clauses into sentences, and we make sentences into larger discourse patterns. The larger patterns, text types, occur on a multidimensional continuum of possibilities, so that speakers and their audiences are always trying to decide what kind of situation they are using language in, and so what words and phrases are most appropriate. This chapter has also introduced the idea that language is part of broader social culture, and that the way we use and understand language cannot easily be separated from the circumstances in which it is used.

Key Terms

allomorph
auxiliary verb
base
bound morpheme
clause
comment
communicative competence
compound words
critical discourse analysis (CDA)
dependent clause
derivational morphology
determiner
discourse
environment
finite clause

free morpheme
genre
given information
grammar
Grice's maxims
head
hierarchy
independent clause
infinitive
inflection
inflectional morpheme
loanword
main clause
modification
morpheme
negation
new information
non-finite clause
noun
NP (noun phrase)
paragraph
participle
past tense
phrase
predicate
prepositional phrase
present tense
root
subject
syntax
text type
topic
verb
verb valency
VP (verb phrase)
word formation

Exercises

A2.1 Make a compound word out of each of the following words by adding another word to it: *apple, boat, care, dog, egg, fare, goat, hair, ice, jelly.* Is there any question whether your compounds should have a space between the two words? NB: the word *bluebird* does not mean the same thing as *blue bird.* Would your compounds mean something different if the words have a space between them (as separate words) or do not (as compounds)?

A2.2 Separate the following words into their component morphemes: *quizmaster, regular, swishy, tripledecker, usurer, vibrated, waterfalls, x-rays, youthful, zebralike.*

A2.3 Name the underlined parts of the phrase pattern in each of the following phrases:

1.	The man in the green suit	jumped over the fence.
2.	Nobody in our town	was over the limit.
3.	Forty-seven barrels of beer	made a heavy load.
4.	A beggar	cannot be a chooser.
5.	The blue sea	made the passenger sick from the waves.

A2.4 Name the verb valency pattern for each of the five sentences in Exercise A2.3.

A2.5 Briefly describe a situation in which you felt you had to violate one of Grice's maxims in order to be polite, or to avoid hurting someone's feelings. Then briefly describe a situation in which you violated one of Grice's maxims for your own benefit (say, to avoid punishment or avoid embarrassment). How are these two situations the same or different, from the point of view of using the language and from the point of view of your personal relations with other people?

Further Reading

Marchand (1969); Adams (1973); Bauer (1983); Stockwell and Minkova (2001). These books are all classic treatments of how words in English are put together. The history of English words is a separate subject, introduced elsewhere in the book. These books provide many more details about the construction of English words than are possible to mention here. A recent textbook on morphology is Lieber (2015).

Quirk, Greenbaum, Leech, and Svartvik (1985); Biber, Conrad, and Leech (1999); Biber, Conrad, and Leech (2002). The Quirk, Greenbaum, Leech and Svartvik grammar is a famous, monumental grammar of English, often called the London School grammar. It is based on materials from the Survey of English Usage. The Biber, Conrad, and Leech grammar is another large-scale production, though the Student Grammar has been cut down to a size usable in university courses. Biber, Conrad, and Leech based their grammar on a large corpus of English, forty million words (this number no longer seems as large as it once did), from which they could both discover and illustrate the grammatical constructions of the language, and also show how different constructions occurred more or less often in different types of discourse. Huddleston and Pullum (2002) is a large-scale grammar based on generative principles.

Biber (1988); Biber, Conrad, and Reppen (1998). Biber's influential work shows that "every text has its own grammar" by demonstrating how particular grammatical constructions occur with different frequencies in different text types. A recent textbook on corpus linguistics is McEnery and Hardie (2011).

Jauss (1977); Jauss (1979: 181–229); Jauss (1982); Derrida (1980: 5–81). Modern discussion of literary genre is bound up with aesthetic movements. H. R. Jauss is the principal genre theorist in the "horizon of expectations" style of analysis that combines social and historical factors in order to discuss genre and changes in genre over time. Jauss begins with Jolles and moves far beyond formalism. Derrida is an acquired taste for many readers, but his witty account of genre is well worth reading once you get the hang of how Derrida writes.

Fairclough (2001); Fairclough (2003). Fairclough is perhaps the scholar most identified with CDA. The approach has been popular because it creates a bridge between language use and social practice, and many literary scholars and linguists are very interested in social practices as they might be related to language. The trick is to keep constantly in mind what effects belong to the language and what effects belong to cultural practices, and so avoid attributing social practices to language.

Hymes (1966: 114–158); Grice (1975: 41–58). The notion of communicative competence was originated by Dell Hymes, who was reacting against the highly formal account of competence and performance set forth by Noam Chomsky. Grice's "cooperative principle" began as a philosophical position, but it has become widely used to explain not only what we assume in a linguistic exchange, but how we often flout the principles in order to achieve our communicative goals. Do you think it would be cruel always to tell the truth?

Words in Use: Meaning and Corpora

In this chapter

Words in use present many more possibilities for meaning than a belief in standards or plain meaning would suggest. C. S. Lewis described how words acquire meanings over time in a process of ramification. He argues that we cannot be satisfied with the contemporary dangerous sense of a word as the meaning that will apply in all times and contexts. Contemporary study of corpora confirms Lewis's insights, and makes it possible to study much more language in a short time than is possible for any individual to experience. Collocational patterns emerge from interactions in every situation of language use which strongly associate particular words. These patterns are different in different situations, which explains why we need to use English differently in them.

A3.1 **Meaning**

As much as many people may wish to find plain meaning in the words of a language, the situation is actually more complicated. What words mean depends on a long historical process, at least for the most common words of English, in which words acquire new meanings over time. English speakers also do not use words in isolation, but instead use them in patterns with other words, and some of these patterns emerge over time to be much more frequent than others and thus condition the meanings of individual words. These meanings can vary for different individual speakers depending upon their personal experience with the language, but words can also carry different meanings according to the places, speech communities, and discourse situations in which they are used: their semantic frequency profiles emerge differently in these different scales of use. Plain meaning, then, is complicated by the multidimensional nature of language in its complex system of interaction between speakers and writers.

A3.2 Ramifications

The literature students of **C. S. Lewis**, a professor at Oxford and Cambridge universities in the middle of the twentieth century, studied **Greats**, the term used to describe works in Greek, Latin, and English, that held a prominent place in the history of Western culture. These students brought their own contemporary understanding of English to these studies, and therein lay a problem: what words mean in contemporary English is not what they used to mean at earlier stages of English, just as our understanding of topics in the world around us today differs from classical authors' understanding of those topics. Lewis found that his students applied the **dangerous sense** of words, the most common contemporary meaning for a word or topic, to their understanding of words from earlier English and the classics, and thereby failed to understand them appropriately. He also found that some contemporary authors committed what he called **verbicide**, what we might know as **spin**, when they repurposed words to make a (usually political) point. If such verbicides were used commonly enough, they might even become the dangerous sense of a word. Lewis argued (1967) that to avoid such misunderstandings, "knowledge is necessary. Intelligence and sensibility by themselves are not enough." In consequence he advocated that his students learn more about the history of ideas in their culture: in other words, that his students should practice **cultural humanism**.

Lewis noted that many common words in English have **polysemy**, a number of meanings, unlike more specialized words in the scientific vocabulary that might have just one meaning. He thought that **ramification** accounted for these multiple meanings, that is, that words changed in meaning over time, not by replacement of one meaning for another, but instead by addition and accumulation. His example is the branching of a tree – literal ramification – where more and more new branches emerge from the trunk and older branches without actually replacing them. Ramification also implies a connection to the past: just as new branches of a tree are connected to the older ones, so new word meanings are connected in some way to the roots of Western culture. The analogy of the tree exactly fits the idea of emergence in a complex system of language, though of course Lewis could not have known about complex systems (they were first described only after his death). Complexity science allows for many variants, many meanings of words, to coexist at different frequencies. Meanings can drop down the A-curve, become less common in the frequency profile of the different possibilities. What Lewis tells us about ramification explains how the history of the language can be related to the range of variant meanings that are available at any one time.

Cultural history remains present in contemporary word meanings. Relatively few branches of a tree completely die and fall away; in the same way, relatively few meanings of words die out completely and become completely obsolete. Rather, in language, particular meanings of words tend to recur in the same contexts, and the original **context** thus protects the older meaning even while new meanings are added in new contexts. As Lewis wrote, different senses "live happily by staying out of each others' way." Good evidence for his argument comes from **puns**, whose humor always comes from invoking the meaning of a word out of its usual context (such as "Politics is like golf: you are trapped in one bad lie after another"). For Lewis, then, the meaning of a word depends on when, where, and how it is used. In this he agrees with one of Lewis Carroll's famous characters, Humpty Dumpty (Figure A3.1) in *Through the Looking-Glass*: "When *I* use a word," Humpty Dumpty said, in rather a scornful tone, "it means just what I choose it to mean – neither more nor less." Because of the possibility of verbicide and the choice of contexts, Humpty Dumpty is literally correct: the same word (1) can indeed mean different things to different people, (2) can mean different things in different typical contexts, and (3) is likely to change its meanings or to develop new ones in the process of ramification. All of this is more complicated than plain meaning would allow.

Lewis provides a good example of what he means in his treatment of the word *free* (Lewis, 1967). He begins his history of the word by saying that it originally presented a contrast with slavery: to be *free*, or *liberal* (from Latin *liber*), was in contrast with being a slave and being servile. Lewis suggests that the behavior of a free person was characterized by generosity and honesty. A slave, on the other hand, was cunning, always looking for a personal advantage. A similar contrast, *frank* vs *villain*, exists in French and was loaned to English: *frank* meant 'acting like a noble' (after the name of the royal group), which in time also meant 'unencumbered, straightforward,' which contrasted with *villain* 'acting like a peasant', which in time also meant 'criminal.' Today, however, after a long period of development, *freedom* is just another word for:

'Nothing left to lose,' as in a song made famous by Janis Joplin (*Me and Bobby McGee*). This represents the dangerous sense of 'able to move, unconstrained,' or as the song puts it, 'nothing left to tie you down.'

'American values,' as in the "freedom fighters" in Central America as described by Ronald Reagan; "freedom fries" (a new context after the September 11 tragedy at the World Trade Center); the "American Freedom Foundation" (an organization for armed service veterans); "Freedom Advocates" (a group that supports property rights); the "US Freedom Foundation" and "The Future of Freedom Foundation" (organizations that lobby for individual "freedoms").

Other coexisting meanings like "Freedom Foundation" (a group fighting drug dependency), "Freedom Foundation" (a Selma, Alabama, community organization promoting African American empowerment), and "Foundation for Freedom" (a group promoting world literacy).

Figure A3.1 Humpty-Dumpty (Tenniel illustration, public domain)

There is some irony for the cultural humanist here in turning "American values" into several causes that may express the cunning and search for personal advantage that historically was believed to characterize the behavior of slaves. The word *liberal* has become a victim of verbicide in both the United Kingdom and the United States, in that it has come to express the political opposite of *conservative*. Neither *liberal* nor *conservative* retains much of its historical meaning when used in political contexts, which are overwhelmingly the most frequent uses of the words today. If we consider the full range of meanings for *free*, the *Oxford English Dictionary* offers twenty-seven meanings for the word as an adjective, eight more meanings for the word as a noun, and three more meanings for the word as an adverb. If we believe Lewis, we should be prepared to encounter any and all of these meanings in particular times, places, and contexts, in historical and contemporary writings. We should not just assume that *free* always means 'unconstrained,' the current dangerous sense, and leave it at that. The history of a polysemous word like *free* gives us strong social connections (whether slavery or American values), which are still here with us in the language because of ramification. We always have what Lewis calls a "simmering pot" of meanings with social values right behind the dangerous sense, and we should be careful about spin, verbicides that look rational but really take social positions.

A3.3 Corpus Analysis

In the mid twentieth century Lewis did not have the means to investigate context very well, but that has now changed. As the Information Age has progressed, the possibilities for **corpus analysis** have greatly expanded. A **corpus** is a body of naturally occurring language (something that somebody has said or written), that exists as machine readable texts (in some computer format), is authentic (from real use, not made up), is sampled (by collecting texts for a reason, according to a plan), and is representative (because of the sampling of a particular population of texts). Historically, projects like the *Oxford English Dictionary* collected **citations**, single sentences illustrating the meaning of a word, stored on paper slips or cards. A citation file is not a corpus because it is highly selected instead of sampled, and thus not likely to be representative of a body of texts. Corpora (the plural form of corpus) can be prepared from written or from spoken sources, although spoken sources are then transcribed, so that corpus analysis consists of computerized counting of words and phrases in a large body of text. Different corpora can represent many different populations of texts: *historical* texts, as in the **Helsinki Corpus**, *regional*, as in the **British National Corpus (BNC)** or the **Corpus of Contemporary American English (COCA)**, *social*, as in the **Bergen Corpus of London Teenage Language (COLT)**, *personal*, as in a corpus of the works of Shakespeare, or *situational by text type*, as in a corpus of financial reports or biology reports. It is difficult to produce a **general corpus**, of British English, say, because it is difficult to create a good sample of all of the language of a large community; the BNC, for example, includes both originally written and originally spoken texts, from many different kinds of writing and speech, and yet it cannot include something from all situations for the use of English. The first modern computer corpus, the **Brown Corpus** of American English, collected texts from fifteen different categories of writing, all published in 1961. The much larger **Cambridge English Corpus** samples from many different categories (e.g., magazines, websites, books, blogs, tweets, newspapers, emails, discussion boards, letters, journals, minutes, novels, agendas, textbooks, proposals, text messages) for written English, plus spoken English, business English, and academic English.

A corpus that seeks to sample widely from numerous categories is called a **balanced corpus**. Corpora can be annotated with part of speech tags (POS tags) to make grammatical analysis possible. One POS tagging system, from the Penn Treebank, uses thirty-six different tags such as NN (noun), NNS (noun, plural), NNP (proper noun), and NNPS (proper noun, plural). Available software can attach these tags to words in a corpus, e.g., "election_NN" or "Clintons_NNPS." Most corpus analysis, however, is based on counting word forms and making frequency lists of how often particular words (or different word forms combined into a single **lemma**, such as *walk/walk/walked/walking* under the lemma WALK) occur in individual texts, in subsets of a corpus, or in the corpus overall. Corpus analysis software will make a word list for an entire corpus, or for any subset down to a single text. All of these word lists will have an A-curve frequency profile; function words are most common, followed by content words. A typical corpus analysis compares the frequencies of words found in two different corpora, or in a part of a corpus as opposed to the whole corpus, in order to say whether the usage of a target word is significantly different in them. Corpus analysis software can show these differences for **keywords**, words that are statistically significantly more common in one corpus than in another, or in one part of a corpus than in the corpus as a whole. Keywords thus can show what is special about the language in particular texts or text types or regions or social groups. The use of computers for this kind of counting is much more accurate and can process much more text than any single reader could manage.

How many words does a single person experience? One study found that both men and women spoke about 16,000 words a day during an average waking period of seventeen hours. If we assume that conversations are roughly symmetrical, then people speak and hear about 2,000 words per hour. At other times, people may be the passive recipients of language from, say, reading, listening to the radio, or watching television. Taking all this together, we can estimate in the roughest of terms that a person may encounter (say, hear, or see) at most about 100,000 words of their language in an average day. Following from this estimate, a person may experience about 36,500,000 words in a year, and over a lifespan of eighty years about three billion words. Another way of thinking about this number is that a community of eighty people may experience about three billion words in one year. We are just now becoming able to collect and store quantities of words of that magnitude in a corpus. The Brown Corpus stored only one million words. Now, however, the Cambridge English Corpus consists of about two billion words. Our best computer resources for the study of words in the language are beginning to approximate the number of words in the life experience of one person, or a year's experience of, say, the residents of a single neighborhood street. In corpus analysis, then, we are able to process in just a few minutes the number of words that one person can experience in a lifetime, or a neighborhood full of people can experience in a year. Corpus analysis makes a big improvement.

Table A3.1 *Collocational Attraction across the Vocabulary*

Node	Top collocate
4%	> 20% (e.g., for *brightly, colored*)
20%	10–20% (e.g., for *angrily, reacted*)
40%	5–10% (e.g., for *advisory, group*)
30%	2% (e.g., for *continental, breakfast*)

Adapted from Stubbs (2001)

Michael Stubbs has illustrated the difference that inspection of corpus evidence can make about Lewis's context. He shows (Stubbs, 2001) that, while the word *surgery* has four different dictionary meanings in British English (briefly, 'medical procedure,' 'branch of medicine,' 'doctor's office,' 'doctor's hours'), the potential ambiguity disappears in actual situations of use. The word *surgery* co-occurs with other words that restrict the meaning, e.g., "undergo surgery," "progress in surgery has made heart transplants possible," "rushed to the surgery," and "she was taking evening surgery." As Stubbs says, "it is not the words that tell you the meaning of the phrase, but the phrase which tells you the meaning of the words." Stubbs based his analysis on a 200-million-word corpus composed mainly of British English. Only the first two of these meanings for *surgery* exist in American English. The Brown Corpus and its replication from the 1990s, the **Frown Corpus** (about two million words combined), have twenty-five tokens of the word *surgery*, always in the company of words like *knee, heart*, and *underwent* that specify which meaning was to be realized in the situation. Thus, the potential ambiguity of *surgery* from its possible dictionary senses is different in Britain and America, but in both places, in practice, the ambiguity disappears in context. This is what C. S. Lewis called "the isolating power of context."

Moreover, Stubbs found unexpectedly high rates of co-occurrence for particular words as **collocates**. If we use a word like *undergo* as our **node** or target word, we can look for the words that occur within a **span** of, say, four words on either side of it, and call the words we find there collocates. Stubbs found that the top twenty collocates of *undergo* from his 200-million word corpus *all* co-occurred with *undergo* at a rate at least 125 times what might be expected by chance. Stubbs provides compelling evidence about other nodes, too, to show that multiple collocates co-occur at extremely high rates with a great many content words.

As Table A3.1 shows, nearly all content words, 94 percent of them (the total of the node frequencies listed in Table A3.1), have strong collocational attraction, at least 250 times more than expected if randomly distributed. A collocational attraction of 1 percent, still 125 times what might be expected, will account for the rest of the content words. This evidence means that we do not just use single words when we talk or write, but we employ words in typical contexts as multi-word units (MWUs). In a MWU the words are not always in the same order, so that "advisory group" and "group that is advisory" both count as the same MWU. Looking for **n-grams**, words in a sequence like bigrams (two consecutive words) or trigrams (three consecutive words), is another way to study collocations, but, unlike MWUs, n-grams do require the words to be in the same order. One more result of strong collocational attraction is **semantic prosody**, the fact that some words acquire meaning from their range of collocates. One example is the word *gossip*, which seems to be something that women do, even though it is perfectly possible for men to engage in the same kind of conversation. Another example is *cause*: most of the collocates for *cause* are negative, like *accident, problem*, or *emergency*, so the word *cause* has come to have a negative quality. You do not want to be the *cause* of anything! So, all the evidence shows that it is a normal feature of language in use that any given word, when considered as a node word, is likely to have multiple collocates with unexpectedly high rates of co-occurrence. Again, the particular words we use with some target word, like *undergo*, provide the "insulating context" that preserves word meanings. Corpus linguistics, then, not only does not conflict with what C. S. Lewis told us, it positively supports it.

One thing that we can do with collocations is to make frequency profiles for them. So, for instance for the node *reckless* we can note (as Stubbs does) that *driving* is a collocate in 19 percent of its occurrences in his corpus, and that *death, causing, admitted*, and *disregard* appear with it 2 percent of the time. If words were distributed randomly, the chance that any particular word would be a collocation for *reckless*, in the 200-million-word corpus used by Stubbs, would be less than 0.01 percent of the time, so it is certainly worth knowing that this profile of words is massively more common than we might have expected. The distributional pattern, which will make an A-curve as you might expect in this book, emerges from the complex system of interactions among speakers. Again as you might expect in this book, somewhat different collocational patterns emerge for every different situation of use, whether in regions, social groups, or text types. Thus, we can use differences in collocational patterns to help us describe the difference between text types, say between academic essays for history classes and academic essays for literature classes. One reason for choosing a major subject in college is to learn the way that people talk in a field of study, which means learning its collocational patterns as much as it means learning the special skills needed for the field. Collocational patterns and MWUs, as much as the different patterns usually described in grammars, help us to understand how English really works. Semantic ramification as described by Lewis and collocational patterns as described by Stubbs are both products of the complex system of language. They are the outcome of emergence.

A3.4 Chapter Summary

Learning about the special qualities of words in use takes us far away from Standard English and plain meaning. It helps to explain how words come to have meaning, not just in logical hierarchies but as a result of a long historical process of ramification. It also explains how context helps speakers of English not to be confused by the different meanings polysemous words have. Corpus analysis helps to show what frequency patterns emerge from the complex system of the language, and thus help us to tell apart the characteristic language of regions, social groups, and text types.

Key Terms

balanced corpus
Bergen Corpus of London Teenager Language (COLT)
British National Corpus (BNC)
Brown Corpus
Cambridge International Corpus
citations
collocate
context
corpus (plural corpora)
corpus analysis
Corpus of Contemporary American English (COCA)
cultural humanism
dangerous sense
Frown Corpus
general corpus
Greats
Helsinki Corpus
keyword
lemma
C. S. Lewis
multi-word unit (MWU)
n-gram
node
polysemy
POS (part of speech) tags
pun
ramification
semantic prosody
span
spin
Michael Stubbs
verbicide

Exercises

A3.1   Look up one of C. S. Lewis's keywords (*nature, sad, wit, free, sense, simple, conscience/conscious, world, life*) in the *Oxford English Dictionary*. Make a note of how many different meanings each word has, and then look at the dates of citations to find out which meanings have been lost, or which meanings have restricted date ranges. NB: each of the numbered meanings may have several subsections, each with its own date ranges.

A3.2   Look up C. S. Lewis's keyword *life* in the *Oxford English Dictionary*. Then consider the word *pro-life* (the motto of the anti-abortion movement in the United States). What meaning of *life* is *pro-life* associated with? Do you suspect spin here, a case of verbicide?

A3.3   Go to the website for the Global Web-Based English (GloWbE) corpus (corpus.byu.edu) and select either BNC or COCA as a corpus to work with. Choose List (it will already be highlighted when you start), put * into the word box, click Search, and observe the display that comes up. Does it look like an A-curve? What kind of words are most common? Are they all words? Make a list of the top ten words. Next, click on Sections and select one text type (spoken, fiction, magazine, newspaper, academic), put * in the word box, and observe the display that comes up. Does it show the same words? Make a list of the top ten words. Next, repeat the process with each of the other text types.

A3.4   Go to corpus.byu.edu and select either BNC or COCA as a corpus to work with. Click on Collocates, and put one of C. S. Lewis's keywords (*nature, sad, wit, free, sense, simple, conscience/conscious, world, life*) in the top entry box, and put * in the Collocates box, then click Search. Are you surprised at any of the collocates that come up? How many of them out of the first fifty occur with your node word at least 1 percent of the time?

A3.5   Go to corpus.byu.edu and select either BNC or COCA as a corpus to work with. Choose List, and put one of C. S. Lewis's keywords (*nature, sad, wit, free, sense, simple, conscience/conscious, world, life*) in the entry box. Then enter a space after the word, and enter either NOUN, VERB, ADJ, or ADV. Click Search. The new list will have your node word followed by a word of the POS type you entered. Does the frequency profile still match an A-curve? NB: if you click [POS] next to the entry box and Insert POS, the corpus will give you all the examples of your word when it occurs as that POS.

Further Reading

Lewis (1967). Here C. S. Lewis talks about a number of keywords like *nature* and *world* as well as *free*, and along the way paints a picture of the kind of cultural humanism studied at Oxford and Cambridge in the mid twentieth century.

Stubbs (2001; 1996). Stubbs is a fine corpus linguist who perhaps has done the most to show how a knowledge of corpus linguistics affects our understanding of language, culture, and literary texts. *Words and Phrases* is more theoretically oriented, while *Text and Corpus Analysis* is more practically oriented. An excellent book for beginners at corpus analysis is Anderson and Corbett (2009).

AntConc, available for download at www.laurenceanthony.net/software.html, is a free, full-featured corpus analysis program. Its developer, Laurence Anthony, offers a number of other helpful programs as well such as TagAnt, which will apply Penn Treebank POS tags to your corpus. Another widely used program is WordSmith Tools, available for sale at www.lexically.net/wordsmith/index .html.

A foundational study in corpus analysis is Biber (1988). Biber uses a set of grammatical tags to develop the idea of dimensional analysis of different text types in English. His more recent textbook is still a fine introduction to the field: Biber, Conrad, and Reppen (1998). A recent textbook on corpus linguistics is McEnery and Hardie (2011).

Glossary

accent   A set of characteristics of someone's pronunciation that may suggest where they come from or with whom they interact.

correctness   The way that people *should* use English based on what is taught in school and included in standardized tests (see prescriptivism).

description   Systematic observation of the facts of language.

dialect   The whole collection of features—pronunciation, lexicon, morphology, syntax, discourse—used by speakers from one place or from one social group (see variety of a language). NB: some people use "dialect" to mean that there is something wrong with the speakers who talk that way.

discourse   The arrangement of chunks of language larger than sentences, as opposed to pronunciation, lexicon, morphology, or syntax.

folk linguistics   Perceptions of how other people talk, bound up with how the perceivers see themselves as speakers of their language (research by Dennis Preston).

generativism   Creation of rule systems, by means of the assumption of a homogeneous speech community, to address our human capacity for speech and to contribute to the description of a "universal" system that people use in the formation of the rule system for their own particular languages (associated with Noam Chomsky).

lexicon   A general term for words and expressions, as opposed to pronunciation, morphology, syntax, or discourse.

lingua franca   A language used for trade or other communication between people who do not speak the same language.

linguistics   Systematic observation of the facts of language, often according to one of the major traditions of such study (structuralism, generativism, systemic functional).

morphology   The association of meaning with "sound shapes," both in words and in the endings we put on words to mark how they work in a sentence.

perceptual dialectology   Perceptions of how other people talk, bound up with how the perceivers see themselves as speakers of their language (research by Dennis Preston).

prescriptivism   The way that people *should* use English based on what is taught in school and included in standardized tests, because people who teach Standard English *prescribe* what we should say or write (see correctness).

rightness The particular kind of English that belongs to people in any particular place and in any particular situation.

slang Words in common usage among some speakers which are not typically used in polite circles.

structuralism Systematic observation of language in which linguists gather information about a language from one or two or some small number of speakers, and then attempt to describe the system of the language from what they say (associated with Leonard Bloomfield).

syntax Aspects of sentence construction, including the arrangement of words and phrases to create well-formed sentences in a language, and a set of rules to describe the arrangement.

systemic functional linguistics Systematic observation of language which focuses on meaning in language and describes a multidimensional framework for getting at the meaning of any utterance from different angles (associated with J. R. Firth and Michael Halliday).

variety of a language The whole collection of features – pronunciation, lexicon, morphology, syntax, discourse – used by speakers from one place or from one social group – a more neutral term than "dialect."

Chapter 2

A-curve Asymptotic hyperbolic curve when observations are placed in order by frequency, formed by a few common observations at the left declining to a long tail at the right of all the rare observations.

complex systems A scientific model that describes the interaction of large numbers of individuals with feedback and reinforcement and without central control, which leads to the emergence of stable patterns.

contingency Any circumstance of the moment to which the operation of a complex system responds and adapts.

culture A general term by which we can designate all the ways that people form themselves into groups and develop particular habits in how they lead their lives.

culture region A spatial area that can be defined when geography and cultural components are brought together for analysis.

emergence The process of development and recognition for patterns and groups as a result of the operation of a complex system.

feedback The sharing of information by participants in a complex system as a consequence of their interactions.

fractal A curve or geometric figure, each part of which has the same statistical character as the whole.

frequency profile The curve that results when observations are placed in order by frequency, notable because observations from different groups may appear in a different order in their own curves.

group formation The way that people associate themselves into groups based on geography and culture.

scaling A pattern that is repeated over and over in every subgroup of the data as well as in the data set overall (see self-similarity, fractal).

self-similarity   A pattern that is repeated over and over in every subgroup of the
data as well as in the data set overall (see scaling, fractal).

Three Body Problem   Name for the property in physics, which Henri Poincaré
proved in 1887, that there is no mathematical solution for what happens to
the position, mass, and velocity of three or more bodies that interact over
time.

Chapter 3

*   A mark that indicates a reconstructed form when prefixed to the form.

Carl Darling Buck   A famous Indo-Europeanist who prepared a famous dictionary
of synonyms from different Indo-European languages.

case   A set of grammatical categories, a different number of them in different
languages, where each category reflects the grammatical function of a word in
a phrase or clause.

Celtic   A branch of the Indo-European language family, of which British and
Welsh are daughter languages.

daisy model   A schematic diagram that shows how the habits of speech that
developed over time within any one of group of speakers would be different from
the habits that developed in any of the other groups.

family tree   A genealogical chart that, as applied to languages, shows historical
relationships between different languages (see stemma).

Germanic   A branch of the Indo-European language family, of which English and
Swedish are daughter languages.

Germanic Sound Shift (Grimm's Law)   A sound change under which some
original Indo-European consonants are said to change systematically into
different consonants in the Germanic branch.

Gilliéron, Jules   An early twentieth-century linguist who said that "each word has
its own history," just the opposite position from the Neogrammarians.

Indo-European   A family of languages which began development about 6000
years ago, and which encompasses most modern European languages.

isolated language   A language that does not have a language family.

Italic   A branch of the Indo-European language family, of which Latin and the
Romance languages are daughter languages.

Kurgan hypothesis   A proposal that the original home of the Indo-Europeans was
in the Central Asian steppes.

language family   A metaphor that represents the simultaneous existence of
populations of speakers in which different language habits have emerged.

linguistic continuum   Consideration of the similarities and connectedness (as
opposed to differences) between languages within branches and between
branches within a language family.

Neogrammarians   The great school of nineteenth-century historical linguists who
promoted a mechanical view of language and said that "sound change operates
without exception."

Nostratic   A proposal for a large historical family of languages of which Indo-
European was a daughter language.

reconstruction   Use of comparisons between modern languages to provide information about what changes must have occurred, in order to predict earlier forms in languages.

Slavic   A branch of the Indo-European language family, of which Russian and Polish are daughter languages.

sound change   The idea that regular correspondences between older forms and newer forms in a language show mechanical differences in pronunciation.

stemma   A genealogical chart that, as applied to languages, shows historical relationships between different languages (see family tree).

umlaut   A sound change under which words pronounced with [e] in one syllable and followed by an [i, ɪ, j] in the next syllable change so that the first syllables are pronounced with [ɪ].

Chapter 4

Angles   A West Germanic group of people among those who came to Britain starting in 449AD and eventually occupied the island.

Anglo-Saxon Chronicle   A historical record maintained in several locations from the ninth century to the end of the Old English period.

Bede   A late seventh-century and early eighth-century monk at Monkwearmouth who wrote the best period history, in Latin, *Historia ecclesiastica gentis Anglorum* (*Ecclesiastical History of the English People*).

British   A language from the Celtic branch of Indo-European, and a people who occupied most of the island of Britain until the West Germanic invasion.

Contemporary English   The period of the English Language beginning in about 1950, from the beginning of the Information Age.

Early Modern English   The period of the English Language from about 1500 to 1700.

England   The name of the largest country on the island of Britain, which comes from the name of one of the invading West Germanic groups, the Angles.

English   The name of the language that emerged on the island of Britain following the West Germanic invasion, which comes from the name of one of the invading West Germanic groups, the Angles.

Frisians   A West Germanic group of people among those who came to Britain starting in 449AD and eventually occupied the island.

gemination   The doubling of any single consonant except *r* when it occurred between a short vowel and an [i, ɪ, j] sound

Gildas   The Romanized British writer who wrote *De Excidio Brittaniae* in the sixth century AD.

Hengest   A West Germanic leader who came to Britain in 449AD, first as a mercenary and later as invader.

Horsa   A West Germanic leader who came to Britain in 449AD, first as a mercenary and later as invader.

Jutes   A West Germanic group of people among those who came to Britain starting in 449AD and eventually occupied the island.

macron   The line modern editors put over a vowel in Old English to represent a long vowel.

Middle English   The period of the English Language from about 1100 to 1500.

Modern English   The period of the English Language from about 1500 to the present.

Old English   The period of the English Language from about 450 to 1100.

period   A conventional division of time thought to represent a state in the development of a language, literature, or other aspect of culture.

Picts   An unRomanized Celtic group of people who lived in the northern part of the island of Britain before the West Germanic invasion.

Prehistoric Old English   The period of the English Language from about 450 to 700.

Saxons   A West Germanic group of people among those who came to Britain starting in 449AD and eventually occupied the island

Scots   An unRomanized Celtic group of people who lived in the northern part of the island of Britain, and who eventually became subject to English government.

St. Augustine   A Christian missionary from Rome who arrived in England in 597 AD.

St. Columba   A Christian monk from Ireland who in 563 AD established an outpost on the island of Iona off the western coast of Scotland.

Vikings   North Germanic raiders who began attacks on the island of Britain in the seventh century, and later established settlements primarily in the northern and western parts of Britain.

Chapter 5

æ (capital Æ)   A letter used in Old English not usually found in modern English writing, called aesc, representing a low-front vowel.

ȝ (capital Ȝ)   A letter used in Old English not usually found in modern English writing, called yogh, representing a <g> or <y> in modern spelling.

þ (capital Þ)   A letter used in Old English not usually found in modern English writing, called thorn, representing a <th> in modern spelling.

ð (capital Ð)   A letter used in Old English not usually found in modern English writing, called eth, representing a <th> in modern spelling.

ƿ (capital Ƿ)   A letter used in Old English not usually found in modern English writing, called wynn, representing a <w> in modern spelling.

ablaut   Change in the stem vowel across the principal parts of a verb paradigm.

accusative   The case corresponding to the object of a sentence.

analytic   A language that uses word order, auxiliary verbs, and prepositions to organize its sentences.

Cædmon   The legendary originator of Old English poetry, as Bede told the story.

cæsura   The pause in the middle between the two half lines in Old English poetry.

codicology   The field that studies the history of how manuscripts were made.

conjugate   The process of understanding both the different endings and changes in the vowel of the stem of a verb.

continental borrowing   Latin words that the Germanic people had already borrowed before they came to Britain.

229

Danelaw A division of the island of Britain where the Vikings held sway, as negotiated by King Ælfred.

dative The case corresponding to what would be represented with the prepositions *to, from* in Modern English.

differential change The principal that a language changes differently over time among the different groups of people who use it, which results in language variation.

diphthongization after initial palatals A sound change in which West Germanic [æ] becomes Old English [ea], and West Germanic [e] becomes Old English [ie] after [j, tʃ, ʃ].

diplomatic edition A modern edition that retains as much as possible of the presentation of text from the manuscript (e.g., no modern punctuation, no macrons).

dual A number, besides singular and plural, that historically had inflections in Old English (two of something, to stand alongside just one or more than two).

emend What editors do to a text to repair what they believe to be errors in the copying of the manuscript.

feminine One of the grammatical genders, which does not correspond to natural gender.

first person One of three categories of person, each of which can be singular or plural, represented by *I, we* in Modern English.

futhorc The set of runes used as a writing system among Germanic groups.

gender Grammatical gender, which does not correspond to natural gender, consists of three classes of words (masculine, feminine, neuter) which have different endings on noun and adjective stems.

genitive The case corresponding to what would be represented with the preposition *of* in Modern English.

gloss A translation into Old English, typically from Latin, added between lines after the first composition of a book.

half line One of the two parts of an Old English poetic line, divided by a cæsura and connected by alliteration of specific consonants or any vowel.

history of the book The field that studies the history of how manuscripts, and later printed books, were made.

illuminated capital The decorated initial capital letter of a section of a manuscript.

illumination Colorful drawings in manuscripts, sometimes separate pictures but often decorations of the initial capital letter of a section of the book.

infinitive One of the principal parts of a verb, represented in Modern English with *to* as in "to go."

instrumental A case with traces in Old English represented in Modern English by the prepositions *with, by*.

interlace An artistic style that connects letters in medieval jewelry and other objects from the early Middle Ages across Northern Europe.

kenning A compound word whose parts together indicate something else, e.g. "whale-road" to mean 'sea.'

Kent The southeastern region of the island of Britain that emerged during the Old English period.

Kentish   One of the four dialects of Old English, found in Kent.

King Ælfred   The English king (born 849, king from 871–899), who defeated the Vikings and negotiated a treaty to divide the kingdom.

majuscule   A letter style often used for inscriptions that features more straight lines than other styles; majuscule forms have become what we now call capital letters.

masculine   One of the grammatical genders, which does not correspond to natural gender.

Mercia   The central region of the island of Britain that emerged during the Old English period.

Mercian   One of the four dialects of Old English, found in Mercia.

minuscule   A letter style often used for glosses; minuscule forms have become what we now call lower-case letters.

mood   A grammatical feature of verbs marked by the use of verbal inflections that allow speakers to express their attitude toward what they are saying, i.e. indicative as statement of fact or subjunctive as statement of desire or potential.

neuter   One of the grammatical genders, which does not correspond to natural gender.

nominative   The case corresponding to the subject of a sentence.

normalize   What editors do to a text to remove dialect differences and other variation in language.

Northumbria   The northern region of the island of Britain that emerged during the Old English period.

Northumbrian   One of the four dialects of Old English, found in Northumbria.

number   A grammatical feature of verbs in which inflections indicate how many people constitute the subject (singular, plural, or in Old English, also dual).

paleography   The history of different letter styles used in manuscripts before the invention of printing.

paradigm   The set of endings for different grammatical states of a noun or verb.

parchment   Specially prepared untanned skins of animals used as a medium to write on and bind into manuscripts.

past participle   One of the principal parts of a verb, represented in Modern English, e.g., as the "gone" form of the verb "to go."

person   A grammatical feature of verbs and pronouns in which inflections or different forms indicate who constitutes the subject (first, second, third).

philology   The history of the transmission of a text as it is copied over time.

preterite   The past tense of a verb.

principal parts   States of the verb that have different forms in the paradigm, including the second person singular present tense, third person singular present tense, the first person singular preterite indicative, the plural preterite indicative, the infinitive, and the past participle.

rune   Symbols from a writing system whose "alphabet" is known for Old English as the futhorc.

second person   One of three categories of person, each of which can be singular or plural, represented by *you* in Modern English.

semiotics   The study of signs and symbols.

stem   The base or root form of a word, to which inflections may be added.

strong   Ideally a different inflection for each slot in a paradigm, in practice just a more differentiated paradigm than a weak form.

synthetic   A language that does not have to have fixed word order because inflections indicate what role each word plays in a sentence.

tense   Indication of time for verbs, such as present or past.

third person   One of three categories of person, each of which can be singular or plural, represented by *he, she, it, they* in Modern English.

uncial   A letter style used in manuscripts where curves were natural for producing with a quill pen, more formal than minuscule.

Watling Street   A name for the old Roman road from London to Chester (on the Welsh border), which formed the boundary between Wessex and the Danelaw.

weak   A set of inflections with a less differentiated paradigm than a strong form.

Wessex   The southwestern region of the island of Britain that emerged during the Old English period.

West Saxon   One of the four dialects of Old English, found in Wessex.

Chapter 6

Ancrene Wisse   Also known as the *Ancrene Riwle*, a manual intended to guide young (noble) women who wanted to retire from daily life and pursue a religious vocation, originally composed in English in the early thirteenth century.

Anglo-Norman   The name of people of Norman heritage who lived in England; also the name of the version of the French language that they spoke.

contingency   New facts of life, changes in the circumstances of daily life, relevant in this book for the speakers of English and other languages.

Domesday Book   An inventory of all the properties and their value across England, commissioned by William the Conqueror.

doublet   Pairs of words for the same thing from two languages (English *swine* vs. *pork*, English *shirt* vs. Norse *skirt*).

ethics   A branch of medieval philosophy in which historical events may be narrated for their didactic value.

exemplum   A brief story with a moral attached.

external history   A record of all of the historical events and cultural changes (see contingency) for the speakers of a language.

fiction   Tales that were not true, or like the truth; frowned upon by the medieval church.

internal history   Changes in lexicon, pronunciation, and grammar of a language.

literature   A modern category of writing not yet present in the medieval period.

Magna Carta   A document that limited the absolute power of the English king and led to the establishment of constitutional law.

Norman   A word that describes the people and the language of residents of Normandy, today a part of France.

Norse   The northernmost branch of the Germanic people, in comparison with the West Germanic English people.

Tower of London   A building still found in London, begun by William the Conqueror in 1078 as a residence and later greatly expanded.

verisimilar   Something like what may have happened even if it never actually happened.

William Caxton   England's first printer.

William the Conqueror   Duke of Normandy who took the English throne in 1066.

Chapter 7

Black Death   An outbreak of plague which occurred in England mainly in 1348–1349 and killed perhaps half of the population of England.

Canterbury Tales   Chaucer's most famous work, in which pilgrims en route to Canterbury each tell tales.

Chaucer   The most famous Middle English author from the end of the fourteenth century (died 1400).

dot maps   Maps from the *Linguistic Atlas of Late Mediaeval English* that show dots where particular features occurred in the texts included in the project.

final e   A representation in Middle English of a reduced form of many inflections in Old English or in etymological situations where another vowel in Old English has been reduced to e.

isogloss   Lines on a map that represent limits of occurrence for particular variants in a language.

Paston letters   Letters written by members (sometimes by secretaries) of the Paston family, landed gentry in Norfolk, between 1422 and 1509.

reduced form   A word in which one of the many inflections in Old English, or in etymological situations, cases where another vowel in Old English has been reduced to *e*.

Chapter 8

auxiliary verb   A verb used in forming the tenses, moods, and voices of other verbs that carry semantic content.

borrowing   Words used in one language, like English, that replicate words used in another language, like French (see loanword).

chain shift   Changes in a vowel system for which the vowels all seem to move in concert with each other.

code   A list of words and a set of rules for how to put them together in a language.

code mixing   The use of words and phrases from one language while mainly using those of another language.

code switching   Changing to the use of words and phrases from a different language when mainly using those of another language.

contractions   The elision of a vowel with replacement by an apostrophe in writing, as in *it's* for *it is*, and sometimes other changes as well, as in *won't* for *will not*.

Francis Drake   An English sailor/pirate who sailed around the world in the late sixteenth century, an expedition that was supposed to attack Spanish possessions in the New World.

Great Vowel Shift (GVS)   A set of sound changes between 1400 and 1700 in which the long vowels ([i, eɪ, ɛ, æ, a] in the front, and [ɔ, o, u] in the back) were raised in a process of vowel rotation.

Jamestown   English colony begun in 1607 in what would later become Virginia.

loanword   Words used in one language, like English, that replicate words used in another language, like French (see borrowing).

long vowel   In English, [i, eɪ, ɛ, æ, a] in the front, and [ɔ, o, u] in the back.

John Milton   Great seventeenth-century English author who wrote *Paradise Lost*.

periphrastic verb   A "helping" or auxiliary verb, especially *do*, whose broad use emerged in Early Modern English, retained in Modern English just for questions (*do you want some?*), negatives (*you don't want any*), and emphasis (*I do want some*).

Plymouth   English colony begun in 1620 in what would later become Massachusetts.

postvocalic r   An [r] after vowels (see rhoticity).

progressive verb   Verbs that use the suffix *-ing* with an auxiliary verb (*I am walking, I was walking*), as an alternative to the simple present tense (*I walk*) or simple past tense (*I walked*).

pull chain   A chain shift in which the vowel at the top of the vowel chart moved and somehow this pulled the others along.

push chain   A chain shift in which the low vowels started to rise and pushed the higher vowels along.

raising   A sound change in which a vowel was pronounced at a higher articulatory position than it had been before.

repertoire   A set of words that speakers of a language recognize and use; the repertoire is different for different speakers and so there can be disagreement about whether a word belongs to a language or not.

rhoticity   The pronunciation of [r] after vowels, which was being lost by some English speakers in the seventeenth century.

Roanoke   English colony begun in 1586 in what would later become North Carolina, later lost.

second raising   Words that had previously been raised one step, like *meat* and *mate*, were raised one more step during the seventeenth century.

Shakespeare   Great sixteenth-century English dramatist and poet.

Spanish Armada   The Spanish fleet that attacked England, and lost, in 1588.

vernacular   A language commonly spoken by the people, as opposed to a learned language like Latin.

vowel rotation   A theory that individual acts of raising tend to raise vowels until they get to the highest position, and then vowels fall along a more centralized track.

wh- relative pronoun   Pronouns like *who, whom, whose* that became popular as starters for subordinate clauses during the Early Modern period.

Thomas Wyatt   Famous English poet (1503–1542) who may have been a lover of Anne Boleyn.

Chapter 9

acrolectal creole   The most English-like variety of an English-based creole.

Age of Enlightenment   The early part of the Modern English period, in which people expected reason and science to explain the world around us.

American Spelling Book   Originally published in 1783 by Noah Webster as part of his *Grammatical Institute*, the book discusses the relationship of sound and spelling in English, and over the course of the nineteenth century became one of the most successful schoolbooks of all time.

ascertainment   The idea that knowledge could be organized and shown to be regular, applied to English beginning in the eighteenth century.

basilectal creole   The least English-like variety of an English-based creole.

British Empire   Territory controlled by British government and commercial interests, which at its height near the end of the Modern period included about one-fifth of the world's population and one-fourth of the world's land area.

creole   A stable native language developed from a mixture of different languages.

Doctrine of First Effective Settlement   The idea that the initial population in an area has great influence on the language that emerges there (see Founder Principle).

Dynamic Model   Proposal by Edgar Schneider that suggests five phases in the evolution of colonial varieties: foundation of the colony, stabilization around the outside norm, nativization, formation of an internal norm, and diversification.

Founder Principle   The idea that the initial population in an area has great influence on the language that emerges there (see Doctrine of First Effective Settlement).

Inland North   The Northern dialect region of the United States, west of New England.

Samuel Johnson   Editor of the first great English dictionary in 1755, a scholarly record of English words as drawn from the best English authors.

Robert Lowth   Author of a famous and long-running grammar in Britain (1762).

mesolectal creole   A moderately English-like variety of an English-based creole.

Midland region   The American dialect region of which Philadelphia was the focal city for settlement and which proceeded west in two broad streams (see North Midland, South Midland).

modernism   An idea that seeks to apply rational, scientific means to reveal the order in the world, or at least to create the appearance of order in rational thought about a more complex reality.

language academy   Institution created to maintain the regularity of the language, e.g. for Italian (Accademia della Crusca), for French (Académie Française), and for Spanish (Real Academia Española), no language academy has been created for English.

James A. H. Murray   First chief editor of the *New English Dictionary on Historical Principles,* later called the *Oxford English Dictionary.*

lexifier   The language that provides much of the vocabulary for a creole (see superstrate).

Lindley Murray   Author of a famous and long-running grammar in Britain (1795).

New England   The eastern part of the Northern dialect region of the United States.

North Midland   The northern part of the American Midland dialect region, whose stream of settlement followed the National Road through Pennsylvania, eventually as far as central Illinois, and the Ohio River valley west from Pittsburgh; its language features mixed to some degree with the speech habits of the Northern region.

Northern region   The American dialect region which occupies the northern tier of states.

Oxford English Dictionary (OED)   Very large historical dictionary of English, begun with a reading program in 1857 and still actively edited, characterized by system and science in editorial principles.

Received Pronunciation (RP)   A name for the British English standard, said to be spoken by graduates of Oxford and Cambridge and adopted by the BBC as its standard form of pronunciation for broadcasting.

Edgar Schneider   Developer of the Dynamic Model (sv) for the process of emergence of colonial varieties of English.

South Midland   The southern part of the American Midland dialect region, whose settlement followed the course of the Shenandoah River south through Virginia towards the Cumberland Gap to enter Kentucky and Tennessee; its language features mixed to some degree with those of the Southern region.

Southern region   The American dialect region which begins in the plantation areas of Virginia and South Carolina, with westward extension.

standardization   An ideology that arose in the Modern period in which speakers believed that there should be a standard form of a language.

substrate   The language that provides the basic grammar for a creole.

superstrate   The language that provides much of the vocabulary for a creole (see lexifier).

Noah Webster   Author of a famous American grammar (*Grammatical Institute*, 1784), a part of which was the *American Spelling Book*.

Chapter 10

acronym   A common test-shortening used in computer-mediated communication consisting of the initial letters of a set of words, e.g. LOL 'laugh out loud'.

Anglicist Hypothesis   The idea that the features of AAVE could be traced to features of English speakers who were the owners or overseers of slaves.

CMC (computer-mediated communication)   A name for all means of sharing information between users using a computer, from bulletin boards to email to social media.

community of practice   Groups of people who are all engaged in the same activity and share linguistic features.

Creole Hypothesis   The idea that African-American English had emerged as a contact language like creoles in the Caribbean.

dense   The quality of a social network in which many people share the same links.

discourse particle   A conditionally relevant word or sound used to direct or redirect the flow of conversation without adding significant content meaning.

edge city   An urban place that is part of a large metropolitan area based on a large city.

emoticon   A graphic device used to convey meaning in computer-mediated communication, such as :) ;) :(.

Estuary English   A variety of English used in the southeast of Britain by educated speakers with some features different from RP.

Information Age   The period of time starting after World War II, named for the rise of telecommunication and later computing.

L1   A speaker's first or native language.

L2   A second language learned by a speaker, whether in school or by other means.

L3   Small bits of a language, not fluency, typically used for trade or other commercial purposes (see use).

mobility   A name for the behavior of people willing to leave their local communities in search of better jobs.

multiplex   The quality of a social network in which people tend to have more than one tie (e.g., the same job, church, and pub).

Northern Cities Shift   A chain shift proposed by William Labov for the Inland Northern region of the US.

pidgin   A language with simplified grammar used among workers with different language backgrounds, not usually a native language.

postcolonial English   A variety of English that develops in a former colony, typically from the British Empire but also in other places like Hawaii.

quotative   A word used to introduce a quotation, like *say* or more recently *like*.

social media   A form of computer-mediated communication designed for social interaction, like Facebook, Twitter, or Reddit.

social network   A set of people in some geographical area who are linked to each other by doing the same jobs, attending the same schools or churches, or other means.

Southern Shift   A chain shift proposed by William Labov for the Southern region of the US.

strong tie   High levels of density and multiplexity in a social network.

suburb   A residential location from which people travel to work in the city.

urbanization   The concentration of higher percentages of the population in cities.

use   Small bits of a language, not fluency, typically used for trade or other commercial purposes (see L3).

weak tie   Low levels of density and multiplexity in a social network.

Chapter 11

codification   Writing down what people say or write, in order to make a grammar or a dictionary of a "standard" language.

Henry Fowler   Oxford-educated schoolteacher and freelance journalist (1858–1933) who brought his own personality and opinions to publication of a famous usage guide, *A Dictionary of Modern English Usage* (1926).

General American   A proxy term for the English of highly-educated Americans, dispreferred because it gives the impression that there is something "general," or common, or popular, about the speech of this group.

grammaticality   The idea that an aspect of usage is a part of the grammar of a language, which is actually a perceptual artifact.

maven   A label that indicates a trusted expert, but when applied to English language experts the word suggests someone who identifies the *correct* bits of language and complains about the wrong ones.

observational artifact   Something that we just perceive to be there, as opposed to something with real existence.

perception   What people notice, even if it is not really there.

plain language rule   The idea that words convey an objective meaning, regardless of the circumstances of their use (associated with Justice Scalia).

plain meaning rule   A term used in England for the idea that words convey an objective meaning, regardless of the circumstances of their use.

prescription   An explicit direction to use (or not use) a particular form of usage, as found in usage guides.

William Safire   Longtime writer (1929–2009) of the popular *On Language* column in the *New York Times*.

usage guide   A collection of prescriptions, many of which are not shared between different guides.

voluntary association   The choice to join a group of like-minded people, such as speakers of Standard English.

voluntary region   An area or place characterized by particular life style choices to which like-minded people can go to live.

Chapter 12

apparent-time research   Measurement of the usage of people born at different times, a substitute for not having actual evidence going back into the past.

Star Trek syndrome   The prediction or expectation that a language like English will become more standardized as time goes on.

Appendix 1

acoustic phonetics   The study of speech sounds that traces the physical qualities of speech sounds and plots them on charts.

affricate consonant   A consonant that begins as a stop and finishes as a fricative.

allophone   One of a set of possible sounds used to pronounce a single phoneme.

angle brackets < >   The symbols used to enclose the letters used as a spelling.

back vowel   A vowel pronounced with the tongue positioned at the back of the mouth.

central vowel   A vowel pronounced with the tongue positioned in the center of the mouth, not high or low.

closed vowel   A vowel pronounced with the mouth mostly closed (see high vowel).

consonant   A speech sound that is articulated with complete or partial closure at some location in the vocal tract.

content   The meaning(s) that we attach to words.

diacritics   Small marks used to indicate gradations of sounds slightly different from the basic phonetic symbols in IPA.

diphthong   Two adjacent vowel sounds in the same syllable.

expression   The physical sounds or appearance in writing by which we recognize words.

fricative consonant   Speech sound made when air passes through a narrowed passage that causes turbulence in the air flow.

front vowel   A vowel pronounced with the tongue positioned at the front of the mouth.

grammar   A set of regularities by which speakers of a language can judge which pronunciations or words or expressions are a normal part of the language.

high vowel   A vowel pronounced with the tongue positioned near the top of the mouth (see closed vowel).

IPA (International Phonetic Alphabet)   The most widely used set of phonetic symbols used to represent a recognizable speech sound.

larynx   An organ that houses the vocal cords, also called the voice box.

letter   Symbols such as those of our Roman alphabet used to spell words.

linguistic sign   A name for the combination of the expression and the content (or the signifier and signified), as in a word.

low vowel   A vowel pronounced with the tongue positioned at the bottom of the mouth (see open vowel).

mid vowel   A vowel pronounced with the tongue positioned in the middle of the mouth, not front or back.

minimal pair   Two words that have a difference of only one sound in their sound shapes.

monophthong   A vowel sound that we consider to occur alone in a syllable.

nasal consonant   A speech sound for which there is a stoppage of the air flow through the mouth and the air escapes through the nose.

native speaker   Somebody who has learned a language at home during the normal period of childhood language acquisition.

onomatopoeia   Words that are supposed to sound like the noises they represent.

open vowel   A vowel pronounced with the mouth mostly open (see low vowel).

phoneme   The range of sounds (see allophone) that make a distinctive difference for telling words apart in a given language or variety.

phonetics   The exact description of speech sounds.

phonetic segment   A recognizable speech sound in a language or variety.

phonetic symbol   Graphic realizations for the exact description of speech sounds (see IPA).

plosive consonant   A speech sound for which the flow of air is briefly blocked at some point.

polysemic   When one word has multiple meanings.

segmental phoneme   A speech sound recognized as a phoneme in a language or
  variety.
semantics   The study of word meaning.
slanted lines / /   Symbols used to enclose speech sounds considered as phonemes
  (see virgules).
square brackets [ ]   Symbols used to enclose speech sounds considered as phonetic
  segments.
stop consonant   A speech sound for which the flow of air is briefly blocked at some
  point.
unvoiced consonant   A speech sound for which the larynx is not in use during
  articulation.
virgules / /   Symbols used to enclose speech sounds considered as phonemes (see
  slanted lines).
voiced consonant   A speech sound for which the larynx is in use during
  articulation, and which has constriction or blockage of the air flow.
vowel   A speech sound for which the larynx is in use during articulation, and which
  has no constriction or blockage of the air flow.
word   The expression and content of a recognizable unit in the lexicon of
  a language or variety.

Appendix 2

allomorph   Each different phonetic realization of the set of sound shapes
  considered to be the same morpheme.
auxiliary verb   A verb used in forming the tenses, moods, and voices of other
  verbs.
base   The basic form of a word to which prefixes and endings can be attached (see
  root).
bound morpheme   A morpheme which must be used in combination with other
  morphemes.
clause   A combination of elements, each of which can consist of one or more
  words, in a set of typical patterns.
comment   The part of the informational content of an utterance that provides new
  information about its topic.
communicative competence   The range of things someone needs to know in order
  to use language well in a community.
compound words   Words composed of more than one word whose content is
  different from the meaning of the component words (e.g. *bluebird* versus *blue
  bird*).
critical discourse analysis (CDA)   A method of study of discourse that focuses on
  the relationship between the author and the recipient of some conversation or
  piece of writing, often regarding a difference in power between them.
dependent clause   A clause that must be associated with an independent clause
  within a sentence
derivational morphology   The process of adding morphemes together to make
  new words.

determiner   A function word like *the* or *a/an* that occurs together with a noun to express the reference of that noun.

discourse   Patterns in language beyond the level of the sentence.

environment   The location of a given speech sound within the sequence of speech sounds, typically the preceding or following sounds.

finite clause   A clause that can be used as an independent or dependent clause in a sentence.

free morpheme   A morpheme that can stand on its own as a separate word.

genre   A term to describe a text type, usually for types that occur in literature or other aesthetic contexts.

given information   The part of the informational content of an utterance that is the topic for later comment.

grammar   A term usually used to describe a set of patterns of syntax, but also used to refer to the whole structural system of a language, including pronunciation and lexicon and discourse as well as syntax.

Grice's maxims   A description of assumptions about language interaction, regarding quality, quantity, reference, and manner.

head   The required part of a noun phrase or verb phrase, to which other optional elements can be associated.

hierarchy   The ordered set of concepts for adequate description of how a language works.

independent clause   A clause that can be used as full sentence.

infinitive   One of the principal parts of a verb, which in Modern English is introduced by *to*, such as *to learn*.

inflection   A bound morpheme that can be added to a free morpheme to adjust its meaning, such as adding *-s* to a noun to indicate that it is plural.

inflectional morpheme   A bound morpheme that can be added to a free morpheme to adjust it with grammatical meaning, like the plural meaning of *-s*.

loan word   An entire word that is borrowed from another language.

main clause   An independent clause, to which dependent clauses may be associated.

modification   An optional element of a noun phrase or verb phrase, consisting of an adjective, an adverb, or a phrase or clause with adjectival or adverbial function.

morpheme   The association of a sound shape with a particular meaning.

negation   A word that confers negative polarity on a verb phrase or clause.

new information   The part of the informational content of an utterance that provides comment about its topic.

non-finite clause   A clause that uses an infinitive or participle for its predicate and does not have a subject.

noun   A word (but not a pronoun) used to identify any of a class of people, places, or things, and which can be used as subject or object in a clause pattern or as the object of a preposition.

NP (noun phrase)   A term to describe one of the functional patterns within a clause, which consists of a noun as head with optional determiner and modification.

paragraph   A section of piece of writing, indicated by a new line, indentation, or numbering.

participle   A principle part of a verb, either the present participle indicated with *-ing* or the past participle indicated with *-ed* or a change of vowel in the stem.

past tense   An inflected form of a verb indicating that the action of the verb occurred before the present time.

phrase   A pattern of words below the level of a clause.

predicate   The part of a clause, typically the verb phrase, that asserts something about the subject.

prepositional phrase   A combination of words that begins with a preposition and includes at least one word, usually a noun, that serves as the object of the preposition.

present tense   An inflected form of a verb indicating that the action of the verb is occurring at the current moment in time.

root   The basic form of a word to which prefixes and endings can be attached (see base).

subject   The part of a clause, typically a noun phrase, that provides a topic on which the predicate acts.

syntax   The patterns in which speakers of a language normally assemble sentences.

text type   A recognizable situation for use of language, either written or spoken.

topic   The part of the informational content of an utterance that provides given information for later comment.

verb   A word that conveys an action or a state or an occurrence, and which can be used as the head of the predicate in a clause pattern.

verb valency   One of the common sequences which are found frequently with particular verbs.

VP (verb phrase)   A term to describe one of the functional patterns within a clause, which consists of a verb as head with optional negation, auxiliary, and modification.

word formation   The composition and content of words

Appendix 3

balanced corpus   A corpus that seeks to sample widely from numerous text types.

British National Corpus (BNC)   A balanced corpus of 100 million words containing written and spoken texts from British sources, composed in the 1990s.

Brown Corpus   A balanced corpus of one million words containing written texts from American sources, composed in the 1960s.

Cambridge English Corpus   A multi-billion word balanced corpus containing written and spoken texts from British and American sources.

citations   Single sentences illustrating the meaning of a word, typically stored on paper slips or cards.

Corpus of Contemporary American English (COCA)   A balanced corpus of over 500 million words containing written texts from American sources, composed starting in the 1990s.

collocate   A word that occurs in proximity to another word (its node).

Bergen Corpus of London Teenager Language (COLT)   A half-million word corpus composed of the speech of teenagers, collected in 1993.

context   The collection of words with which a particular target word with a particular meaning is typically found.

corpus (plural corpora)   A body of naturally occurring language (i.e., something that somebody has said or written) that exists as machine readable texts (i.e. in some computer format), is authentic (i.e., not made up, from real use), is sampled (texts included for a reason, collected according to a plan), and is representative because of the sampling of a particular population of texts.

corpus analysis   The study of corpora, typically to establish quantitative parameters of texts and corpora with a view to comparison of such parameters.

C. S. Lewis   A professor at Oxford and Cambridge in the middle of the twentieth century who developed ideas about polysemy, context, and ramification.

cultural humanism   Study of the history of ideas in Western culture, as exemplified in the traditional curriculum at Oxford and Cambridge.

dangerous sense   The most common contemporary meaning for a word or topic, which may not be the meaning of a polysemous word in context.

Frown Corpus   A balanced corpus of one million words containing written texts from American sources, composed in the 1990s in replication of the Brown Corpus.

general corpus   A sample of all of the language of a large community, difficult to create because it is not possible to include texts from every text type of a language.

Greats   Works in Greek and Latin and also English that held a prominent place in the history of Western culture, a curriculum at Oxford and Cambridge.

Helsinki Corpus   A balanced corpus of 1.5 million words containing written texts from Old English, Middle English, and Early Modern English.

keyword   A word that is statistically significantly more common in one corpus than in another.

lemma   Different word forms combined into a single entry, such as *walk/walks/walked/walking* under WALK.

Michael Stubbs   Corpus linguist who supplied quantitative evidence that supports C. S. Lewis's idea of context.

multi-word unit (MWU)   The idea that we do not just use single words when we talk or write, but employ words in typical contexts.

n-gram   Words in a sequence.

node   A target word, for which one observes words that occur within a **span** of words on either side, for the purpose of finding collocates.

polysemy   The state of a word having a number of meanings.

POS (part of speech) tags   Markings in a corpus that identify the function of a word within a clause.

pun   Humorous usages that invoke the meaning of a word out of its usual context.

ramification   Lewis's idea that words change in meaning over time, not by replacement of one meaning for another, but instead by addition.

semantic prosody   The meaning that some words acquire from their range of collocates.

span   A set of words on either side of a target word, for the purpose of finding collocates.

spin   The use of words repurposed from their historical meanings in context to make a (usually political) point.

verbicide   The use of words repurposed from their historical meanings in context to make a (usually political) point.

References

Adams, Valerie. 1973. *An Introduction to Modern English Word-Formation*. Oxford: Blackwell.

Algeo, John. 2009. *Origins and Development of the English Language*. 6th edn. New York: Wadsworth/Cengage.

Alim, H. Samy. 2006. *Roc the Mic Right: The Language of Hip Hop Culture*. London: Routledge.

Allen, Judson. 1971. *The Friar as Critic: Literary Attitudes in the Later Middle Ages*. Nashville: Vanderbilt University Press.

Allen, Judson. 1982. *The Ethical Poetic of the Later Middle Ages*. Toronto: University of Toronto Press.

Amodio, Mark, ed. 2005. *New Directions in Oral Theory: Essays on Ancient and Medieval Literatures*. Tempe: Arizona Center for Medieval and Renaissance Studies.

Anderson, Wendy, and John Corbett. 2009. *Exploring English with Online Corpora*. London: Palgrave.

Bailey, Richard. 1996. *Nineteenth-Century English*. Ann Arbor: University of Michigan Press.

Bailey, Richard. 2012. *Speaking American*. New York: Oxford University Press.

Bailyn, Bernard. 1986. *The Peopling of British North America*, New York: Vintage.

Baker, Peter. 2012. *Introduction to Old English*. 3rd edn. Oxford: Blackwell.

Barber, Charles. 1993. *The English Language: A Historical Introduction*. Cambridge: Cambridge University Press.

Barber, Charles, Joan Beal, and Philip Shaw. 2012. *The English Language: A Historical Introduction*. 2nd edn. Cambridge: Cambridge University Press.

Baron, Dennis. 1990. *The English-Only Question: An Official Language for Americans?* New Haven: Yale University Press.

Bauer, Laurie. 1983. *English Word Formation*. Cambridge: Cambridge University Press.

Baugh, Albert, and Thomas Cable. 2012. *A History of the English Language*. New edn. London: Routledge.

Bede. 1994. *The Ecclesiastical History of the English People*. Trans. Judith McClure and Roger Collins. Oxford: Oxford University Press.

Benedictow, Ole J. 2004. *The Black Death 1346–1353: The Complete History*. Woodbridge: Boydell Press.

Benskin, M., M. Laing, V. Karaiskos, and K. Williamson. 2013. *An Electronic Version of A Linguistic Atlas of Late Mediaeval English*. Edinburgh: The Authors and The University of Edinburgh. (See McIntosh et al., 1986.)

Bessinger, Jess, and Diane Bornstein. 1973. *A History of the English Language*. Audio recording. New York: Caedmon.

Biber, Douglas. 1988. *Variation across Speech and Writing*. Cambridge: Cambridge University Press.

Biber, Douglas, Susan Conrad, and Geoffrey Leech. 1999. *Longman Grammar of Written and Spoken English*. London: Longman.

Biber, Douglas, Susan Conrad, and Geoffrey Leech. 2002. *Longman Student Grammar of Written and Spoken English*. London: Longman.

Biber, Douglas, Susan Conrad, and Randi Reppen. 1998. *Corpus Linguistics*. Cambridge: Cambridge University Press.

Bickerton, Derek. 1990. *Language and Species*. Chicago: University of Chicago Press.

Blair, Peter Hunter. 2003. *An Introduction to Anglo-Saxon England*. 3rd edn. Cambridge: Cambridge University Press.

Bloor, Thomas, and Meriel Bloor. 2013. *The Functional Analysis of English*. 3rd edn. London: Routledge.

Boberg, Charles. 2010. *The English Language in Canada*. Cambridge: Cambridge University Press.

Bomhard, Allan. 2011. *The Nostratic Hypothesis in 2011*. Washington, DC: Institute for the Study of Man.

Brewer, Charlotte. 2007. *Treasure-House of the Language*. New Haven: Yale University Press.

Buck, Carl Darling. 1949. *A Dictionary of Selected Synonyms in the Principal Indo-European Languages: A Contribution to the History of Ideas*. Chicago: University of Chicago Press.

Burkette, Allison. 2001. The Story of Chester Drawers. *American Speech* 76: 139–157.

Burkette, Allison, and William A. Kretzschmar, Jr. 2018. *Exploring Linguistic Science*. Cambridge: Cambridge University Press.

Burrow, J. A., and Thorlac Turville-Petre. 2005. *A Book of Middle English*. 3rd edn. Oxford: Blackwell.

Cameron, Deborah. 2012. *Verbal Hygiene*. London: Routledge.

Campbell, Alastair. 1959. *Old English Grammar*. Oxford: Clarendon Press.

Cassidy, Frederic, Joan Hall, and Luanne von Schneidermesser, eds., 1985–2012. *Dictionary of American Regional English*. Cambridge: Harvard University Press.

Chapman, Don. 2009. Lost Battles and the Wrong End of the Canon: Attrition among Usage Prescriptions. Paper presented at Studies in the History of the English Language 6, Banff, Canada.

Chaucer, Geoffrey. 1987. *The Riverside Chaucer*. Larry Benson and F. N. Robinson, eds. 3rd edn. New York: Houghton Mifflin.

Clackson, James. 2007. *Indo-European Linguistics: An Introduction*. Cambridge: Cambridge University Press.

Commager, Henry Steele. 1958. Noah Webster 1758–1958, Schoolmaster to America. *Saturday Review* 41 (October 18): 10–12, 66–67.

Crystal, David. 1995. *The Cambridge Encyclopedia of the English Language*. Cambridge: Cambridge University Press.

Crystal, David. 2003. *English as a Global Language*. 2nd edn. Cambridge: Cambridge University Press.

Curzan, Anne. 2014. *Fixing English: Prescriptivism and Language History*. Cambridge: Cambridge University Press.

D'Arcy, Alexandra. 2007. *Like* and Language Ideology: Disentangling Fact From Fiction. *American Speech* 82: 386–419.

Derrida, Jacques. 1980. The Law of Genre. Trans. by Avital Ronell. *Critical Inquiry* 7: 5–81.

Di Jamiekan Nyuu Testiment. 2012. Kingston: Bible Society of the West Indies.

Dinneen, Francis J. 1967. *An Introduction to General Linguistics*. Washington: Georgetown University Press.

Durkin, Philip. 2009. *The Oxford Guide to Etymology*. Oxford: Oxford University Press.

Durkin, Philip. 2014. *Borrowed Words: A History of Loanwords in English*. Oxford: Oxford University Press.

Eckert, Penelope. 2000. *Linguistic Variation as Social Practice*. Oxford: Blackwell.

Fairclough, Norman. 2001. *Language and Power*. London: Longman.

Fairclough, Norman. 2003. *Analysing Discourse: Textual Analysis for Social Research*. London: Routledge.

Fisher, John. 1995. *The Emergence of Standard English*. Lexington: University Press of Kentucky.

Foley, John M. 1985. *Oral-Formulaic Theory and Research: An Introduction and Annotated Bibliography*. New York: Garland.

Fortson, Benjamin W., IV. 2010. *Indo-European Language and Culture: An Introduction*. 2nd edn. Oxford: Wiley-Blackwell.

Fowler, Henry. 2015. *Fowler's Dictionary of Modern English Usage*. 4th edn. Jeremy Butterfield, ed. Oxford: Oxford University Press.

Fulk, Rob. 2012. *An Introduction to Middle English*. Peterborough, Ontario: Broadview.

Garner, Bryan. 2009. *Garner's Modern American Usage*. 3rd edn. New York: Oxford University Press.

Giles, John Allen, ed. and trans. 1841. *The Works of Gildas and Nennius*. London: James Bohn.

Golding, William. 1955. *The Inheritors*. New York: Harvest.

Görlach, Manfred. 1991. *Introduction to Early Modern English*. Cambridge: Cambridge University Press.

Gould, Stephen Jay. 2003. *The Hedgehog, the Fox, and the Magister's Pox: Mending the Gap Between Science and the Humanities*. New York: Three Rivers Press.

Grice, Paul. 1975. Logic and conversation. In P. Cole and J. Morgan, eds., *Syntax and semantics 3: Speech acts*: 41–58. New York: Academic Press.

Harriot, Thomas. 1951. *A Brief and True Report of the New Found Land of Virginia*. Facsimile of 1588 document. Ann Arbor: Clements Library Associates.

Hawking, Stephen, and Leonard Mlodinow. 2010. *The Grand Design*. New York: Bantam.

Holland, John. 1998. *Emergence: From Chaos to Order*. New York: Basic.

Holm, John. 2000. *An Introduction to Pidgins and Creoles*. Cambridge: Cambridge University Press.

Huddleston, Rodney, and Geoffrey Pullum. 2002. *The Cambridge Grammar of the English Language*. Cambridge: Cambridge University Press.

Hughes, Arthur, and Peter Trudgill. 1983. *English Accents and Dialects*. 3rd edn. London: Edward Arnold.

Hymes, Dell. 1966. Two Types of Linguistic Relativity. In William Bright, ed., *Sociolinguistics*. The Hague: Mouton, 114–158.

Jauss, Hans Robert. 1977. *Alterität und Modernität der mittelalterlichen Literatur*. Munich: Wilhelm Fink.

Jauss, Hans Robert. 1979. The Alterity and Modernity of Medieval Literature. *New Literary History* 10: 181–229.

Jauss, Hans Robert. 1982. *Toward an Aesthetic of Reception*. Trans. by Timothy Bahti. Minneapolis: University of Minnesota Press.

Johnson, Ellen. 1996. *Lexical Change and Variation in the Southeastern United States 1930–1990*. Tuscaloosa: University of Alabama Press.

Kachru, Braj. 1992. *The Other Tongue: English Across Cultures*. 2nd edn. Champaign: University of Illinois Press.

Kachru, Braj. 2017. *World Englishes and Culture Wars*, Cambridge: Cambridge University Press.

Kachru, Braj, and Yamuna Kachru. 2009. *The Handbook of World Englishes*. Oxford: Wiley-Blackwell.

Kaiser, Mark, and V. Shevoroshkin. 1988. Nostratic. *Annual Review of Anthropology* 17: 309–329.

Keene, Derek. 2000. Metropolitan Values: Migration, Mobility, and Cultural Norms, London 1100–1700. In Laura Wright, ed., *The Development of Standard English 1300–1800*. Cambridge: Cambridge University Press, 93–114.

Kortmann, Bernd. 2001. In the year 2525 . . . Reflections on the Future Shape of English. *Anglistik* 12: 97–114.

Kretzschmar, William A., Jr. 1992. Caxton's Sense of History. *Journal of English and Germanic Philology* 91: 510–528.

Kretzschmar, William A., Jr. 2009. *The Linguistics of Speech*. Cambridge: Cambridge University Press.

Kretzschmar, William A., Jr. 2010. The Development of Standard American English. In Andy Kirkpatrick, ed., *Handbook of World English*. London: Routledge, 96–112.

Kretzschmar, William A., Jr. 2011. Language and Region. In Rajend Mesthrie, ed., *The Cambridge Handbook of Sociolinguistics*. Cambridge: Cambridge University Press.

Kretzschmar, William A., Jr. 2015. *Language and Complex Systems*. Cambridge: Cambridge University Press.

Kretzschmar, William A., Jr. 2016. Roswell Voices: Community Language in a Living Laboratory. In K. Corrigan and A. Mearns, eds., *Creating and Digitizing Language Corpora*. London: Palgrave, 159–176.

Kretzschmar, William A., Jr., Virginia G. McDavid, Theodore K. Lerud, and Ellen Johnson. 1993. *Handbook of the Linguistic Atlas of the Middle and South Atlantic States*. Chicago: University of Chicago Press.

Kretzschmar, William A., Jr., and Merja Stenroos. 2012. Evidence from Surveys and Atlases in the History of the English Language. In Terttu Nevalainen and Elizabeth Traugott, eds., *The Oxford Handbook of the History of English*. Oxford: Oxford University Press, 111–122.

Labov, William. 1972. The Logic of Non-Standard English. *Language in the Inner City:* 201–240. Philadelphia: University of Pennsylvania Press.

Labov, William. 1981. Resolving the Neogrammarian Controversy. *Language 57:* 267–309.

Labov, William. 1994. *Principles of Linguistic Change: Internal Factors*. Oxford: Blackwell.

Labov, William, Charles Boberg, and Sherry Ash. 2006. *Atlas of North American English: Phonetics, Phonology and Sound Change*. Berlin: Mouton de Gruyter.

Ladefoged, Peter, and Keith Johnson. 2014. *A Course in Phonetics*. 7th edn. Stamford: Cengage.

Lapidge, Michael, John Blair, Simon Keynes, and Donald Scragg, eds. 2013. *Wiley-Blackwell Encyclopedia of Anglo-Saxon England*. 2nd edn. Oxford: Wiley-Blackwell.

Lester, Mark, and Larry Beason. 2012. *The McGraw-Hill Handbook of English Grammar and Usage*. 2nd edn. Columbus: McGraw-Hill Education.

Lewis, C. S. 1967. *Studies in Words*. 2nd edn. Cambridge: Cambridge University Press.

Lewis, Carenza. 2016. Disaster Recovery: New Archaeological Evidence for the Long-Term Impact of the 'Calamitous' Fourteenth Century. *Antiquity 90:* 777–797.

Lieber, Rochelle. 2015. *Introducing Morphology*. Cambridge: Cambridge University Press.

Lippi-Green, Rosina. 2011. *English with an Accent; Language, Ideology, and Discrimination in the United States*. 2nd edn. London: Routledge.

Lord, Albert. 1960. *The Singer of Tales*. Cambridge: Harvard University Press. 2nd edn. 2000, Stephen Mitchell and Gregory Nagy, eds. Cambridge, MA: Harvard University Press.

Mandelbrot, Benoit. 1982. *The Fractal Geometry of Nature*. San Francisco: Freeman.

Mandelbrot, Benoit, and Richard Hudson. 2004. *The (Mis)behavior of Markets*. New York: Basic.

Mantel, Hilary. 2009. *Wolf Hall*. London: Holt.

Mantel, Hilary. 2012. *Bring Up the Bodies*. London: Holt.

Marchand, Hans. 1969. *The Categories and Types of Present-Day English Word Formation*. 2nd edn. Munich: Beck.

Marsden, Richard. 2015. *The Cambridge Old English Reader*. 2nd edn. Cambridge: Cambridge University Press.

Mathews, Mitford. 1951. *A Dictionary of Americanisms on Historical Principles*. Chicago: University of Chicago Press.

McArthur, Tom. 1992. *The Oxford Companion to the English Language*. Oxford: Oxford University Press.

McConnell, Ruth. 1979. *Our Own Voice: Canadian English and How it is Studied*. Toronto: Gage.

McEnery, Tony, and Andrew Hardie. 2011. *Corpus Linguistics*. Cambridge: Cambridge University Press.

McIntosh, Angus, Michael L. Samuels, and Michael Benskin. 1986. *A Linguistic Atlas of Late Medieval English*. Aberdeen: Aberdeen University Press.

Millward, Celia. 1989. *A Biography of the English Language*. New York: Wadsworth/Cengage.

Millward, Celia, and Mary Hayes. 2011. *A Biography of the English Language*. 3rd edn. New York: Wadsworth/Cengage.

Milroy, James. 1992. *Linguistic Variation and Change*. Oxford: Blackwell.

Milroy, James, and Lesley Milroy. 2012. *Authority in Language: Investigating Standard English*. 3rd edn. London: Routledge.

Milroy, Lesley. 1987. *Language and Social Networks*. 2nd edn. Oxford: Blackwell.

Milton, John. 2013. *The Complete Poetry of John Milton*. John Shawcross, ed. New York: Anchor.

Mitchell, Bruce, and Fred Robinson. 2011. *A Guide to Old English*. 8th edn. Oxford: Blackwell.

Mitchell, Melanie. 2009. *Complexity: A Guided Tour*. Oxford: Oxford University Press.

Modiano, Marko. 1999. Standard English(es) and Educational Practices for the World's Lingua Franca. *English Today* 15(4): 3–13.

Moore, Samuel, Thomas Knott, and James Hulbert. 1972. *The Elements of Old English*. 10th edn. Ann Arbor: Wahr.

Moore, Samuel, and Albert Marckwardt. 1965. *Historical Outlines of English Sounds and Inflections*. Ann Arbor: Wahr.

Moore, Samuel, Sanford Meech, and Harold Whitehall. 1935. Middle English Dialect Characteristics and Dialect Boundaries. *Essays and Studies in English and Comparative Literature* 13: 1–60. Ann Arbor: University of Michigan Press.

Mufwene, Salikoko. 2001. *The Ecology of Language Evolution*. Cambridge: Cambridge University Press.

Mugglestone, Lynda. 2000. *Lexicography and the OED*. Oxford: Oxford University Press.

Mugglestone, Lynda. 2005. *Lost for Words*. New Haven: Yale University Press.

Murray, Elizabeth. 1977. *Caught in the Web of Words*. New Haven: Yale University Press.

Nevalainen, Terttu, and Helena Raumolin-Brumberg. 2016. *Historical Sociolinguistics*. 2nd edn. London: Routledge.

Nielsen, Hans F. 1989. *The Germanic Languages: Origins and Early Dialectal Interrelations*. Tuscaloosa: University of Alabama Press.

Ogilvie, Sarah. 2012. *Words of the World*. Cambridge: Cambridge University Press.

Parkes, Malcolm. 1993. *Pause and Effect: Punctuation in the West*. Berkeley: University of California Press.

Peters, Pam. 2004. *The Cambridge Guide to English Usage*. Cambridge: Cambridge University Press.

Preston, Dennis. 1989. *Perceptual Dialectology: Nonlinguists' Views of Areal Linguistics*. Dordrecht: Foris.

Preston, Dennis. 1993. Folk Dialectology. In Dennis Preston, ed., *American Dialect Research*. Amsterdam: John Benjamins.

Preston, Dennis, and Nancy Niedzielski. 2000. *Folk Linguistics*. Berlin: de Gruyter.

Pryor, Francis. 2004. *Britain BC: Life in Britain and Ireland before the Romans*. London: HarperCollins.

Pryor, Francis. 2005. *Britain AD: A Quest for Arthur, England and the Anglo-Saxons*. London: HarperCollins.

Pryor, Francis. 2006. *Britain in the Middle Ages: An Archaeological History*, London: HarperCollins.

Pyles, Thomas, and John Algeo. 2004. *Origins and Development of the English Language*. 5th edn. New York: Harcourt Brace Jovanovitch.

Quirk, Randolph, Sidney Greenbaum, Geoffrey Leech, and Jan Svartvik. 1985. *A Comprehensive Grammar of Contemporary English*. London: Longman.

Rickford, John, and Russel Rickford. 2007. *Spoken Soul: The Story of Black English*. New York: Wiley.

Robins, R. H. 1997. *A Short History of Linguistics*. 4th edn. London: Longman.

Robinson, Orrin W. 1992. *Old English and its Closest Relatives: A Survey of the Earliest Germanic Languages*. Stanford: Stanford University Press.

Russell, J. C. 1972. Population in Europe, 500–1500. In Carlo Cipolla, ed., *The Fontana Economic History of Europe: The Middle Ages*, 25–70. London: Collins/Fontana.

Sanchez-Stockhammer, Christina, ed. 2015. *Can We Predict Linguistic Change?* Helsinki: University of Helsinki, VARIENG.

Saussure, Ferdinand de. 1986. *Course in General Linguistics*. Charles Bally and Albert Sechehaye, eds., with the collaboration of Albert Riedlinger. Trans. and annotated by Roy Harris. La Salle, IL: Open Court.

Scalia, Antonin, and Bryan Garner. 2012. *Reading Law: The Interpretation of Legal Texts*. Minneapolis: West.

Schneider, Edgar. 2007. *Postcolonial English*. Cambridge: Cambridge University Press.

Schneider, Edgar. 2011. *English Around the World*. Cambridge: Cambridge University Press.

Seidlhofer, Barbara. 2011. *Understanding English as a Lingua Franca*. Cambridge: Cambridge University Press.

Shakespeare, William. 2013. *The Complete Works of Shakespeare*. David Bevington, ed. 7th edn. London: Pearson.

Smith, Jeremy. 1996. *An Historical Study of English*. London: Routledge.

Stockwell, Robert, and Donka Minkova. 1988. The English Vowel Shift: Problems of Coherence and Explanation. In D. Kastovsky and G. Bauer, eds., *Luick Revisited: Papers Read at the Luick Symposium at Schloss Lichtenstein*. Tübingen: Gunter Narr, 355–394.

Stockwell, Robert, and Donka Minkova. 2001. *English Words: History and Structure*. Cambridge: Cambridge University Press.

Stubbs, Michael. 1996. *Text and Corpus Analysis*. Oxford: Blackwell.

Stubbs, Michael. 2001. *Words and Phrases*. Oxford: Blackwell.

Swanton, Michael. 1998. *The Anglo-Saxon Chronicle*. London: Routledge.

Tacitus. 2010. *Agricola and Germania*. James Rives and Harold Mattingly, eds. and trans. London: Penguin.

Tagliamonte, Sali. 2011. *Variationist Sociolinguistics: Change, Observation, Interpretation*. Oxford: Wiley-Blackwell.

Tagliamonte, Sali, Alexandra D'Arcy, and Celeste Rodríguez Louro. 2016. Outliers, Impact, and Rationalization in Linguistic Change. *Language* 92: 824–849.

Tagliamonte, Sali A., and Derek Denis. 2008. Linguistic Ruin? LOL! Instant Messaging and Teen Language. *American Speech* 83: 3–34.

Tiersma, Peter M., and Lawrence M. Solan, eds. 2012. *The Oxford Handbook of Language and Law*. Oxford: Oxford University Press.

Townend, Matthew. 2005. *Language and History in Viking Age England: Linguistic Relations between Speakers of Old Norse and Old English*. Turnhout, Belgium: Brepols.

Upton, Clive, William A. Kretzschmar, Jr., and Rafal Konopka. 2001. *Oxford Dictionary of Pronunciation for Current English*. Oxford: Oxford University Press.

Upton, Clive, and William A. Kretzschmar, Jr. 2017. *Routledge Dictionary of Pronunciation for Current English*. London: Routledge.

Wade, Nicholas. 2006. *Before the Dawn: Recovering the Lost History of Our Ancestors*. New York: Penguin.

Watkins, Calvert. 1985. *The American Heritage Dictionary of Indo-European Roots*. Boston: Houghton Mifflin.

Watkins, Calvert. 1995. *How to Kill a Dragon: Aspects of Indo-European Poetics*. Oxford: Oxford University Press.

Werner, Valentin. 2016. Overlap and Divergence: Aspects of the Present Perfect in World Englishes. In Elena Seoane and Cristina Suárez-Gómez, eds., *World Englishes: New Theoretical and Methodological Considerations*. Amsterdam: Benjamins, 113–142.

Whitelock, Dorothy, David Douglas, and Susie Tucker, eds. and trans. 1961. *The Anglo-Saxon Chronicle*. New Brunswick, NJ: Rutgers University Press.

Whorf, Benjamin. 1956. *Language, Thought, and Reality: Selected Writings of Benjamin Lee Whorf*. John B. Carroll, ed. Cambridge, MA: MIT Press.

Wilson, Joycelyn. 2007. Outkast'd and Claimin' True: The Language of Schooling and Education in the Southern Hip-Hop Community of Practice. Unpublished dissertation, University of Georgia.

Winchester, Simon. 1998. *The Professor and the Madman*. New York: HarperCollins.

Winchester, Simon. 2003. *The Meaning of Everything*. Oxford: Oxford University Press.

Winthrop, Robert C. 1964. *Life and letters of John Winthrop : Governor of the Massachusetts-Bay Company at Their Emigration to New England*. Boston: Ticknor and Fields, 37–39.

Wolfram, Walt, and Eric Thomas. 2008. *The Development of African American English*. Oxford: Wiley-Blackwell.

Wright, Laura. 1996. *Sources of London English: Medieval Thames Vocabulary*. Oxford: Clarendon Press.

Wright, Laura, ed. 2000. *The Development of Standard English 1300–1800*. Cambridge: Cambridge University Press.

Wyatt, Thomas. 2015. *The Complete Poems*. R. A. Rebholz, ed. London: Penguin.

Zelinsky, Wilbur. 1992. *The Cultural Geography of the United States: A Revised Edition*. Englewood Cliffs, NJ: Prentice Hall.

Websites

www.007.com Official James Bond site

www.cambridge.org/us/cambridgeenglish/better-learning/deeper-insights/linguistics-pedagogy/cambridge-english-corpus Website for the Cambridge English Corpus

corpus.byu.edu Website for Global Web-Based English (GloWbE) that offers collections of texts from twenty countries where English is spoken

www.daredictionary.com Website for the *Dictionary of American Regional English*

www.dchp.ca/dchp2 Website for the *Dictionary of Canadianisms on Historical Principles*

doe.utoronto.ca Website of the *Dictionary of Old English*

www.helsinki.fi/en/researchgroups/varieng/corpus-of-early-english-correspondence Website for Corpus of Early English Correspondence

www.imdb.org IMDb site about movies and television

www.lap.uga.edu Website for the American Linguistic Atlas Project

www.laurenceanthony.net/software.html Website for AntConc

www.lel.ed.ac.uk/ihd/elalme/elalme.html Website for *An Electronic Version of A Linguistic Atlas of Late Mediaeval English* (see also Benskin et al., 2013)

www.lexically.net/wordsmith Website for WordSmith Tools

www.oed.com Website for the *Oxford English Dictionary*

proenglish.org Website advocating English as an official language

www.santafe.edu Website for the Santa Fe Institute

soundsofspeech.uiowa.edu Website for sounds of American English

www.usenglish.org Website advocating English as an official language

Index

Bold terms are key words, italicized entries are words discussed as words in the text.